Economics for the Disinterested

and

Why there are no Aliens

Lutz Jacoby

2015

Published in 2015 by Little River Design Pty. Ltd.

Little River Design Pty. Ltd.

PO Box 3161

Newport VIC 3015

lrd17@bigpond.com

www.littleriverdesign.com.au

ISBN: 978-0-9944051-2-8

Cover art by Lutz Jacoby

Contents

An Early Interlude: Inequality and Socialism.................................... 11

Back to Trading and Transactions 13

A Bit of History.. 17

Some Theory... 21

So let's Analyse... 22

Opportunities 30

Buying and Selling 31

Supply and Demand – Take II 34

An Interlude... 36

Another Interlude 41

Revisiting Circulation 45

Econometrics... 47

Saving your Money... 48

How Government Spoils the Economy............................... 52

Yet Another Interlude.. 65

The Law of Multiplication of Subordinates 67

The Law of Multiplication of Work.................................... 68

Back to Government Interference..................................... 69

An aside from 1921 77

An Economics Tragedy 80

Now the Government some more 83

Whose money is it? 94

Where does Money come from? 95

What About Inflation... 103

Foreign Trade.. 106

The Concept of Comparative Advantage........................ 108

Reserve Currency... 110

The Trouble with Banks 111

Shadow Finances 118

Capitalism 121

Foreign Trade Again... 125

Government Again.. 126

Economic Cycles 128

Thinking Large... 136

Profits?.. 137

Circulation Again... 139

People who Made Theories.. 143

A Word About Marx.. 175

Private Equity, Capitalism's Secret Weapon................... 181

Away with Banks.. 182

GOLD.. 191

Bitcoin... 195

The War on Cash.. 198

A Minor Fantasy... 203

Our Biggest Enemy? The UN! 210

The End of Democracy?.. 215

Personalisation 219

Preface

I claim no formal economical education at all, but have spent a lot of time thinking about what is really required from economic knowledge. We are not taught anything relating to economics in grade school and are let into the world full of incidental knowledge – mostly misleading or false – with very little guidance as to where to seek out more information. What is presented in newspapers is usually slanted by ideology of one type or another and what's more, judging from the goings on in the world recently and also in the past, economic knowledge does not give you any advantage in dealing with the economy.

I make no claim to originality for any of the views expressed here but hope that in some cases I may succeed in giving a little insight into subjects not readily available to a general readership. The object was to elucidate a number of principles and propositions which are in the realm of modern and classic economics. Included are some thoughts that have arisen over time due to seeming fallacies and omissions in the popular presentation of economic news and views. This does not preclude the outlining of some opinionated statements which the reader is welcome to disregard or write to me about. I also hope to be forgiven for some small phrases which were lifted from other writings where these described what I was explaining in a manner that could not be improved upon.

I am trying to make light of these economic matters since in the face of the huge and intrinsic power of government in collusion with banks there is nothing the ordinary citizen can strive for, except to protect themselves as much as possible. We have the opportunity to choose a government every so many years, but a large portion of the electorate is uninformed about economic matters and does not have the resources or inclination, perhaps, to correct this.

The chapters are laid out in a somewhat sequential manner, but any section or portion thereof can be passed over as there is repetition in the information to keep the main points in the reader's mind.

Most of our life is spent with only mundane financial issues: generating an income through wages or salaries, from business or government handouts. Then we need to balance this with our desires as to how to spend this income for maximum effect. The majority of the population does this quite well as they go through life buying a house, cars and looking after the children's education. Sometimes, however, when following the news from around the world one gets the impression of being surrounded by madmen, of living in an asylum. A lot of the news doesn't make sense and economic discussions seem irrational and divorced from what we do in our lives. Some of the explanations and descriptions in this book should at least allow the reader to understand a little of the ongoing developments and form an opinion on financial news topics.

Looking back over my research for general economic information it is interesting to note that I had no preconceived notions about economics in general, except that what I had been exposed to up to then seemed distinctly unsatisfactory. All through the 70s and 80s there had been spikes and crashes and economic turmoil, and always some bright spark said they knew exactly what to do about it – but no-one ever managed to improve or even predict what came next. With both the crashes of 1987 and 2008 costing me and others dearly I was prompted into seeking some background, a little deeper than what was being offered in the news – most of which was obviously slanted and edited to conform to ideology. As I gathered more information and researched economic history it became apparent that the prevailing economists of the 20th century were living in a dreamsphere, ignoring harsh realities and denying people's reactions to changes. Along with government spokesmen, central bank officials and the business community these economists strived to maintain a status quo whereby the population was kept complacent and compliant, to be used and exploited and deprived of their investments. A lot of the people involved in the big companies playing with our money were just simply lying about the state of things to maintain their advantage and allow them to syphon off funds.

4

All that ordinary people want is simply to be left alone to pursue their own path to happiness (or not), yet there is a constant barrage of rules and regulations and interference to prevent them doing so, and the attitude that only the government knows how to get you to your happiness prevails.

While researching and learning more about economics, two very particular realisations sprung to the foreground and, apart from general terminology and definitions, this book is very much about these as a result. The first is one that is quite difficult to make people understand, and as you read the book the proposition will become clearer. For the last several decades there has been an attitude that it is the government's responsibility to encourage people to spend more, buying goods and services, and this is referred to as the demand economy. It is an extremely seductive proposition and so plausible that it is hard to argue against it (many thanks to the Catallaxy Files writers for making me aware). It implies that the government should force people to spend more in order to make the economy stronger – this is accomplished by either giving them money, discouraging savings or by printing money directly to increase the pool of available funds. The fallacy in this is quite simple: These funds are not used to create, grow or manufacture things, but they are simply a feel-good directive. Were we to concentrate on the supply of goods by encouraging manufacture or production, then workers need to be employed and these workers get paid *for actually producing goods to fill shelves.* Now a supply of goods is available to be purchased, *but by people who have produced something in turn.* Now note the difference: The government gives away money to people to spend, but nothing is produced – OR – industry is supported, not by hand-outs, but by changes in restrictive laws, reduction in taxes, by proper funding arrangements and by less onerous employment conditions (Unions take note), which allows more workers to be paid as they are producing goods, which other productive workers will then buy. It takes a while for this concept to sink in and most economists and bureaucrats have not and probably will not understand the meaning here.

The second realization is a lot more straightforward, but carries some complex implications. It is imperative to understand that all government revenue can only come from you directly or indirectly, that is from each individual in the society they live in. Be it from personal income tax, from fees and charges on services, sales taxes, excise taxes and import duties: The only one who supplies a government with funds is you – the individual citizen – either now or by a future generation. Recently there have been arguments that large corporations are not pulling their weight, are not paying appropriate amounts of company tax. Money that corporations earn is not magic currency that doesn't affect you as an individual and society. Corporations are there to produce goods or render services and earn an income. This income is not whisked away to corporate heaven; it is paid to shareholders or re-invested in the corporation. This means if the corporate tax burden is increased, the costs of the goods and services have to be adjusted upwards to enable the corporation to still be viable, and keeping in mind that the corporation must be solvent by law. So ignore all the arguments and discussions about tax revenue, all you hear in the news and read in the editorials – the individual is the only tax payer one way or the other.

So if a government wants to balance the books they either have to cut spending or raise your taxes – there is no other way.

The critical mind reviewing this text may point out that there seems to be a lot of negativity in the descriptions and tales accumulated here. The intent is more to make the reader who is new to some economic learning aware of the sort of thing that goes on in the world. A lot of information is simply not disseminated in the popular press and a lot of this serves to protect governments, banks or even specific persons. It should also serve to question and investigate any economic policies that are being promulgated in society, most are simply not in favour of the populace, but serve the government or large institutions like banks. In particular the large banks have been in control of the monetary system since the mid-1800s and are only and sincerely interested in their own welfare regardless of what the population may think.

6

There are no footnotes since readers may find them disruptive, but there is a bibliography for those who want to extend their awareness or to follow up on books mentioned here. A lot of the older texts are freely available to read on the web.

Melbourne 2015

The Cast – in Order of Appearance

The Entrepreneur	the most important member of the cast
The Shovelmaker	our first entrepreneur
The Grasshopper	prefers gallivanting to gathering
The Ant	gathers stuff for the winter
The Socially Minded	gives away his surplus
Johan Palmstruch	issued the first bank notes
Aristotle	Buyer = Seller
Reagan and Thatcher	Supply economics
Hipolito Yrigoyen	Argentinian President - overthrown
Juan Peron	Argentinian Socialist President
C. N. Parkinson	Work fills whatever time is available
D. J. Boudreaux	Government realist
King John	Magna Carta Man
Alan Greenspan	Federal Reserve Chairman and obscurant
Helga	runs a bar and issued Drinkbonds
David Ricardo	addresses capital
Ben Bernanke	just another Federal Reserve Chairman
John Stuart Mill	most brilliant economist of 19th century
Richard Cantillon	first proper market analyst
Jean-Baptiste Say	so called Say's Law
Thomas R. Malthus	investigated population & consumption
Adam Smith	most famous enquirer into wealth
Claude Frederic Bastiat	saw things that were unseen by others
John Maynard Keynes	extremely influential 20th century socialist
Ludwig von Mises	Austrian School pillar of thought
Carl Menger	free market economist of 20th century
Friedrich A. Hayek	economics and government analyst
Karl Marx	not an economist
Satoshi Nakamoto	Bitcoin inventor and pseudonym
Maurice Strong	Secretary General of 1992 Earth Summit
Christine Figueres	UN climat change official
Alex de Toqueville	French traveller
Alfred Lord Tennison	quite a poet

The only good government is one that leaves you alone.

8

In order to understand anything about anything it is always best to start with basic principles. To understand economics one needs to go a step further back…

In the Beginning, (Genesis 1:1/1:25) there was a whole lot of stuff in a ball, but it didn't actually do anything. Then, suddenly one bit of stuff decided to replicate itself, and we still don't why or how this actually happened – usually deferred to alien influence.

Anyway, this bit of matter found there was enough extra matter around to reassemble into a new bit exactly like itself. The new bit now carried the same knowledge and carried on replicating.

The rest is the history of life.

You can now follow through history what went on. An example: the green stuff determined how to use solar energy, water, carbon dioxide and some other useful minerals to make more complex items, essentially an improvement on the original simple replication process. Once the news was out, there was no stopping this process and things replicated and developed into what is now known as palaeontology. Later we will see how economic procedures replicate this process.

There was, however, always one condition that stopped the process: When the particular configuration had run out of one of the materials required. Keep this in mind.

If we now take a great leap into the human age we find a direct comparison. After many eons of nomadic existence living hand to mouth and only hunting and gathering, humans developed a system of agriculture by which they could assure themselves of continuing replication without getting involved in nasty details of cell division, etc. The principle was the same as always: Take a few ingredients, add sunshine and water and a little supportive care and presto – there was your food. Humans, being the way they are, would always strive next to reduce their workload – or increase production for the same workload. This led to tools. Spending a lot of time making tools was

9

not a good idea for the farming type, and soon others made and offered tools in exchange for food. You can see where this is leading. For example, a shovel maker didn't just want to buy food from one farmer who had only wheat and asparagus available. So next time he got a debit voucher for wheat to the value of one shovel. He could now trade this for tomatoes from a guy who needed wheat. This system was called *bartering,* but done by noting credit against one another – there was no money yet. We need to keep the term bartering as an ideal sort of term since trading did not take place just like that one item for another. In small societies debts from consumption tended to be accumulated and then later paid off with an equivalent item. Thus expenditures on one part would appear as a debt to someone else until cleared.

This shovel maker needs to be accepted as the first *entrepreneur,* which is very important to define as a first premise for economics. Up to now we have been seeing what is called subsistence farming: All your efforts all year round are expended in just putting enough food on the table to keep the family happy. If the entrepreneur does not appear at this first stage we have no products, we will have no items for bartering and there will not be an economy. This entrepreneur was the first individual to produce something in excess of what he personally needed and allowed others to use his product to support their lives. Whether this was a farmer, a manufacturer or a fisherman, this step defined the first free trade in society, and by free trade we mean that no one so far interfered with his endeavours.

Entrepreneur derives from the French language as someone who *undertakes* something new, an economic activity with the aim of doing business and generating an income. As a side effect, any such undertaking will produce a certain upheaval in the economy which may be very minimal like the invention of the paper clip, or almost devastating as in the invention of the steam engine.

We have many historical examples of the opposite to this path, where people lived under circumstances with food and minimal shelter abundant, which allowed all to live reasonable lives without needing shovels or much else. Under these circumstances no shovels were invented, no entrepreneur ever appeared and society happily carried on without ever developing any further. Money would be unnecessary, ownership of things was not restricted to individuals and everyone shared what was there. This is the case of the natives of central South America for example. However, when man moved to areas where life was not so easy and required planning and foresight, having an economic arrangement was inevitable.

An Early Interlude: Inequality and Socialism

We must note here that as soon as man settled down from a living-off-the-land in a nomadic lifestyle to a settled type of early farming, the concept of income inequality rears its ugly head. Now it is assumed that in the first instance everybody had a couple of goats or sheep or maybe tilled a patch of land for growing of grains. In an effort to secure the future when there may be less abundance it is the surplus of production that counts. And, in the spirit of human endeavour, some marked differences will appear immediately. Some individuals will be more concerned or industrious, investing heavily in the support of their products. Others may say 'no worries' and sit back and relax most of the time. Over the passage of time the more industrious will have accumulated a far larger amount of goods to secure the future while others will only have little. When hard times come, the latter will be forced to purchase for his needs from the former. But since he is unlikely to have much in way of assets his life becomes more difficult. For those who have followed the recent spate of 'stop inequality' calls in the media it is good to know that there is nothing new or recent about this situation. Richard Cantillon in his *Essay on the Nature of Trade in General* from about 1734 mentions for example that if a landowner divides his estates evenly among the population, after a time only a few will have substantial holdings. This is still relevant today as there will always be those who are more industrious (or lucky as well) and those who will always be scrounging for support. There will be some unlucky individuals who

11

arrive at this point through no fault of their own and do require looking after by those around them. Aesop's fable of the ant and the grasshopper is a perfect story illustrating the conundrum of inequality and how to deal with it.

One summer's day a Grasshopper was hopping about, chirping and singing to its heart's content. An ant passed by, bearing along with great toil an ear of corn he was taking to the nest.

"Why not come and chat with me," said the Grasshopper, "instead of toiling that way?"

"I am helping to lay up food for the winter," replied the ant. "and I suggest you do the same."

"Why worry about the winter?" said the Grasshopper, "there is plenty of food around." The ant went on its way and continued its toil. When the winter came the Grasshopper had no food and found itself with pangs of hunger while the ants were distributing food every day from what they had collected in the summer, and the Grasshopper finally understood: It is best to prepare for days of necessity in the future.

That may be the end of the fable, but in the real world you don't let people just starve when you can help. It raises what is called the *Samaritan's Dilemma*. People of a kind and decent disposition don't wish to allow others to suffer, especially if helping them would be a small sacrifice. But providing charity may foment moral hazard, thereby leading to more people needing help. In this case the next step is for the ants to engage the grasshopper in work to earn his food and understand that nothing comes for free. Once the menial work was being done by the employed food seekers, it gave the food collectors more free time, and in typical fashion this was not wasted but used to further development of goods, to make them finer, better and invent new goods. In effect this was an initial barter of labour for goods.

This is also where socialism is such a disappointing proposition. Say, the farmer earlier who grows tomatoes and potatoes and works harder than his neighbours will invariably have a surplus. He now has several choices how to utilise this surplus. If he is a socially minded so-called do-gooder he would give his surplus to all his neighbours who are not doing as well and he would be loved by all and probably elected to run the place. Unfortunately in doing so he is not actually doing anyone any favours at all since they will become dependent on his supply and will starve if one year his harvest is not as great as thought. The society around him will basically stand still and remain slaves to circumstances. His second choice would be to conclude that he doesn't really have to work as hard as all that and stake back his endeavours to match his requirement. Now the others are left out and all will still be subject to the circumstances around them. The third choice is the one that actually does some good to everyone. The farmer markets his surplus, engages the people in the village and increases his output. He can now invest to increase his plantations and generate sufficient produce to trade with other villages for building supplies for example. He will now need a means of transport and engage drivers and warehouse workers and suddenly the whole village is busy generating wealth, everybody is happy and has means of supporting themselves and that is the role of the entrepreneurial system as compared to the socialist system.

Back to Trading and Transactions

So far, so good and it made sense for everyone's survival. The point here is that once upon a time man was free and from these first steps a system of economics developed in order for these people to get along and live together. It must be emphasized here that this system developed itself based on human behaviour and was not imposed from the outside or controlled by anything but individual decisions as to what is good for each person's own self-interest. This may sound a bit harsh, but we need to keep in mind that during free barter each participant needs to arrive at the conclusion that they have made the better bargain – from their point of view.

Thus the whole of economics is simply this: Two entities trading –

buying and selling – whatever it is that needs to be exchanged. This is the only underlying factor, whether it is two individuals making a sale or large corporations arranging million Dollar contracts – every time it is exchanging one good or service for another in a transaction. The world is completely saturated with this activity all day every day in all places from going shopping for food to travelling; even going to work for somebody is such a transaction. What the government does are transactions and what the central banks do are transactions. Even collecting taxes is a transaction in that the government takes your money and uses it to look after your country's safety and welfare – whether you agree or not. Some of these transactions may not be in the form of actual money but can be in the form of credit – for example in the purchase of a car or a house or large investment. In this case the seller finances your purchase instead of you laying out the money and this can also be a third party rather than the seller. But we need to keep in mind that this credit has been created on the spur of the moment, because it is not actual money generated from productivity. It is more like a thought bubble but contains the reality that the credit amount must be repaid at some time in the future. The amount of credit in the world far outweighs the amount of actual funds in existence and this makes credit at the same time a most useful and the most dangerous arrangement and the implications of this will be dealt with later in the book.

But back to bartering for now. In keeping with the bartering of items, eventually something was needed to allow an easy transfer of these credit vouchers, and since other smaller objects proved to be easier to keep and carry around people decided on the value of such items and started using them in their society. One of these items used to be the Cowrie shell, which was widely used in the Pacific region and parts of Africa until fairly recently.

In the distant past, for example during the Sumerian period in Mesopotamia, there is plentiful evidence that direct bartering did not take place in that sense, but that all transactions were captured by scribes, and endless lists of who owned and owed what have been found. Each bartered item was assigned an equivalent worth in silver and written down as such so that for example a bushel of grain was worth one shekel in silver. The silver did exist somewhere, but was not traded as money in coins, only the equivalent values were recorded resulting in a system of debt records. It is interesting to note that credit seems to have mainly been handled by the temples, who acted as a quasi-bank loaning money and collecting interest, some of it at what today would be considered usurious levels of 20% or more. There existed also small clay tokens with representations of jars of beer, loaves of bread and all manner of animals which were an indirect form of money in a way as they could be called for from the issuer. The idea of charging interest seems to have been based on the procreation of animals – say someone lent 10 sheep for a year to someone else, they would expect to receive back more than 10 since they would have had offspring in the meantime. As a side effect this lending of items led to the invention of the earliest calendars which were required to capture the length of time that something had been lent out.

Since the shovel maker and many others needed metals for their products, small pieces of metal had a definite value in accordance with the grade of difficulty of obtaining them. As a result everyone agreed that some small amounts of things like copper, iron and later bronze were useful in the exchange of goods equivalency. The remains of this type of value exchange are still with us today in the usage of the word pound in a number of languages. It refers back to a time when the exchange was accomplished by trading a pound of copper, iron, lead etc. or equal portions thereof and in ancient Rome this copper pound was divided into 12 ounces. It is important to note here that at the time of the trade the metal was actually weighed to ensure that you received the correct value and, although this tended to be cumbersome, it provided confidence.

As once again business was roaring, a lot of people required items to show off their good standing – and also to prepare for possibly worse times in the future or putting something aside for their offspring so they would be grateful and look after the parents in their old age! And, sure enough, some materials proved to be just what was needed to fulfil this desire – silver and gold. They could be made into jewellery; they were easily carried or hidden and were universally acceptable as members of society grew generally wealthier. This coin making endeavour was usually taken over by the powers that be, whatever the governing body was, and few were democratic. Thus governments would issue coins with imprinted identification stamps, usually to the glorification of the 'Supremo'. These coins were to become known as *currency*. [Medieval Latin *currentia,* literally: a flowing, from Latin *currere* to run, flow]

And of course this is where the term pound sterling originated, representing a pound of silver of a known fineness and bearing a stamp. But even at this point things were not as simple as all that. Since the government tended also to incur debt the temptation was there to gradually reduce the content of the coins by either reducing the weight, or by alloying the metal with lesser content and consequently allowing other debtors to also reduce their debts by such deceit. This subsequently resulted in a form of inflation since the population quite well understood that money had lost some value every time. If once there was rock solid confidence in the coinage when metal was weighed during a trade, we now have abandoned this confidence to the greed of government by controlling trade in its favour. And not much has changed since that moment. The so-called Federal Reserve looks after that aspect very fastidiously.

And finally, underlying all this trading activity is an important consideration: there must be an acceptance of the concept of *private property*. If the person who possesses an item to be traded does not have ownership of that item, no trade can take place and all human prosperity is stifled. This for example is why many societies based on communistic principles will not prosper simply because nobody can trade individually, only the state can accept your product on their terms. And what's more, this private property principle must be guaranteed by the government at hand, it is the one thing that is most useful about having decent governance.

An extension to this thought is the proposition that in fact the main purpose of a government for the economy is to provide protection for the business activities. The government must establish a legal system to protect the property and the revenue of businesses, as well as individuals. Laws must be developed and enforced to protect from illegal activities, to support contracts and ensure fair dealing between traders inside and outside of the country. This is also presuming that the society has at least a modicum of integrity and morals, insofar as the attitude to corruption, blackmail and bribery is concerned. A society cannot thrive where taxes and revenue are used for personal enrichment and to support only those connected to the government while ignoring support for the population and business.

And ultimately, that is the totality of what a government should be concerned with: a legal system for internal and external security and the guarantee of private property. Anything beyond that can be looked after by the population directly.

A Bit of History

One year, a wheat farmer reaped a lot more wheat than he expected and had lots extra. He now wanted to show off and ordered an automatic, solar powered and chromed shovel to impress others. Other farmers also had a good time and bought more fancy shovels, so that the shovel maker now received a lot more wheat credits and looked around for something extra as well. Some clever individual noticed all this additional income and saw all the wheat credits the shovel maker had and made a proposal: Let me look after all this credit for you, for a modest fee, and if I can use it you'll get an *interest* from that.

Interest is a thing that works both ways: If someone has surplus funds these can be made to work and produce an income through generating interest. In order to make this proposition profitable the funds must actually be used to produce something else of value, since the money itself is of no use at all. Thus these funds get loaned out to someone who needs them to create more value through their endeavours, and this entity will have to pay a premium above the

17

interest offered to the depositor of the funds. The difference goes to the arranger of all this, nowadays usually a bank. The difference is the banks profit and is called the *spread,* usually between ½ and 1%.

In order to use the farmer's funds to generate more income and to register this credit the person invented a piece of paper which was to represent so much value, or equivalent values of commodities. While at this point the coins or pieces of paper still represented a material value and had the intrinsic value of the metal or the amount of product written on the paper, a time soon arrived when this became divorced. That is when governments interfered and issued pieces of paper of their own. This government money not backed by gold is called *fiat money* and exists because the population must accept that its value is what it claims to be.

The earliest record of paper money comes from China, they tended to be ahead of others in those days. The first paper banknotes appeared in China about 806 AD. The first use of paper was for letters of credit which needed to be transferred over large distances, a practice which the government quickly took over from private concerns. This practice was referred to as "flying money" because it was so light and could blow out of one's hand. The first paper money was, strictly speaking, a draft rather than real money. A merchant could deposit his cash in the capital, receiving a paper certificate which he could then exchange for cash in the provinces. The government soon used it for the forwarding of local taxes and revenues to the capital. The printed notes were normally military scrip or other emergency measures issued in dire circumstances, but for the most part these notes disappeared quickly. The first real use of a paper money system was in Szechwan province, an isolated area subject to frequent copper shortages (which is a component of bronze). It had reverted to an iron currency of coins, and paper was a welcome option. Iron banks sprang up to facilitate the trade, and the government was quick to take over the profitable enterprise. As always where money is concerned everyone wanted to get into the act and by the 15th century paper notes were being issued irresponsibly so that their value rapidly depreciated and inflation soared. Additionally, forgeries became more common and trust in the currency deteriorated. Paper money was abandoned by 1455 and next reappeared in Europe in 1661.

By this time banks abounded in Europe but all used solid materials that were kept in storage or interbank notes, an early version of a check. The first issuer of paper money was Sweden, where in 1661 Johan Palmstruch's *Stockholm Banco* introduced the first banknotes, but still based on deposited copper and silver plates at the bank. The difference was that these notes were on printed paper forms in round denominations and without specifying a depositor, a deposit or any interest demand. The notes were payable to bearer, possession of the note was sufficient to constitute a claim to the bank. Finally, the notes were issued by an institution having the status of a central bank. Other European countries soon followed the Swedish lead and in 1694 the Bank of England was established and was soon printing "running cash notes". These notes were initially handwritten on Bank paper and signed by one of the Bank's cashiers. They were made out for the precise sum deposited in pounds, shillings and pence. However, after the recoinage of 1696 reduced the need for small denomination notes, it was decided not to issue any notes for sums of less than £50. Since the average income in this period was less than £20 a year, most people went through life without ever coming into contact with banknotes.

The recoinage of 1696 was an early example of government interference and the subsequent unintended consequences. The problem of monetary confidence had been developing through the late 1600s and came to a head in 1696 when the standard of coins had deteriorated to such an extent that the government was receiving a fraction of the coin value as indicated by the coins. The problem lay in the use of minted silver and gold coins which over time had been clipped, thus reducing their weight as indicated. Poor quality stamping produced coins that were off-centre and even the addition of milling around the edges was no guarantee that the coin was full weight. Coins could be clipped or shaved around the edges and still continue in circulation. The cuttings were melted and sold as bullion.

What used to be a minor nuisance became critical in 1696 when about half of the indicated weight of total coinage was simply no longer there. At times the bullion price of silver exceeded the indicated coinage value and complete coins were melted down and sold as bullion; for example in Holland where the bullion price was higher than in England. At the time England was at war with France and it was imperative to maintain revenue to support the war.

A very high powered team including William Lowndes, John Locke, Isaac Newton, Charles Davenant and others were tasked with resolving this impasse. After much discussion and writing, the decision was taken to re-establish the original value of the silver coin and reissue new specie via the Bank of England, in preference to a devaluation of the silver coins in accordance to their usage value. This was to take place in a specific short time frame to collect all old coins and reissue new ones of correct weight. Not all business was carried out using coins, there was already an appreciation of the value of credit present and most daily transactions were recorded on Tallies and Bank Notes, the first admission of paper money. What happened next would be perfectly predictable with hindsight: Everybody desired the new coins, the system was unable to deliver new species as the demand rose, and there was a 'run' on the Bank of England. The silver was mainly tied up in returned clipped coinage and the Mint was unable to deliver sufficient coins – the total value of specie in circulation was greatly reduced. Thus, soon after the final date of recoinage, the Bank of England was forced to default on its commitments to Continental creditors and any confidence in English credit evaporated. Only with additional support from the Dutch government became it possible later that year for payments to resume.

Up to this time gold had been a secondary medium and silver had been used almost exclusively for daily transactions. With the new coins being ordered the ratio of value to the gold Guinea changed drastically and the Guinea became overvalued trading as high as 30shillings. Over the ensuing years the Guinea had to be progressively revalued until it finally fixed at 21shillings. During this time the importance of silver diminished greatly and gold became the only standard in the realm. Despite all efforts the outflow of silver continued and in 1774 another recoinage took place, this time to combat the deterioration of the gold coins.

It was not until England introduced the gold standard in 1816 that the paper represented an equivalent material value backed by a reliable government.

Some Theory

Now for the economics bit: all of this is really run by smoke and mirrors. Imagine for a moment the shovel maker just stored his shovels in a shed, or the farmer kept all his grain in a silo. Nothing happens. The system only works if there is *circulation* of value. There is only this one underlying secret to the economy: money must circulate. The wages you earn enable you to buy things you need and want, which in turn enables others to earn money for their own expenditures. If we stop spending the whole thing falls apart! And as downturns in the economy have shown, it doesn't take much loss of confidence to affect the spending pattern of the population. Even a 5% - 7% reduction in spending removes sufficient funds from circulation to force some businesses that are marginal to close and you'll see the For Rent signs going up in High Street. It is now immediately obvious, if the population has a low confidence in the government they have elected, people will become more cautious and spend more carefully. Usually when this occurs the government will try and improve their image with spectacular new plans and programs after which the normal outcome is more uncertainty and more restraint in spending.

Since this book approaches economics from a lay perspective it is important to keep in mind how economic studies started. Back when people bartered there was no formal 'economy' and everyone got on with one another, well mostly. People simply decided what they wanted to do in life and how to make a living and then proceeded down that path. It was only when others, usually governments at first and then large corporations and banks started to interfere with this process that such a thing as an economy was defined and then required analysing and dissecting and book writing. Much like the lawyer's trade, the importance of the economist was an artificially created undertaking. In this context it is important to understand that an 'economy' as such, as a single unit, does not exist; there are only individuals that make up an economy by acting in voluntary unison and cooperation. A lot of abstract economic thinking always seems to want to analyse an economy as a whole and guide or direct this entity, and invariably this does not work simply because the individuals respond each in their own unpredictable way and not as an economic whole.

When spending ones valuable time analysing economical and financial matters it is important to keep in mind what money is: a financial good, an item of trade. When we started, the shovel maker needed food which he got from people who produced food, and with whom he traded shovels. Now he needs some tiles for the roof, but the tiler has no need for shovels, but he still needs to buy food. The monetary note or item, piece of gold, silver or copper that intercedes at this point is simply a surrogate product that stands in for the value of goods you have produced until you can then trade for the item you really wanted. On the other hand that surrogate product is still just another good to be traded and has no intrinsic value: only that what the users assign to it. So, if these money items become more abundant their value will lower accordingly and we have what is called inflation. More about that later.

As an additional novel advantage a key benefit of the involvement of money is that it makes possible the calculation of profit and loss as well as future allocation of resources by entrepreneurs thus leading to greater economic progress.

So let's Analyse

The whole basis of traditional economics seems to be based on the presumption that people desire an unlimited amount of stuff while offering as little as possible in return. In between these extremes lies the area of negotiation. Thus economics also becomes a study of human behaviour and a social science. Unfortunately it is also assumed that people's behaviour in this endeavour is rational, and, as the world around us proves, this is not always the case. Anyone who has invested in the stock market in the past will tell you that it runs on madness and is driven by greed and fear – fear of losing your money, fear of not making as much on your investment as Joe down the road, fear that the government will do something stupid and ruin your life, and so on. People are also assumed to act only in their own self-interest, but they don't necessarily know what is best for their self-interest, resulting in some pretty irrational behaviour in the economy. We will also learn that economic theories abound on all sides and are all considered equivalent, depending on whom you are listening to.

Underlying this is the economic concept of *scarcity*. This points out that no matter what you are looking at, there is only a limited supply of it. The best example is time, which is most definitely limited and therefore one must make sure it is used efficiently when trying to generate an income. So scarcity refers to such as insufficient resources, goods, or abilities to achieve the desired ends. The term is actually a relative one, as scarcity can have different underlying reasons. There is a basic scarcity of things that are just not there in large quantities as gold and diamonds and this is reflected in their price (not value!). Then there are things that have only relative scarcity related to abundance of either availability or location. Water is scarce in the desert but not in the tropical jungle. Then there is a perceived scarcity as is happening with oil and gas supplies. As these are being used the cry went out that we would be running out of both, but when more pressure was applied it turns out that both are now again abundant due to new technology and more effort in finding resources. There is a variable scarcity for example in food stuffs. When the weather is favourable there is usually a glut of food and when some disaster happens food will become scarce as it cannot be stored indefinitely. When a new invention or device is placed on the market at first it will be scarce since there is high demand and limited production resulting in a high price. As the item permeates the market and competitors appear it will become abundant and the price will adjust accordingly. Finally there is an imagined scarcity such as with very expensive fine wine: most people would not be able to tell if a wine was really so good as to be worth $3000 a bottle, but for those who can afford this it presents a scarcity as truly there are only a few bottles available.

In economic terms the use of *scarce* always refers to the fact that there may be lots of a particular good, but it is limited and needs to be valued to be able to trade.

We can now see where a kind of 'pure' economy came from and how over time it became perverted. The early stage of bartering presented the first stage of a 'free enterprise' system, although it was not an imposed system in that sense – it was simply individuals acting in their own self-preservation and self-interest. This self-interest lies at the core of all economic thinking, if this thinking is kept on a rational level. To deny self-interest as a core principle leads into a delusional world and to destruction in the real world for those who subsequently suffer under imposed systems of economic autocracy. Free enterprise has allowed the human genius to roam freely and create wealth and prosperity at a scale previously unknown in history. The famous Samuel Johnson quote: *"There are few ways in which a man can be more innocently employed than in getting money"* sums up the reality of self-interest very well indeed. This is not to say that things always work out in the best reality, but the vast majority functions well. However, it is these few instances of free enterprise slipping up that provided the wedge for interference by authorities trying to impose their will upon society.

A concept required at this point is that of 'supply and demand'. No other concept has caused more excitement amongst economists and produced more varying interpretations and arguments. Whole theories on economies have been created out of nothing around this concept and more fallacies swirl around this simple thought. Looking back at the shovel maker we saw that he makes the shovels by his

24

own hand and sells them to the people who need one. That is the supply side. If nobody wants his shovels he is out of business again and has wasted his efforts. If they become immensely popular he will need to employ people to help him make more shovels. Of course he can help his case by publicising his wonderful shovel and spread quotes from people who have been happy with his product. He cannot fundamentally alter the fact of how many people are actually in a position to want one of his shovels. If you live in an apartment it is unlikely you'll need a shovel, if you don't care for gardening or are not gaining a living in agriculture it will be impossible to sell you a shovel. So the basis of the market is the total possible demand for shovels and this demand cannot be increased by an increase in the supply of shovels, regardless of price. Since this man also needs to live he will take the income from the shovels and purchase some grain. The demand for shovels now becomes his demand for grain and many other goods – supply and demand are the two sides of the interaction, they are in essence equivalent.

The consideration that goes hand in hand with this demand is that of a fair price. Shovels must be made and sold at a price that allows the manufacturer a decent living and at the same time the shovel must be priced so that the potential buyer does not think he is being overcharged. This approach was recognised as early as ancient Greece when Aristotle spent a lot of verbiage on a theory of economics in society. He realised here for example that the just price is the harmonic mean of the maximum the buyer is willing to pay and the minimum the seller is willing to accept, which nowadays seems quite rational and obvious.

Above all it must be understood that nothing can happen until there is a supply. First the entrepreneur must generate a product to put on the market and then the demand establishes itself accordingly. We only establish the power to purchase if we have produced and sold something in order to acquire the means to engage in consumption. Most current economic wisdom seems to be based on the idea that if you give people money they will create demand and in turn supply. This is a fallacy: The investment to make products must be made before a demand can appear. A demand for goods is not a demand for labour. Or in the words of John Stuart Mill: "...*to purchase produce is not to employ labour; that the demand for labour is constituted by the wages which precede the production, and not by the demand which may exist for the commodities resulting from the production.*" This may be difficult to comprehend, but it simply says that the investment money must be spent to create goods – only when they have been created can they be sold. This investment consists of three components: The cost of the property where the work is undertaken, the cost of the labour and materials required to produce the goods and the revenue stream for the entrepreneur. It is pointless to give someone money to purchase goods that have not been created, since the people that need to invest money are the ones that provide the supply first. If the money is not available to make goods no amount of demand can create them. This topic will come up again later, so be prepared.

Consider this example: The government gives everyone $1000 to stimulate the economy, to create demand. The people now go out and look for goods to purchase. If these goods are on the shelves, then the money to make them has already been spent and no new value is added by buying them with taxpayer's money. If these goods are not there, they cannot be created by the people who have been given free money simply demanding them. Where will the new supply of goods come from after the stimulus money has been spent? First of all money has to be invested to create goods to put on the shelves before anyone can have a demand – otherwise your shelves will be bare. Furthermore the money the government gives away is only tax revenue, and once again we are talking redistribution from one part of society to another. The people who had to give up tax money could have easily spent these funds for their own purposes.

Finally, you cannot create demand without first creating value adding supply. Governments have no idea how to create value so virtually everything they spend money on cannot add to demand or supply. This is why the stimulus has failed everywhere it has been tried.

Income and wealth are not distributed - they are created and earned by their creators.

Just to recap what we have here: Demand refers to how much (quantity) of a product or service is desired by buyers. The quantity demanded is the amount of a product customers are willing to buy at a certain price. Supply represents the quantity of a product that is on offer in the market. The quantity supplied refers to the amount of a certain good producers are willing to supply when receiving a certain price. Price thus is a reflection of supply and demand. Let's also keep in mind that these market exchanges are voluntary and peaceful which makes them infinitely preferable to coercive or enforced methods of distribution such as proposed under socialist or communist systems.

The meaning of *prices* in the market cannot be emphasized enough. Prices are generated to reflect the underlying realities of the market; prices inform producers and consumers about how best to coordinate their actions with each other and also to give incentives to countless producers and consumers to adjust and coordinate their actions with each other. The budding economist *must* understand that prices are what drives the whole world in a predictable manner. How billions of people all looking out for their own interests will function together in cooperation to supply all of us with our daily needs and fill the shelves continuously. None of this would happen if prices were imposed by decree or by sellers on buyers, such as happens under price controls, rationing or as is happening with minimum wage laws.

The whole system of how this works seems a very fragile one. The investors are required to put up funds for products that will only be on a shelf much later. For staples such as food and drink this is fairly straightforward - the population needs certain things continually. For more complex items of consumption the entrepreneur carries the risk that they may not sell as well as expected or not at all. Yet, throughout history the vast majority of businesses have got it right and humanity has always been provided with what is desired and only a small percentage of products have failed entirely, usually because something better was there already or appeared at the same time such as the Beta video recorder or the 8-track cartridge. The underlying reason for this is because of the *structure* of demand, which means that the exact amount and type of goods that are demanded by the market are supplied by the businesses. As long as the market is free, that is uninhibited by government or union distortions, history has proven that it gets it right almost all the time. It is rare for shortages to impede supply, usually due to some meteorological nastiness or something like uncontrolled strikes. Over time and sometimes quite rapidly the market changes and all the participants must react to compensate. Technology advances, social attitudes change and affect whole sections as happens in the clothing industry continually for example. In this case the change is solely based on the buyer's preferences and they can be fickle.

In the words of Ludwig von Mises:

The real bosses, in the capitalist system of market economy, are the consumers. They, by their buying and by their abstention from buying, decide who should own the capital and run the plants. They determine what should be produced and in what quantity and quality. Their attitudes result either in profit or in loss for the enterpriser. They make poor men rich and rich men poor. They are no easy bosses. They are full of whims and fancies, changeable and unpredictable. They do not care a whit for past merit. As soon as something is offered to them that they like better or that is cheaper, they desert their old purveyors. With them nothing counts more than their own satisfaction. They bother neither about the vested interests of capitalists nor about the fate of the workers who lose their jobs if, as consumers, they no longer buy what they used to buy.

During the Reagan/Thatcher years the term 'supply side economics' was a constant companion in the media and caused reams of discussion and also a lot of vituperation by its opponents. The theory is quite simple once again: Support those that produce a supply of goods. This can be done in three ways: reduce taxes on corporations, reduce regulatory oppression on companies and use monetary policy to control money supply. Sounds all very straightforward. The underlying thought is that if life is made easier for these companies, their owners and managers will try to expand the business with more goods or better goods and increase turnover. When taxes are lowered the additional money is put back into a company to increase business and employ more workers. If regulations are eased it will make a better business case and the changes can be introduced more rapidly, not having to wait for many different government levels and departments to agree and give their permission. And if the money supply is appropriate it will be easier to borrow financing for production and for expansion. There is also a confidence aspect that arises when companies feel the government is actually behind them and gives support for this expansion and any improvements. All this will lead to lower unemployment since the economy is speeding up.

The opponents of supply side economics maintain that only the consumer drives the market and that only demand stimulates production, and – when this demand falls – only government intervention in the form of stimulus money can overcome this downturn in activity. The flaw in this thinking is that all the goods that a stimulus demand may remove from their shelves have already been made and paid for – there is no additional activity since the manufacturers of those goods will need to invest more money up front to produce more goods and pay their employees, and, if economic conditions are not positive, he is unlikely to do so. The workers who earn an income by producing goods can now spend their income on items produced by other workers in other enterprises. The upshot is that the stimulus money has not put the incentive where it was required – it is just a feel good exercise and shows that the government is doing something. The government cannot stimulate the economy; it can only move money around. To allow some people to spend more money it will make others spend less, and politicians insist they know how to differentiate between people who should have more and those who should have less. Apart from causing injustice here, bureaucrats cannot know the needs of people intimately. The perfect example has been the recent 2008 crisis where all the stimulus money in the world has not reduced unemployment in the USA or Europe. This type of thinking is based on treating an economy like a single organism or a machine that can be controlled in its entirety, but there is no such organism, an economy consists of individuals acting on their own behalf inside the boundaries created by the same ruling elite, and each individual will react differently to a particular situation.

Just to reinforce the importance of this thought: When entrepreneurs are encouraged to invest money in business, more goods are made available and wealth actually increases. Through the production of goods their employees have earned money they can now spend other goods. If you apply stimulus money by giving it away, it becomes a simple redistribution and no goods are produced and no wealth is added. That is the difference!

Opportunities

Since hardly anyone has unlimited funds to obtain all the things they want in life, certain decisions have to be taken, that is, what do I spend my money on and how much should these items cost. The term *'opportunity cost'* refers to this process. It means what an individual would forgo in order to obtain a certain desired item. Obviously, depending on the necessity and usefulness of the item to be purchased most of the time this is not difficult. The farmer needing a shovel has to buy one. His circumstances may lead him to buy a low cost shovel if he has little funds or a more expensive one if funds are available. If he decides to buy the more expensive one, he has to forgo some other thing that the extra money could have purchased. When it comes to items that are not necessities, the struggle for these funds becomes very noticeable in the form of advertising. Whether you buy chewing gum or another soft drink becomes life or death for commercial manufacturers; which company can convince you their automobile gives you more value makes or breaks that product.

This opportunity cost is of course a relative thing, different for each individual and changeable during someone's life. If the person earns more or less, at some stage the opportunity cost will change depending on his circumstances. With a much higher income the person will invariably raise the threshold and splurge on more expensive holidays or higher value personal toys.

Buying and Selling

Let's now look a bit closer at the process of what happens between a buyer and a seller. There seems to be an opinion about stipulating that this process only happens between equals, i.e. people of equal wealth. That may be the case where the shovel maker and the farmer trade directly and in turn then trade with a chicken farmer: all are in the same stratum of society. But, as things develop in that society, some people are much better at production and at trading and become much wealthier than others. This does not remove them from the trading cycle, it simply widens the field for their trades. Having more money to spend allows the wealthy to purchase luxuries others can't afford. Surplus funds may be invested in collecting new art in the form of paintings or sculpture, in turn enabling a poorer artist to buy food and more materials. Thus wealth spent allows a lot of very specialized knowledge to be supported such as in building yachts or gardening or the architectural industries. Some of this spending is not always obvious as to its extent. Let's say a couple goes to the opera or a concert, expending maybe 500 Dollars simply for their entertainment. To some this reeks of elitism and wasted money that could have been better spent on humanitarian improvements or supporting some homeless. Following the path of what is behind the scene results in quite a different picture. The income derived from a large number of people joining together for their 'entertainment' supports first of all the existence of the venue and all its employees and support staff. It supports the lives of the performers and stage hands and all their families. Next in line are people who coach and guide the performers throughout their life as well as the artisans who manufacture and constantly improve the instruments used by the performers and these in turn need the support of the suppliers of high

31

quality and specialized materials for the manufacture, and so on.

What really matters in trade is more a consideration of relative value. A person with limited means must carefully consider where the money is spent and what the priorities are. Take the case of a poor person being given the opportunity to buy a good iron and ironing board. To others it may seem a mundane necessity not to be worried about too much – it is simply acquired. To the poorer person it may represent an opportunity to now offer a service of ironing the clothes of others and being able to earn a modest living from this. So the actual value to that person is much greater than what a $200 iron and ironing board represents sitting in a shop. Now simply scale this up to larger business and we find similar circumstances. Sometimes there are reports about enormous amounts of income generated by large mining or manufacturing companies and the public usually believes that these are excessive and we would all be better off if prices were generally lower instead. What is not seen here is the amount of money that has been invested to realize the enormous income that is required. The investment for mines runs into billions of Dollars, it takes many years for a large mine to come on stream and all this investment needs to be financed in the intervening non-productive period.

This leads us to a term used when large sums are expended for a business and that is the ROI – *Return on Investment*. In its simplest form this is the ratio of a gain realized against the original investment. So if $500 is invested and the gain is $50, the ROI is 10%. Taking an investment say for a large mining project the sums become more complex. There is the ongoing cost of investing in the project, the financing cost and the nowadays very large costs of complying with governmental and environmental regulations. There are always surprises in large projects such as weather not cooperating or strikers not cooperating. When the project is completed there is no immediate payout. There will be operating costs to mine the ore, shipping costs to bring it to the customer and maintenance costs of the equipment. Against this there will be revenue in a steady stream, if all goes well. The installation will now be written off over a certain period of time, say 20 years, and the difference between the revenue stream and the operating costs is now the return on the investment. All the risk lies with the operator of the mine and ultimately the outcome will be a positive cash flow producing a net income. This income will be taxed by the government. Next there will be a multitude of shareholders, and for a large corporation the number of outstanding shares will be in the hundreds of millions or over even billions. These will need to have dividends paid out otherwise the share price will fall and it will become more difficult for the company to obtain financing. Any money after that is usually paid back into the company for improvements and productivity increases, or for the next project..

Looking at another example taken from the automotive industry, a similar investment is necessary. Currently it requires an outlay of about a billion Dollars to bring a new model to the market, and again financing this has to come from the manufacturer. This model will remain on the market for 5 years without a major change and so the production line has to finance $200 million per year. If the market will accept 100 000 cars per year the cost burden per vehicle is $2000 to recoup the investment, which for a vehicle costing $40 000 represents 5% of the sales price and this makes for a good business case. Should the market turn away from this product, the burden on the vehicle will increase and quite quickly lead to a loss situation, and this is what has happened for example to the Australian motor industry where an influx of more imported models and a change in buyer preferences led to a total collapse of the motor industry. It is nowadays imperative for a motor vehicle company to operate in many markets simultaneously to maintain the sales volume and allow financing of future products as well.

On the other side the relative value argument is identical: in the case where a large wealthy corporation requires the services of specialised knowledge, an individual or a much smaller company will have bargaining power to the extent that the use of that knowledge is far more valuable to the corporation's future business income than to the individual possessing it. Therefore it is advantageous for the corporation to pay a good fee to the individual for that specialised knowledge. This applies nowadays in particular to certain computer programming work, which has become quite specialised, so that different industries need very narrowly trained individuals to manage their particular concerns. In order to concentrate on their expertise, the mining industry requires detailed analysis of the soils and geology. Thus an independent and experienced geologist with good equipment can command large fees for supplying reliable information about the availability of raw materials to be mined.

Supply and Demand – Take II

The law of demand states that, if all other factors remain equal, the higher the price of a good, the fewer people will demand that good. The number of items that buyers purchase at a higher price is lower because, as the price of a good goes up, the opportunity cost of buying that item has increased. As a result, people will naturally avoid buying a product that will force them to forgo the consumption of something else they value more.

Similar to the law of demand, the law of supply demonstrates the quantities that will be sold at a certain price. The law of supply states that the quantity of a good supplied (i.e., the quantity owners or producers offer for sale) rises as the market price rises, and falls as the price falls. This simply implies that a producer will increase supply if he can make a good profit and look for something else to make if the profit on current production is inadequate. On the demand side the buyer will purchase more of a product at a lower price than at a higher price, which also means that more people can afford an item at a lower price or to buy it more frequently.

A commonly cited example is the so-called pork (or hog) cycle. There is a fixed supply of pork in the market and supply balances demand and as this is quite steady and predictable, the producers make a good profit at this level. As others notice this, more suppliers begin to enter the market and to compete they have to offer the product at a slightly lower price while still making a good profit.

Now the total supply of pork has increased and according to the law, the price will come down. Since it takes a few months to breed up a marketable weight of hog, quite suddenly the market now floods at a certain later time and the prices crash. This forces some producers out of the market until a new equilibrium has been found – just to be disturbed again by the next cycle and so on. Oddly enough whole tomes of books have been produced just analyzing and expanding on theories derived from this cycle, so if you want to pick up a book about the pork cycle or supply in general they should be quite reasonably priced.

Since supply and demand are closely interrelated, the effect of the system produces what is called *equilibrium*. Nobody wants to pay more than an item's realistic worth and no manufacturer wants to produce goods that are too expensive for that product. In a free market this automatically comes about since an equilibrium price (also known as a *"market-clearing"* price) is one at which each producer can sell all he wants to produce, and each consumer can buy all he demands. Naturally, producers always would like to charge higher prices. But even if they have no competitors, they are limited by the law of demand: if producers insist on a higher price, consumers will buy fewer units. The law of supply puts a similar limit on consumers. They always would prefer to pay a lower price than the current one. But if they successfully insist on paying less, as would happen if there are price controls, suppliers will produce less and some demand will go unsatisfied.

Human labour is also a form of product in supply and demand and it is regulated by the income generated for the individual. When left to market forces, the cost of labour, that is the individual's income, will also find its equilibrium. Each manufactured item contains a component of labour as part of its selling price along with the cost of raw materials, overheads and profit. If any component of these is artificially altered the product will face difficulties in matching demand. These interferences can be tariffs, taxes, monopolies, unions and even criminal elements or minimum wage laws.

An Interlude

With all this business and making money going on, we need to introduce another concept that Adam Smith made a great deal of in his book 'The Wealth of Nations', and that is the *division of labour*. Our shovel maker above needs a number of components for his product: there would be the metal shovel portion, a wooden shaft, a handle and some fastening part to attach the shovel to the handle. If he were to make all parts himself it would take a long time and he would need to be knowledgeable in woodworking, in steelmaking and smithing and in screw or rivet making as well. Behind these components are further steps of iron ore mining, smelting and refining, of wood felling and lumber preparation and so on. The end result is simply that people need to co-operate and specialize where everyone contributes a share and receives a share in return. Ultimately the shovel maker is more of a shovel assembler, although he may have specified exactly via drawings and specifications the parts he requires. The mining is done by one group of individuals who then deliver the ore to the smelter people who produce raw metals and later make alloys from this. These now need to be rolled and manipulated so that other products can be made from the steel. The road for the wooden handle is similar, from growing and felling trees to treating the wood to cutting and later, using machines to shape the piece of wood like a handle in this case. The shovel maker alone could probably only produce a single handle and a single metal shovel part in a day and could not possibly have the machinery required to make these parts. So the division of labour comes about naturally in a society. The ultimate form is the production line such as for automobiles. Even here what you see in an assembly plant is only the last step of assembling the vehicle - all components have been more or less pre-assembled in other locations and are simply delivered at the right time to be fitted to a car. There is a wonderful short film about this process on the web called *I, Pencil.*

Thus, when we hear that competition is ruining society, it is once again one of these fallacies that abound in the economic world. All the participants have to *co-operate* to be able to generate products at all. The only competition is in the open market end where the manufacturers are forced to maintain their supply, their quality and plenty of innovation against others, who would offer more to the consumer. This works in favour of the consumer and of society as a whole by producing an ever increasing stream of quality products and new innovative items to make everyone's life better or easier or more fun.

This line of thought can even be extended a little further and include the situation where the anonymity and impersonality of the market will lead to unexpected co-operation, since even people who dislike one another are led to work together for mutual benefit. In the words of Milton Friedman:

"The great virtue of a free market system is that it does not care what colour people are; it does not care what their religion is; it only cares whether they can produce something you want to buy. It is the most effective system we have discovered to enable people who hate one another to deal with one another and help one another."

Thus the market process actually leads to everyone having an equal opportunity, even those who are unpopular and unpleasant, and so the market becomes an instigator of social peace.

When all the participants in a country are working together and producing things and consuming things, it becomes necessary to determine exactly how much is being produced. The basis for this is called the *Gross Domestic Product* or GDP for short. As we have already seen, as soon as we have a quantification of something, arguments start about what that means. As a starting point, it is a measure of all the monetary value of final goods and services, that is, those that are bought by final users, produced in a country in a year. It counts all of the output generated within the borders of a country. GDP is composed of goods and services produced for sale in the market and it also includes some nonmarket production, such as defense or education services provided by the government. The calculation is done following an internationally established process as contained in the *System of National Accounts*, 1993, compiled by the International Monetary Fund, the European Commission, the Organization for Economic Cooperation and Development, the United Nations, and the World Bank.

More importantly, in order to compare year to year GDP accounts, the monetary value needs to be adjusted for inflation every year. This 'real' GDP allows us to see if the growth in output has been due to increased productivity or simply an increase in prices. GDP is measured in the currency of the country, and to compare the GDP of different countries the values are usually converted into US Dollars at the rate for that year. However, for a more realistic comparison of the living standard for each country, what must also be adjusted is the purchasing power of each, that is, what is the cost to purchase the same quantity of goods and services under local conditions.

Ultimately the value of GDP is still a very relative thing and lends itself to abuse by the powers in charge of its calculation. Firstly there can be no absolute value for any item, only a value at one market price for everything sold. But if there is a sudden popularity for bananas and their price doubles it would show up at higher production value, but it would still be the same amount of bananas except valued more highly – there would not have been an increase in production. Since all government services are included, if civil servants get a 5% increase in salary, surely it cannot be said that this portion of GDP has increased by 5% as well, as these employees could not and would not actually increase productivity. If there is a severe drop in demand for government services, all these employees are still there, 'producing' something at their desks, and are counted regardless of the output. It is much more the case that government services has no value in the first place, being there to obstruct, harass, harm and make itself generally obnoxious to business and the general population.

Looking a little closer at the government component of GDP, it becomes counterproductive to the real evaluation of the economy. Say a country produces $1000 of real goods and $200 are taken away in taxes and spent by the government, then the GDP calculation will show GDP = $1200. It consists of the $1000 of goods and $200 of whatever the value of the government service is. If now the government spends $100 less next year, then the GDP will decline to $1100, even though the real goods manufactured are still $1000. Makes sense? Now, if we were to say that the GDP has no input from the government, then in the first case it would become $1000 minus the taxes of $200 and a net GDP of $800. When now the taxes are reduced by $100 the proper net GDP would become $900. Surely this must be a more realistic evaluation because it accounts for the actual goods available to be used in society. What the government spends does not add value to the economy, but removes the availability of these goods. (Thanks to J.T.Salerno)

Then there is the question of how to split the intermediate products, say steel beams. The steel manufacturer has certainly a large output of high value which is not used up immediately. A portion will sit and be eventually be used in building something else with a higher value, but is now counted doubly, and it is doubtful whether a GDP calculation could separate these items reliably. Where services such as a tennis or windsurfing school are included, one cannot reliably say that something has been added to the output of the country regardless of how many people are interested in learning these sorts of capabilities.

It is also doubtful if GDP has any meaning when we consider the quality of the measured product. There is no indication if the products have been of any use or are even desired by the people. In the old communist systems of the USSR and East Germany large GDP numbers were always presented at each 5-year plan, with total disregard whether anything was on the shelves or all the citizens had all they needed for daily life. If a company is bailed out by the government such as was the case with General Motors, Chrysler and some of the steel industry, this will show up as an increase in GDP even though nothing additional was actually produced.

The calculation is also influenced by the relationship between import and export which are added and subtracted from the GDP calculation. This makes no sense at all as the products that were exported were actually produced in the country of export. Whether the products imported could have been manufactured in that country is unknown, but either way, this does not mean that less was produced in the country. The money that is used to purchase imports always comes back into the country through other trade or financing as it cannot be used anywhere else as a currency.

Ultimately it leads to the conclusion that the GDP determination is a fairly random number generation in the service of the government. What it really should show is the actual increase in the production of useable goods and the allowance that can then be made to increase the money supply in accordance with that increase, much as the shovel maker would have more funds available if he makes more shovels – and sells them. But, as we will see later, the creation of money under the current system does not relate to the production of goods in the first place, since it is based on the creation of debt alone.

The abuse of the GDP value shows most readily in the quarterly statistics issued by some government authority. The economy, by definition, is only doing well when there is an increase in GDP in every calendar quarter, and the economists agonise over fractions of percent increases or decreases, regardless of whether anything has been achieved in this time. Should, heaven forbid, the quarterly result show a negative growth result for two quarters in a row, the economic astrologers will immediately call for something to be done, resulting in more strange government interference. During a real downturn businesses would have to slough off some fat, reduce staff and realign their goals in order to turn around any fall in revenue. This is the normal business cycle and prepares everyone for the stronger growth ahead. Companies that cannot handle downturns have bad management and need restructuring or elimination to make room for better business formulas - and that is what a free market is meant to achieve. Where governments meddle in the process, they distort the market and prevent this periodic cleansing that is necessary for an efficient market to operate.

Another Interlude

It is interesting to note that in South America, in particular in Argentina due to the century-long destructive government interference in the economy, the principle of bartering has once again sprung up. People are going to markets with their wares and products and use a bartering coupon to obtain products and 'sell' products.

Argentina is actually an interesting, but very sad case of economic mismanagement. Arising from the Spanish Empire, a society was established consisting of an oligarchy of leading families, immensely powerful, on a land, the Pampas, that produced grain in abundance and fed large numbers of cattle. These families ruled and controlled the economy and politics of the country. They encouraged immigration from Europe to supply an educated work force, and they supported free trade. This oligarchy required a stable central government with as little as possible involvement in economic matters as possible. Foreign investment was not opposed and, for example, a British railroad was a welcome addition to the infrastructure. Towards the end of the 19th century an investment bubble developed in South America and a lot of money flowed into the area, and of this a lot was being borrowed. The Argentine government also borrowed heavily in the 1880s which culminated in a financial crisis in 1890, the 'Baring Crisis'. Although this was overcome, it opened the door for a variety of political forces to begin competing for power.

The crisis developed along very modern lines. Argentina started borrowing funds for infrastructure projects such as roads, railways and land improvements, which should have led to increased economic activity and improved revenues. These projects took longer than expected and required extensive funding so that additional borrowing was required, not only to service existing loans but also to support ongoing expenses. In turn, more money was printed and inflation set in, which made the loans still more expensive. The largest proportion of these loans was carried by the house of Baring in London, which eventually had to approach the British government for help to prevent failure. A consortium of the Bank of England, Bank of France and Russia's central bank eventually salvaged Barings, but the effect of the crisis reverberated throughout the Western World.

Renewed political forces now came to be prominent in Argentina and electoral laws were introduced and revised, and new political parties came to power. The Great Depression of the 1930s hit Argentina very hard, as their exports were mainly focused on beef and grain and agricultural products where demand had slowed dramatically. The elected government of Hipolito Yrigoyen was overthrown in September of 1930 and replaced by a conservative military grouping. His government had concentrated on supporting the new urban and industrial classes at the expense of the older conservative families. A military junta took over with great public support and instituted an almost fascist regime until 1945. Neither period from 1916 to 1930 nor from 1930 to 1945 was economically successful, due to a concentration of very narrow interests which left Argentina vulnerable to market forces.

During the war a new player, Juan Peron, began to build a new support base among the working classes, and in his position as Secretary of Labour and Social Welfare introduced improvements in working conditions, wages and social services, health and pensions. He was briefly detained by the military as his ambitions become clear, but a popular mass uprising brought about his release. He then married Eva who was to be at his side and highly visible to the electorate. Peron won the election in 1946 and began a hard left-wing regime, nationalizing banks and railways and increasing social spending. His wife Eva was chosen to represent the largesse of the administration and put in charge of distributing benefits to the poor. She subsequently developed a near saintly image among the population. After her death in 1952 Juan Peron stayed on and won another election and finally, due to his attack on the Roman Catholic Church and increasing repression, another military coup became inevitable in 1955. Political fortunes now swing back and forth between Peronista factions and the military and all the time the economy is neglected and the country becomes increasingly impoverished. The reader is welcome to explore some more the convoluted history of what should have been a highly successful society, but for exploitation of populism combined with repressive regimes, leading to the current status of a very depressed economy. Before 1914 Argentina counted among the top 10 wealthiest countries in the world, and now trails neighbours such as Chile and Uruguay. The main reasons lie in the circumstances of development. Unlike other countries early in the 20th century Argentina did not industrialise significantly and relied on commodities only. At the same time the elites were not interested in a good system of popular education, preferring to maintain a society of workers. This made it difficult to adjust to modernization. After the impact of the depression, Argentina instituted more protective commercial layers which restricted free trade with the world, just as the world was liberating international trade, especially after the 1947 GATT agreements. Perversely, even though the country has had a refreshed democratically elected government since 1989, nothing was learned from the past. Interventionism has once again stifled the economy and prevents agriculture and industry from expanding, because of export controls and lack of investment. Political greed and short term thinking keeps the country on a downward spiral. Argentina is the ultimate example of how not to run an economy.

Bartering started seriously after the last crisis in 2001, where once again the government was unable to fulfil its debt payments and limited withdrawals and froze individual bank accounts. This was probably due to interference of bad advice from the IMF by proposing to peg the Peso to the US Dollar. This very bad idea, combined with government irresponsibility and endemic corruption, led to the value of the Peso increasing with the value of the Dollar and thus reducing export revenue. This, combined in turn with severe cutbacks in government wages and pensions, scared people into withdrawals through fear of returning inflation. Many of the poor were left only with direct trading through barter, and avoiding all the middle men and taxes. Interestingly, bartering has also commenced in Spain and Greece due to the severe European misalignment of currencies.

We have on the opposite side of the spectrum the colony of Hong Kong. This island was first ceded to Britain in 1842, and later in 1898 Britain leased more territory from China. Hong Kong acted as a trading base for Britain but was never an economic power house. This changed after WWII when a lot of mainland Chinese returned to Hong Kong after the Japanese occupation, then followed by more migration after the communist takeover of China. Since there were essentially no politics to distract the population from making money, that is what they did. The British administration had a very simple tax system consisting of a flat tax that cannot exceed 16% for individuals and 17.5% for companies. Thresholds are quite high and thus only about 40% of the population pays any tax at all. The total tax burden is also low at around 20%, as there are no taxes on dividends and interest (excepting financial institutions or firms supplying goods or services on credit), there is no sales tax, no capital gains tax, no succession taxes, no payroll tax and neither are perks from business taxable. The tax code was established in 1947 and there have been very few changes to it, in fact it is only 200 pages long. Compare this to the typical OECD tax codes which run into many thousands of pages, depending on who you ask and who you order a copy from. For example the US tax code is variously quoted as low as 3500 pages and as high as 80 000. The Hong Kong government has additional income from stamp duty on property sales, taxes on some imported luxury goods and petroleum products, and additionally there is interest income from the accumulated surplus the government has amassed. Hong Kong is the freest society of all and the inhabitants are happy with the conditions, including a low spending government – total government expenditure is at or below 20% of GDP. As a result per capita GDP has risen from $2000 to over $25 000 since 1947. Thus it proves that a society can run very well without much government interference and become extremely prosperous. The argument can be made that there still is not a lot of support in the form of welfare, pensions and so on, but their society does not so far clamor for it. It can also be said that a lot of taxation of the middle classes in other countries is just to give benefits to the middle classes to stimulate popularity.

Revisiting Circulation

The whole of the financial sector, as we have seen, certainly leaves an endless scope for strange concepts and weird thinking. Starting from the simple statement that money needs to circulate to make an economy viable, somewhere along the way a clever head invented the concept of *Velocity of Money*. This term refers to the number of times a defined amount of funds is spent repeatedly. Let's say you've earned a Dollar and you spend it on some food. The grocer receives the Dollar and sooner or later spends it on petrol for his truck. The station owner then sometime later buys himself a case of wine and so this Dollar – in the view of this strange theory - is passed on from receiver to the next receiver. The strange part now is that we need to predict how fast this passing on takes place in a given period of time, for example how many times does it pass hands in a year.

The first reaction would be that for the most part this would be quite random, since we really don't know how soon a particular individual feels like spending his income. If the money changes hands quickly the velocity would be high and the demand on money would be low, since it moves quickly to satisfy everyone's desires. If money moves slowly through the economy by not as much as is available at any one time, the demand for money therefore would increase as it has now become rare.

What determines this velocity then? There are two factors available: the GDP of the country and the money supply available. In effect the GDP is dependent on how much money is available to produce a supply of goods and services. If there is a low money supply the velocity will have to increase to manage the GDP expectation. If the money supply is large the money can become 'lazy' and doesn't need to circulate as much to produce the same amount of GDP. So velocity is GDP divided by the money supply and this actually contains some good news. In conforming to Keynesian fashion, governments everywhere have been doing what is called Quantitative Easing (QE), that is printing money to give away. The usual effect of this would be inflation, since by supply and demand an increase in supply lowers the price and this applies to money as well. But, as it so happens, at the same time this money is being created, its velocity has slowed down and the money that is entering the market is being used less often. This means people are probably reducing debt or saving more money rather than wildly spending it and so a natural balance has taken over and inflation is still relatively low. Whether this will stay so is uncertain and once again all theorising one can do tells us nothing about the future. It is, however, safe to assume that all this additional money will eventually start circulating more quickly and then inflation will catch up.

This line of reasoning once again also contains the seed of its own destruction. We talk about money circulating when in fact the money, being an intermediary, only represents the circulation of goods and services. The money in itself is passive and the activity of the individuals is what really matters here. The implication is then that all of a sudden all goods are being traded at a different rate from some time earlier, which is most likely unlikely. The outcome is that even such esoteric analysis only confirms the fact that the market above all depends on the confidence the population has in the present circumstances.

There is another factor that makes the validity of the velocity concept dubious: It does not account for the creation of credit. Remember credit is created on the spur of the moment and is in fact uncontrollable in the short term. So the implication can be that the velocity is quite high, when in fact it is only a period of high credit creation, leading to excessive spending, usually in turn leading to a hangover when the money becomes due. At that time people will really have to trim spending in order to repay debt and the velocity would slow again, even though there is plenty of money around, but it is being spent differently. There is also a case where a house or a car is traded several times during a year. This looks like a lot of economic activity, but the economy has not created anything or increased wealth, just a lot of dust. All in all, as a concept velocity of money doesn't seem to have much usefulness. So what shall we make of the following story from the internet:

A visiting tourist stops at a motel, and lays a $100 bill on the desk saying he wants to inspect the rooms upstairs to pick one for the night.

As soon as he walks upstairs, the motel owner grabs the bill and runs next door to pay his debt to the butcher.

The butcher takes the $100 and runs down the street to retire his debt to the pig farmer.

The pig farmer takes the $100 and heads off to pay his bill to his supplier, the Co-op.

The guy at the Co-op takes the $100 and runs to pay his debt to the local prostitute, who has also been facing hard times and has had to offer her "services" on credit.

The hooker rushes to the hotel and pays off her room bill with the hotel Owner.

The hotel proprietor then places the $100 back on the counter so the traveler will not suspect anything.

At that moment the traveler comes down the stairs, states that the rooms are not satisfactory, picks up the $100 bill and leaves.

A 100 Dollar bill has passed through 6 hands. No one produced anything. No one earned anything. However, the whole town now thinks that they are out of debt and there is a false atmosphere of optimism and glee.

Econometrics

More terminology coming up. When economists pretend there is science involved then we get into big words like this. It is the application of statistical and mathematical theories to economics for the purpose of testing hypotheses and forecasting future trends. Economic models are generated and then tested using statistical methods. Results from this are then compared to real world data. There are a number of tools in play such as probability, statistical inference, regression analysis and time series methods. Fairly esoteric mathematics is used to interpret collected data and support decisions for the real world, not only necessarily economic decisions. Any decision that deals with the allocation of scarce resources falls into this category. This could be as varied as a decision on a student taking a second degree instead of entering the work force or to help a company decide whether to make a certain investment to generate more income. Some more direct information can also be derived such as a relationship between the value of the US Dollar against changes in oil prices or to show if a change in minimum wage affects employment of some sections of society. Econometrics is an immensely useful tool and is extremely valuable for government and corporations to ensure that resources are used effectively.

Saving your Money

However, don't stop reading yet, there are some more complications, some more juicy bits to come. All of us think about the future and worry – as we should. The natural thing is to put aside some of the earnings for various other reasons: to have an income later in life, to have something to fall back on when things aren't that rosy, or simply to obtain something more expensive and saving up for it. It is important to note that this is money that has already produced some goods or services, and savings is not money removed from the economy, it is simply funds applied in a different manner. Savings technically remove some funds from the circulation introduced previously, but this isn't necessarily a bad thing, since generally savings rates are low, currently about 2% - 3% of income. We are talking here of after tax and non-pension fund savings, and this used to be much higher at about 5 – 7% some decades ago. It would be interesting to evaluate if the loose financial policies of the governments in the last 40 years have gradually led the population to think that saving money just isn't worth the deprivation of desirable goods.

The normal route would be to give this 'saved' money to an institution such as a bank, a savings group or other investment house for safekeeping and to earn some more revenue. In turn these institutions are required to produce an income for you and at the same time for themselves, and this is generally done by lending the funds to another entity who needs some additional funds over what they have available to achieve their aims in life. This pool of savings is used to finance such things as new buildings, company expansions and also to support individuals in home ownership.

In theory this is a good thing. Instead of sitting idly under your bed these funds now support others again in their work, allow companies to increase their revenue and employ more people and finance your house. The funds are thus returned into circulation, and notice here that they are used to increase wealth in the community. Increasing wealth is an incredibly important concept and a reality we enjoy living with. Simply using an individual's labour plus some available raw materials something of use is produced, which enables more individuals to occupy themselves making more useful things.

For many centuries in the past interest rates for loans were not allowed or were ethically objectionable. This presents a problem for the owner of the funds as they would like to earn something from their assets, much as renting a property will bring a rental income. After all money is just another commodity and its loaning out should produce some incentive, just as a vehicle rental or a land lease would produce an income. On the other hand, autocratic regimes in antiquity had no qualms about collecting usury charges from the population for their 'services'. There is a good article on money

lending in history by Yaron Brook at The Objective Standard web page: *The Morality of Moneylending.*

Time for another little diversion: A lot of people misunderstand what an asset is and what represents a liability. In short: an asset is something that generates revenue for you and a liability is something that demands spending from you. Many proud owners think because they have a fancy boat or a very expensive vehicle that these represent assets. When analysed, however, there is no revenue to be had – only expenses for upkeep, for insurance premiums, for running costs when you want to use it, and on top of all that the value usually depreciates over time and through your use. If the same amount of money were invested in a business, a bank or some other capital item that you can rent out, it would then be an asset because you derive an income from the investment. One has to be very careful with this differentiation and many people don't understand why they have little money available when they have all these wonderful and expensive 'assets'.

Along the same line we keep hearing of the 'wealthy' people, who have amassed great sums of money on their own behalf, and who are said to be worth many billions of Dollars. Certainly some of this wealth will be available to them in spendable funds, but the vast bulk will be in investments, that is, shares in their companies or other people's companies, investments in properties or investment funds. The point here is that money itself has no value; it only has potential value, which is realised when you purchase something. All the investments in funds or companies can vary and will go down as well as up, and in any case don't represent anything except a number to look at. If you have a car you can drive it, if you have a beautiful painting you can admire it every day, but a large percentage of a shareholding at best gives you a small say in the running of the company. We also need to understand the difference between price and value. The price of something is what the two participants in a transaction agree upon – it is totally relative. If you want to sell your shovel and nobody wants to buy shovels, then it has no value at all, regardless what you think its price is. A value is the subjective worth of a good or service as determined by people's preferences and the tradeoffs they choose to make given their scarce resources; therefore value is inherent, but is a relative term for the worth something represents to its owner.

Now back to your savings – we claimed that these funds would create wealth in the community. This is true as long as the investments are used to enhance existing assets, or to create new assets, essentially the use of the funds increases income at some point. Thus a manufacturer has enlarged his facilities and can increase output and employ more people in the factory. Or a large building has been erected and new space can be leased out for other businesses to carry on. All of these developments generate more revenue and are thus classed as assets. When you now look back at a world with only empty space as compared with buildings, factories, roads and so on, it becomes obvious that the wealth of the whole community has increased. People have worked hard, used their time wisely and used their investments wisely and the reward is a world with things in it that keep everyone in the circulation loop, which continuously redistributes that money to everyone's satisfaction.

The original importance of savings must be appreciated in that it allows capital to be generated. Capital is referring to the means of production, that is plant and equipment, and not only of the products on the shelves, but also the machinery and equipment required to make the equipment for production and the raw materials. The mark of a capital item is that it is used to generate an income. Your personal vehicle is not capital, but if you use it for your sales trips it becomes capital. It is important to realise that money is not capital, since it cannot be used in the production of a good directly, although it can be used to purchase items of production, which then become capital, but in the money state that decision has not yet been made. Again, we need to note how the socialist mentality has defined a 'capitalist' incorrectly as somebody who is immensely rich (usually implying undeservedly so), while originally as defined as far back as 1878 by John Stuart Mill, capital was the basic requirement for production without referring to wealth or even the term 'capitalist'.

It must be noted that the current low interest rates offered by banks run totally counter all economic wisdom. Since people realise that

51

they can't get ahead through savings, most money has been diverted into housing investment, driving up prices in that sector. The corollary of this is that less money is available for capital investment by business, and that, if these lower rates don't actually produce the intended effect of increasing business loans for capital investment, it must be said that the whole economic direction of fiscal stimulation is an abysmal failure. As a side effect we also have untrammelled growth in consumer debt because 'interest rates are so low'.

We need to introduce a couple of distractions to this arrangement to complete the picture of an economy. There are outside influences such as trade with other countries and we will address this below. The more important spoiler here is the influence of government.

How Government Spoils the Economy

At the outset the idea of government was most likely a good one. Image yourself part of a largish tribe of early settlers in a farming environment. Probably a communal society where everybody has some assignment: tilling fields, gathering wood, hunting and fishing and so on. Since disputes invariably break out amongst people in groups, it is a good idea to have an administrative team, usually of the Elders, to do what planning is necessary, to guide the tribe generally with wisdom (!) and to resolve disputes. These persons do not physically contribute to the accumulation of wealth but perform an ancillary function in that they assure the smooth operation of the whole arrangement – as long as they act benevolently.

We have maintained this type of structure in the current guise of a business company. An executive team manages the operations and all the 'tribe' members fulfil their respective responsibilities to the benefit of all concerned.

Being so successful these tribes prospered and grew and with them grew the administration. Eventually they became city states and the simple administration morphed into a government and thus politics was invented. The larger state required more administration, land became individually owned, roads were required and a policing authority became installed. All this required funding and the administration needed to spend a lot of time developing means of extracting this revenue from the population. Early forms of this were to simply collect some of the grain and store it in government silos. Since a commodity like wheat or rice or maize was universally a necessity, this achieved two aims on behalf of the administration: It gave them a means of paying bureaucrats, soldiers, police and themselves, plus it gave them a means of controlling the commodity. By withdrawing or releasing the wheat it affected the market and a crude form of price control was possible. From the benevolent angle grain can be stored and kept for times when the harvests were insufficient. The government could now pass out rations to the population to keep the peace and give themselves a good name. Note here that the government did not actually contribute to the wealth creation, for that it depended on the mass of lowly farmers and workers.

One would think that a group of people wanting to create a government was driven by some rationality and avoid creating too much of a government, but, as history has proven, once the devil is out of the bag, he cannot be constrained. Having installed a government the population loses the strength to contain it. Quoting the brilliant and unjustly maligned social philosopher Herbert Spencer in his book *The Man Versus the State* from 1884, well worth a read by the way:

What, then, do they want government for? Not to regulate commerce; not to educate the people; not to teach religion; not to administer charity; not to make roads and railways; but simply to defend the natural rights of man – to protect person and property – to prevent the aggressions of the powerful upon the weak – in a word, to administer justice. This is the natural, the original, office of a government. It was not intended to do less: it ought not to be allowed to do more.

Another common way for the government to create revenue for itself was through ownership of land. Any land owned by the government could be either leased or given to those currently favoured in the government's eyes. In either case the land would be leased out for agricultural production and thus produced an income stream for both the owners and the government. This is still the case in China where the government owns all land and just leases it to the population.

There are essentially two kinds of land ownership in China, state ownership and collective ownership. Rural land, or housing land and the household contract farmland, is collectively owned. Farmers are part of the collective community and have property rights to their land, but with restrictions. According to Article 152 of China's Real Right Law, housing land holders are entitled to possess and use collectively-owned land to build houses and related facilities. In 2002, the Law on Land Contracts in Rural Areas of China was promulgated for the purpose of granting farmers long-term and guaranteed land-use rights and safeguarding the legitimate rights and interests of the parties to land contracts in rural areas. According to Article 20 of the Law, the term of contract for arable land is 30 years.

According to the Institute for Urban and Environmental Studies, Chinese Academy of Social Sciences, there are ambiguities in farmers' property rights to rural land in Chinese law. The 30-year contract term does not mean farmers enjoy full property rights, as for example the right of possession or transfer. The calls for "more property rights" are an attempt to allow farmers to transfer their land freely in the market. Farmers will benefit from the reform as land is the means of production for them. Chinese farmers, though they are entitled to possess and use land, do not have full ownership. It is impossible for Chinese farmers to mortgage their land for loans. Therefore, the top priority is to clarify who the true holder of the rural land rights is. Farmers' rights over their land have been strictly prescribed. For example, household contract farmland is only for farming, but when a family moves to a city to work, they are not allowed to lease their farmland to others. Any attempt at land reform will be a very difficult undertaking, as local governments rely on their power to take and sell land to increase their revenue. (Ref.: *china.org)*

When traveling through a country like Egypt one cannot but be impressed by the imposing structures created during the reign of the pharaohs and their architectural achievements. However, when looking more closely, the problem you find is that the society was essentially static for three millennia! This may be a good thing for those in power but does little to advance the general wealth of the society. So we find that the tools for farming remained mainly wood and stone tools, and later copper was used for stone masonry, but the methods of transport were mainly the donkey or people dragging sleds through the sand. Metals were used but restricted to the upper classes because of the cost of smelting and refining. None of the wealth was used to develop better methods of metallurgy nor was there any interest in improving the lot of the common people. The masses were simply there to be available for major religious projects when these were decided, and since the pharaoh was god, most of the effort was expended to provide appropriate tombs for the pharaoh so he could pass on into the afterlife properly equipped for splendour. Their main advances were in the invention of papyrus for their tomb designs, mathematics for architecture and very advanced embalming methods. Similarly, in more recent times, large palaces and spectacular arenas were constructed in countries such as Bulgaria and North Korea for the aggrandisement of the ruling elite, and all the while the population was starving.

Although all this happened long ago we can draw some conclusions from their form of government. Firstly, the government will take what it feels society can bear without overthrowing the administration. The Boston Tea Party is an example of when things went too far. The background here is that the UK government created a Tea Act in 1773 that allowed the East India Company, then in dire financial strife, to export their unsaleable stores of tea to the colonies at preferential conditions, and without taxes for the colonial merchants. Ultimately this would undercut local production and impose a monopoly when the competition was bankrupted. Next a general boycott started against British tea whereupon the UK tried to force landing of tea in American harbours, resulting in the famous night where some 150 patriots dumped all the tea from British ships into the harbour. Although the situation with colonies was more complex than that, the amazing realisation to be made here is the total idiocy of the British government to force such a minor matter to the point of ultimately causing the War of Independence.

Secondly, we can conclude that a government is not the best arbiter for wise dissemination of funds. If we look back to the beginning of the story you find that people traded amongst themselves for items they made. If someone made a thing that rotated earth and collected earthworms it would be very desirable for fishermen, but the market is limited to those fishermen and so becomes self-regulating. If this machine simply rotated earth and then told you how much earth has been rotated (but didn't do anything useful) nobody would buy it and there would not be such a machine since it adds no value. Governments are exempt from this rule and can spend funds on whatever they see fit, regardless of an added value. This is how you get such completely wasted arrangements such as a Climate Change Department, a Waterways Authority, desalination plants and reports such as the Levenson Enquiry into the press.

The expansion of government 'services' was quite extensive in the earlier part of the 20th century and led to the institution of authorities for the generation of power, distribution of gas, management of waterways, hospitals, ambulances, liquor stores, rubbish collection, health insurance, rail and bus services, air lines, telecommunications, airports and so on – the list is endless. What has been missed here is that the government should not be in business at all. The government should only be responsible for those areas directly involved in administering a country. The extra layers of bureaucracy increase the costs and overheads for any endeavour and prevent competition from improving or even replacing a particular service. Opponents of privatisation will often cite the fact that some businesses are a revenue earner for the government and that the investment of the proceeds will bring lower revenue than the business did before privatisation. This is a spurious argument, since the government's job is not to generate its own revenue and thus compete with private businesses; it must generate revenue from taxes and spend this revenue to run the country, one year at a time. After privatisation the new business will also generate an income and pay taxes. The price of the product will most certainly decrease and the consumers of that product will have funds to spend on other goods and services which in turn will also generate tax revenue. The people most annoyed by the privatisation process are the unions as all civil servants seem to be unionised by force removing more or less any opportunity for better efficiency.

One main fallacy in government thinking - and this is followed by large sections of the learned economic community – is the belief that buying things leads to economic growth. The thought is that, if someone buys something without first producing something of similar value, this will create jobs. Going back to our shovel maker it is obvious that people have to eat even while their time is spent growing food for future demand. But if someone is employed by the government to rotate earth for no reason or to dig and fill holes, nothing of value is produced and the wealth of society is actually diminished since those people could have been growing food for example. (Think of government departments such as 'The Human Capital Officers Council', 'Office of Minority Health' or the 'Advisory Council on Historic Preservation' all exercises in time-filling futility). Ultimately the removal of these people from the labour pool reduces production and demand; a customer can only buy what someone has produced and make work programs do not increase supply of goods. This connects well with financial stimulus policies: If the government injects large amounts of cash into the economy this will stimulate spending and increase economic activity. This sort of reasoning is simply saying that if I take $1 from A through taxes and give it to B to spend, we have stimulated the economy. What has been achieved is a socialist redistribution. A is

57

presumably someone who pays taxes and B someone who doesn't or pays very little – otherwise he would not be eligible for stimulus money.

What is really happening is that the government actually borrows money from A and gives it to B and expects a different outcome: that we are all better off. This again is nonsense since taxes on A must be raised tomorrow and when the government announces this, A will reduce his spending accordingly. Additionally, this sort of stimulus spending and forward balancing of the books inevitably will lead to more inflation and we are all worse off while the government gets to pay back debt in inflated currency at a lower absolute cost.

While we are here, let's consider taxes some more. As we saw above some tax money is useful for such matters as defence, foreign relations and the general administration of the country and its infrastructure. But ultimately the inhabitant of the country is contracting an authority to look after certain things for him. Ultimately it is in the best interest of that inhabitant that he should receive the best deal for his money. So here one has to consider very carefully where the best interest lies: if you give a contract to a private company to carry out certain works or look after certain endeavours you at least have some say in the matter of accomplishing this. If you give this contract to the government they simply say "Trust me", and you have no further say until the next election, where these take place. If one follows government development it becomes obvious that government grows and grows, the number of so-called 'civil servants' and bureaucrats increases constantly and the government explains this by claiming to offer more services to the population. But a closer look will show immediately that we are again in the realm of redistribution. The largest portion of this tax money will be spent on social services, welfare and subsidies to companies or whole sections of society and none of this spending produces one grain of new goods or wealth. The whole idea of the European Union started as a way of distributing farm subsidies and controlling food production. The largest portion of the US subsidies pool is spent on farming simply to keep the agricultural community on side. This amounted to $179 billion in 2010, compared to 'only' $94 billion in Europe. Note that this money does not produce any food or anything at all, in many cases it is handed out to prevent food from being produced to maintain price levels!

And so it goes with most of government spending: it does not add value to the economy, money is spent on maintaining government departments that employ people to look busy but not produce anything, not add to the wealth of the country. Government spending essentially is our money spent by someone else and diverted into areas of their preference. Some of these coincide with what we want, most don't, and yet governments seem to think that using our money in this way magically adds to the total wealth available, which is really a monstrous form of deception. Additionally, if taxes must be increased to pay off debt, that limits the cash available to finance further private-sector growth, which is by far and away the largest source of growth for the economy.

There is a wonderful outline of this concept of spending by Milton Friedman: *"There are four ways in which you can spend money. You can spend your own money on yourself. When you do that, why then you really watch out what you're doing, and you try to get the most for your money. Then you can spend your own money on somebody else. For example, I buy a birthday present for someone. Well, then I'm not so careful about the content of the present, but I'm very careful about the cost. Then, I can spend somebody else's money on myself. And if I spend somebody else's money on myself, then I'm sure going to have a good lunch! Finally, I can spend somebody else's money on somebody else. And if I spend somebody else's money on somebody else, I'm not concerned about how much it is, and I'm not concerned about what I get. And that's government. And that's close to 40% of our national income."*

When following economic events we need to separate stocks from flows. *Stocks* are all the assets already in existence (much like stock in a warehouse). A small addition is made each year through construction, goods and services, and this addition to the stocks is the *flow* of funds. The spending of money itself does not enrich an economy, it depends on the capital you have available and how this is used to enrich the country. For each expenditure we need to assess if any value is being added – exactly as you would spending your own money on projects or investments – you don't want to be poorer next year! Spending money on green schemes, on most renewable energy programs (all subsidised) or propping up industries that are not viable, all fail the test to show they add more to the economy than they use on implementation. Welfare spending is very well if the country can afford it, but it is a luxury and adds nothing to the stock.

As a result governments are constantly fighting windmills. It will look at the surrounding reality and then imagine what a perfect and ideal situation should look like – in the government's political imagination – and then create laws to bring this about. This invariably fails on several accounts. First there is a certain inertia in the society to move away from what the people consider a good arrangement and the people will quietly revolt by doing things their way and defending their situation against government imposition. Secondly the imaginings of the government lead it to looking for the greener grass on the other side of the fence and in their minds introduce what are considered small changes, and these fall afoul of the law of unintended consequences. It will be impossible to predict what the people affected by the changes will do in reaction to the new situation, and generally the government will have presented a case that seems to benefit everybody, but ultimately falls into the 'to-good-to-be-true' category. You can't please all the people all of the time and, whatever the change, some will benefit and some others will be worse off. So if the plan were to incentivise some sort of social improvements whether in housing, pensions or employment one would need to ask first if the market will accept this as a useful product. If there are subsidies involved, the participants will simply take the money and run, and this has happened in all the various alternative energy schemes, such as wind turbines, nodding ducks, solar power and even geothermal energy. A perfect current example is the creation of the expensive new electric car from the Tesla

Corporation. It seems that this is a wonderful product, and there is no denying it is a good car, but its existence depends entirely on the collection of money from the purchase of zero emission credits from other motor car manufacturers. The original Tesla motors factory was obtained by a joint venture deal with the Toyota Corporation's old facility in California and both vehicle and battery manufacturing was supported by large tax incentives and even federally supplied funds, and a 465 million Dollar loan. Companies should be left to their own devices to make it in the market place, and a lot of taxpayer's money would be saved did these loans and federal subsidies not exist. The government is not in the business of starting up companies and competing with the banks for loans. Furthermore, a company showing government backing has an unfair advantage for further financing over a competitor who is going at it alone. The precedent for the Tesla was called Solyndra, which was set up to produce a novel type of circular solar cell with improved efficiency. Amongst other investors the government in August 2009 supplied a loan guarantee of 535 million Dollars and for whatever reasons, the company declared bankruptcy in September 2011. The funds came from the Department of Energy's green energy funds all arising out of the 787 billion Dollar stimulus money issued in 2008. There are many other loans this department made and probably some are doing good things. The point remains that the government should not get involved in lending and supporting industry, since only private money will be able to establish if there is a business case to be accepted.

By interfering in the market and pushing various schemes the government is essentially trying to make the population behave differently, that is to fall into line with institutional thinking – and that just doesn't work. All that seems to be achieved is the destruction of what a free market would give to society. Government has learned to work together with corporations and banks that are then granted privileges in turn. This is maintained in a variety of ways through tax concessions, subsidies, intellectual property regulation, trade restrictions, land appropriation, building codes and restrictions on the working population with minimum wages imposed, penalty rates and work practise restrictions. All of these prevent the individual from making their own arrangements for their working life, and all this is done with the 'best intentions' of protecting worker's rights, but is in fact preventing them from working under their own conditions.

The most astonishing thing about government behaviour is that no administration learns from all the previous mistakes from all around the world. The temptation of the approach that 'we know best' and the support for the party line is so overwhelming that all rational thought goes out the window and is replaced by ideology. A favourite world problem is the constant harping by authorities that there is not enough water of the potable variety in the world and that we must all conserve by using less water all the time. This is complete nonsense and it is unbelievable that any population anywhere would put up with it. The sun heats the ocean and evaporates water which forms clouds which in turn fall back onto the earth. Admittedly, a lot of this falls back onto the ocean and is of no use to us. Admittedly we cannot control when and where rain will fall in useful areas. But the situation that no one will admit to is that we do not manage this rain very well at all. In particular where green groups have the upper hand in stopping reservoirs and diversions, and some places prohibit any collection of water due to some dubious green preservation schemes. About 110 000 cubic kilometres of rain falls every year on the earth, and of this about 40 000 falls on land. We manage to transport oil and gas in pipelines over thousands of kilometres to the market, so why not with water? The main problem seems to be that most groups seem to think that water is free, which may be the case if you can collect water regularly yourself in a high precipitation area. Water needs to become a commodity and would be priced according to market demand. Let the household compete with the farmers and the industry and the situation would change rapidly. Both the industry and farming can well do with recycled and reconstituted water if it is competitive with pipeline water for example. Households would stop letting their taps and showers run at leisure if there was a proper cost attached.

Another totally political problem is the use of nuclear energy for electricity generation. You would think that the green component of society would be enthralled by a system that produces vast amounts of energy cheaply and from miniscule amounts of material without any emissions at all. A small amount of Uranium of about 75kg will produce 1000MW of electricity for about 3 years as a rough guide and at this point it is depleted but not unusable. There are ways of reprocessing this remainder after or even during the generation period of the reactor. Uranium is freely available all over the world and quite easy to process. In many instances it could be a by-product from other mining such as copper. There have been some nuclear accidents over the years, and this has caused a negative impression of the safety of nuclear plants which is totally unwarranted. There are currently over 430 nuclear power plants operating around the world but only ever three major accidents in commercial plants: in 1986 Chernobyl in the USSR, which was due to an inappropriate operating procedure and the only one with known direct fatalities; in 1979 at Three-Mile-Island in the USA, which was a contained melt-down and only very small amounts of radioactive material escaped; in 2011 at Fukushima in Japan, when the nuclear plants were flooded by an enormous tsunami with no directly attributable fatalities, however, a substantial amount of contaminated material was released, mainly into the ocean. This must surely represent a safety record ahead of almost any other industry and yet there seems to be no political will to further advance nuclear installations in the OECD, apart from France which already is over 75% nuclear energy supplied.

The total idiocy of the populist driven governments was once again displayed for all to see when Germany, after the Fukushima episode, ordered all nuclear plants to be decommissioned and replaced with coal fired power plants. France's President also proposed to shut down half of nuclear supplies over the coming years, even though no accidents had occurred in either country.

On the economic front there are also many examples of refusing to learn from the past, the foremost of which is the constant drive to increase the tax burden of a country. Every time taxes have been lowered and restrictions on business eased, the outcome has been to increase tax revenue since more business will be created. The only thing higher taxes achieve is to discourage new businesses and to reduce expansion of existing business. As they say: The best tax system is to make poor people richer and not rich people poor.

Subsidies on products also belong in this category since they distort the market and undermine the economy. Subsidies represent at best redistribution and at worst a total loss of the funds. The money is applied to a small section of the economy and the rest of the population has to pay for it. Subsidies inevitably contain an opportunity cost, because of the subsidy an item will cost more and this money could have been spent better elsewhere. Subsidies are a classic example of seen versus unseen. A subsidy for farmers has very visible effects: farmers see profits rise and hire more employees. The invisible costs include what would have happened with all of those dollars without the subsidy. Subsidies have to be taxed from individual income, and consumers are hit again when they face higher food prices at the grocery store. So-called renewable energy is the current worst form of a subsidy. Enormous amounts have been spent in the Western countries to alleviate an imagined problem with carbon dioxide in the atmosphere. The hidden outcome is that the price of electricity rises and of course affects mostly the lower income earners who can least afford the additional expense and will be forced to cut back on other necessities like food and clothing. Subsidies may also encourage continued inefficiency among producers when the operation of free market forces might result in a more efficient allocation of resources. Unfortunately, subsidies are generally introduced by a government to buy some more votes.

The only certainty we have about governments learning from the past, if they could, would be that all the shenanigans of governments throughout history have proven that only by staying out of the way of the productive population can the situation be improved. The less a government interferes with the economy the better off we are all –

but this seems to be too difficult a lesson to accept.

And if you think that all this is a grand new revelation, consider this:

""The budget should be balanced, the Treasury should be refilled, public debt should be reduced, the arrogance of officialdom should be tempered and controlled, and the assistance to foreign lands should be curtailed, if Rome becomes bankrupt People must again learn to work instead of living on public assistance" Cicero, 55 BC - So, evidently we've learned nothing in the past 2070 years. " (Thanks to Mannkal Foundation)

Yet Another Interlude

As we are speaking of government growth another interlude makes it rewarding to recall the article by Cyril Northcote Parkinson as a humorous essay published in *The Economist* in 1955. Parkinson had extensive service in the Civil Service and mulled over the situation that for example the Colonial Office was expanding while the number of British colonies was shrinking and the British Admiralty continued growing as the number of ships was diminishing.

This is the article with the latter part of the analytical portion omitted:

"It is a commonplace observation that work expands so as to fill the time available for its completion. Thus, an elderly lady of leisure can spend the entire day in writing and despatching a postcard to her niece at Bognor Regis. An hour will be spent in finding the postcard, another in hunting for spectacles, half-an-hour in a search for the address, an hour and a quarter in composition, and twenty minutes in deciding whether or not to take an umbrella when going to the pillar-box in the next street. The total effort which would occupy a busy man for three minutes all told may in this fashion leave another person prostrate after a day of doubt, anxiety and toil.

Granted that work (and especially paper work) is thus elastic in its demands on time, it is manifest that there need be little or no relationship between the work to be done and the size of the staff to which it may be assigned. Before the discovery of a new scientific law—herewith presented to the public for the first time, and to be called Parkinson's Law—there has, however, been insufficient recognition of the implications of this fact in the field of public administration. Politicians and taxpayers have assumed (with occasional phases of doubt) that a rising total in the number of civil servants must reflect a growing volume of work to be done. Cynics, in questioning this belief, have imagined that the multiplication of officials must have left some of them idle or all of them able to work for shorter hours. But this is a matter in which faith and doubt seem equally misplaced. The fact is, that the number of officials and the quantity of work to be done are not related to each other at all. The rise in the total of those employed is governed by Parkinson's Law, and would be much the same whether the volume of the work were to increase, diminish or even disappear. The importance of Parkinson's Law lies in the fact that it is a law of growth based upon an analysis of the factors by which that growth is controlled.

The validity of this recently discovered law must rest mainly on statistical proofs, which will follow. Of more interest to the general reader is the explanation of the factors that underlie the general tendency to which this law gives definition. Omitting technicalities (which are numerous) we may distinguish, at the outset, two motive forces. They can be represented for the present purpose by two almost axiomatic statements, thus:

Factor I. — an official wants to multiply subordinates, not rivals; and

Factor II. — officials make work for each other.

We must now examine these motive forces in turn.

The Law of Multiplication of Subordinates

To comprehend Factor I, we must picture a civil servant called A, who finds himself overworked. Whether this overwork is real or imaginary is immaterial; but we should observe, in passing, that A's sensation (or illusion) might easily result from his own decreasing energy—a normal symptom of middle-age. For this real or imagined overwork there are, broadly speaking, three possible remedies

(1) He may resign.

(2) He may ask to halve the work with a colleague called B.

(3) He may demand the assistance of two subordinates, to be called C and D.

There is probably no instance in civil service history of A choosing any but the third alternative. By resignation he would lose his pension rights. By having B appointed, on his own level in the hierarchy, he would merely bring in a rival for promotion to W's vacancy when W (at long last) retires. So A would rather have C and D, junior men, below him. They will add to his consequence; and, by dividing the work into two categories, as between C and D, he will have the merit of being the only man who comprehends them both.

It is essential to realise, at this point, that C and D are, as it were, inseparable. To appoint C alone would have been impossible. Why? Because C, if by himself, would divide the work with A and so assume almost the equal status which has been refused in the first instance to B; a status the more emphasised if C is A's only possible successor. Subordinates must thus number two or more, each being kept in order by fear of the other's promotion. When C complains in turn of being overworked (as he certainly will) A will, with the concurrence of C, advise the appointment of two assistants to help C. But he can then avert internal friction only by advising the appointment of two more assistants to help D, whose position is much the same. With this recruitment of E, F, G and H, the promotion of A is now practically certain.

The Law of Multiplication of Work

Seven officials are now doing what one did before. This is where Factor II comes into operation. For these seven make so much work for each other that all are fully occupied and A is actually working harder than ever. An incoming document may well come before each of them in turn. Official E decides that it falls within the province of F, who places a draft reply before C, who amends it drastically before consulting D, who asks G to deal with it. But G goes on leave at this point, handing the file over to H, who drafts a minute, which is signed by D and returned to C, who revises his draft accordingly and lays the new version before A.

What does A do? He would have every excuse for signing the thing unread, for he has many other matters on his mind. Knowing now that he is to succeed W next year, he has to decide whether C or D should succeed to his own office. He had to agree to G going on leave, although not yet strictly entitled to it. He is worried whether H should not have gone instead, for reasons of health. He has looked pale recently—partly but not solely because of his domestic troubles. Then there is the business of F's special increment of salary for the period of the conference, and E's application for transfer to the Ministry of Pensions. A has heard that D is in love with a married typist and that G and F are no longer on speaking terms—no one seems to know why. So A might be tempted to sign C's draft and have done with it.

But A is a conscientious man. Beset as he is with problems created by his colleagues for themselves and for him—created by the mere fact of these officials' existence—he is not the man to shirk his duty. He reads through the draft with care, deletes the fussy paragraphs added by C and H and restores the thing back to the form preferred in the first instance by the able (if quarrelsome) F. He corrects the

English—none of these young men can write grammatically—and finally produces the same reply he would have written if officials C to H had never been born. Far more people have taken far longer to produce the same result. No one has been idle. All have done their best. And it is late in the evening before A finally quits his office and begins the return journey to Ealing. The last of the office lights are being turned off in the gathering dusk which marks the end of another day's administrative toil. Among the last to leave, A reflects, with bowed shoulders and a wry smile, that late hours, like grey hairs, are among the penalties of success.

One of the most poignant illustrations of this unchecked growth has been the Transportation Safety Authority (TSA) in the USA. Founded as a reaction to the September 11 attacks it was started in November 2001 and in typical fashion grew exponentially to now over 60 000 (!) employees and a budget of over 8 billion Dollars. The security of the travellers is no longer an imperative, but the continuation and expansion of the bureaucracy is. The TSA has been shown to be somewhat ineffective on numerous occasions where items have been left undetected and many more where it has become obvious that many of the officers simply exert chicane on the travelling public by exerting authority, a typical condition for low level authoritarian uniforms. There are now many calls to abolish this authority and revert to private companies under individual contracts to carry out security checks.

Back to Government Interference

For those old enough, the crisis times of the early 1980's will not be remembered fondly. Interest rates shot up very suddenly and many a home owner had to simply walk away from their house since they could no longer afford the mortgage payments, and they could not sell the house since it was now worth less than they had originally paid. What had led us there was once again government interference through the Reserve Bank of America. Quite a while before this particular crisis became noticeable, the groundwork had been laid through the invention of the Federal Savings and Loan Insurance

Corporation (SLIC) in 1934. This entity was to insure deposits at savings and loan companies up to $100 000 in a similar fashion to the Federal Deposit Insurance Corporation (FDIC) which was set up to protect deposits in banks. The unseen problem lurking in this arrangement was the lack of risk assessment – any S&L was insured regardless of how risky their investments were. A private insurance company offering the same protection would adjust premiums according to the risk that was covered and the higher premiums would automatically preclude some investments from being insured. The government does not see things in a rational way and so all institutions were covered equally. This went reasonably well until in 1979 the new fed chairman Paul Volcker started with a revised monetary policy, the discussion of which requires another chapter. As a result interest rates soared during the next two years and mortgage defaults increased and with the S&L insurance scheme in place it was easier for a lot of these small banks to declare bankruptcy rather than trying to solve their problems or merge with other institutions. Payouts soared over the next decade until in 1989 the SLIC was integrated into the FDIC. Unfortunately by this time the American taxpayer was into over $160 billion of bailout money. The real problem was not the actual situation of the S&Ls funding, but the continued interference by the government in their affairs. A lending institution of this type borrows short and lends long, that is, depositors of funds usually leave these for a shorter period in the bank, a matter of at most a few years. Lending for mortgages extends over much longer periods usually decades. Thus if a mortgage is locked in at a low rate the bank is forced to borrow at higher rates than the mortgage offers and the bank starts losing money. If now, as happened, the government controls the rates of the mortgages to enable politically useful low mortgage rates, the institution has no choice. To add to the woes of the institutions there was also the so-called *Regulation Q* introduced in 1933 and 1935, which set a limit on the amount of interest a bank could pay on deposits. Once again the intentions were good and were meant for example to prevent small banks to simply re-deposit their own deposits with larger banks, and instead support local economies with their lending. But, as we know too well, the unintended consequences always get you again. All was not too bad as long as the deposit interest market rate that banks would normally offer was below the ceiling as determined by the regulation, and this held until about 1966. Then Congress decided to extend the regulation to the Savings & Loan banks as well. This move had the dual purpose of halting an escalation of interest rates paid on deposits and simultaneously expanding mortgage credit, particularly for the S&L banks. For that purpose the ceiling for the S&Ls was set higher than for banks. This did not attract more business to the S&Ls since the differences were very small and the big banks developed new non-financial attractions for customers such as gifts, vouchers and more outlet locations. After more tinkering finally in 1986 Regulation Q was also abandoned.

Governments are known for such irrational behaviour that history abounds with useful examples. The most poignant of these occasions was after the crash of 1929. Again, the government believed it was the only source of wisdom and proceeded to act unilaterally to overcome the crisis.

The crash of the stock market in 1929 did not cause the Great Depression. It did cause a lack of consumer confidence and destruction of wealth, which caused consumers to be more cautious about spending. The biggest contributor of the Great Depression that followed was the government meddling in the economy. Even Ben Bernanke later declared: *"Economists now recognize the cause of the Great Depression was failed government policy."*

To better understand what happened we need to start well before the crash. After the First World War a serious sense of optimism set in over the ensuing years. As always the war had advanced technology and airplanes were becoming commercially viable, Henry Ford invented the production line and great new buildings were planned and constructed. Over the decade of the 1920s a social and economic euphoria set in and everybody was caught up in it. For the most part this was justified since industry boomed and confidence in the economy was great. This decade made America the wealthiest nation in the world. Interest rates for brokers were in the 4.5% to 5% range all throughout, so financing was a fairly easy proposition. One of the newest instruments was the offering of hire-purchase contracts. The purchaser could buy something with a deposit and then pay the loan off in installments, including an interest payment. Hire-purchase was easy to get and people took up the contracts without any real concern for the future – it became a matter that if you wanted something you just went out and got it. Since in those days most everything was still made manually a lot of people got paid for their work and went out and spent money on acquisitions in turn, thus adding to the accumulation of production on credit. New products excited the consumer and everything from cars to washing machines, refrigerators, radios and telephones became the drivers for production. Essentially what followed later on was a credit crisis as stocks were to a large extent bought on margin as well, and all the credit extended removed funds from circulation and reduced demand for goods greatly.

One of the problems that were neglected during this euphoria was the plight of the farming community. During the war prices for foodstuffs was good and consumption extensive so farmers were rewarded with high incomes. The destructive ravages of the war on European soil which reduced food production there provided an opportunity for the American farms to make up for the shortage. This dropped off dramatically after the war and incomes shrunk due to an oversupply of food and the consequential fall of prices. Many farmers had in this time purchased more land and farm machinery on credit, believing that the boom would just continue, and they were caught out badly when prices fell and many were dispossessed of their businesses. At the same time the government had become involved in a trade war with Europe. After the war European farm production rose again and Europe introduced import tariffs on foodstuffs to protect the farming community. In turn the USA also introduced tariffs and all trade with the outside world was reduced. Tariffs on imports have the effect of increased prices internally as there is a lack of competition from cheaper imports. All these above factors in the end became a part of the problems leading to the depression of the 1930s.

Nevertheless, as the decade went by, confidence and optimism prevailed and the stock market rose from around 70 in 1921 to peaking at 381 points by 1929, neglecting totally that there should be solid earnings data behind stock prices.

The first signs of trouble should have been obvious to the thinking investor, when interest rates for brokers started rising in late 1928 going over 6%. In early 1929 the rate hit 10% briefly and later rates above 10% were common. Since an interest rate reflects the risk of the loan involved, the market saw the problem coming. In early 1929 the first sign of an actual devaluation came when on 25th March a sell-off started, led by nervous investors, and the first casualties were those with large margin calls. However, with the support of some banks and a promise of money being available for financing, the market once again set off on an upward trend. The market reached its record high on September 3rd at 381.2 and began falling the next trading day. Then during September and early October more voices were pointing out that the market was unsustainable and resembled a 'speculative orgy', and finally on October 18th the drop began seriously. Every day thereafter confidence decreased and panic increased until finally on October 24th the market fell by 11% at the opening. Intervention by a group of banks and financiers slowed the fall over the next few days, but on October 28th (Black Monday) the Dow lost 13%, and again on Tuesday October 29th 16 million shares changed hands, many stocks were simply unsellable and the market lost another 12%. The Dow continued to decline over the time following, until the bottom of 41.22 was hit on 8 July 1932, despite several rallies during that period which all failed to arrest the decline.

This was one of those occasions where a failure of what may have been regarded as a free market gave the government and the politicians an excuse to impose their will with the intent of correcting the situation. Ultimately all were caught out by the unintended consequences and the lack of looking for 'what is not seen'. This is disregarding the fact that politicians of various persuasions had already interfered in a free market through the control of trade and monetary policy before the crash occurred. The main failure was the totally unrestrained credit availability and the complete disregard of any financial analysis regarding the performance of companies. Over $8.5 billion was out on loan, more than the entire amount of currency circulating in the U.S. at the time. Despite this most horrifying example of a bubble crashing, in 2001 the exact same situation led to the dot com crash, with the zealots profoundly proclaiming 'if you don't get in now you will never be able to profit from this expansion in internet businesses'.

Although only about 16% of the people were actual investors in the market in 1929, the repercussions were much larger than this would indicate. Confidence went out of all business for a while, banks went bankrupt and many companies had to close their doors. Credit availability contracted severely, and far less money was available to maintain business as usual. With large numbers of unemployed demand for goods shrank accordingly and the whole of the economy contracted. What followed is again very contentious and many tomes have been written on the subsequent events and the causes of the following depression, which lasted throughout the 1930s, but some actions undertaken were clearly unhelpful in restoring confidence and supporting businesses. The first action was that of other countries who started a run on the US Dollar, which forced the Federal Reserve to increase lending rates directly into the path of the downturn. Then came more protectionism through the Smoot-Hawley Act. This raised tariffs for imports once again, for some commodities by as much as 70%, sparking trade wars, crippling international trade and reducing US exports, thus reducing GDP.

In 1928 a new monetary policy had been introduced, the Real Bills Doctrine, requiring that all currency or securities have material goods backing them. This policy resulted in US money supply falling by over a third from 1929 to 1933. Money now became scarce and many banks and companies failed simply by being unable to ensure extension of credit to continue operating. The failure here is compounded by the government resisting any attempt to help the failing banks, resulting in severe losses for depositors.

In the background of all this activity there was also a push to maintain the gold standard. This implied that countries, who had abandoned the gold standard during the First World War to allow more funds for the war to become available, were now returning to the gold standard in order to combat inflation from money printing. Both the US and France were particularly aggressive in increasing their gold reserves and eventually both had reserves far in excess of their currency requirements. This led to a shortage of gold in the world and indirectly contributed to the deflationary pressure that followed the 1929 crash. Where a currency is tied to a fixed price of gold an increase in the value of the currency is required to acquire more gold. As a result the currency will become more valuable with respect to all the goods available and the price of these goods will go down – a deflationary pressure. As it turned out the effect of this was so intense that the gold standard collapsed again in 1932. The decline in the money supply in the US between August 1929 and March 1933 brought on higher interest rates and a contraction in money supply. This led to the demise of many hundreds of small banks and the subsequent loss of savings from individuals. It is astounding that during all this time the Federal Reserve, which had been created only 15 years earlier and specifically to deal with financial instability, did nothing to support the economy by releasing funds to the banks at lower rates to avoid the panic. The exact reasoning behind all these actions is now probably lost forever, but provides good fodder for many speculative dissertations and publications. The outcome is clear, in that various inept government policies combined to turn a simple market adjustment into a full blown depression lasting for 10 years.

And then there was the issue of taxes. In the 1920s, Treasury Secretary Andrew Mellon championed a series of income tax cuts that reduced the top individual tax rate from 73 percent to just 25 percent by 1925. As rates fell, the U.S. economy boomed until the stock market crash in 1929. Ignoring this information, and to help in balancing the budget in an election year, in 1932 President Hoover radically changed course from the low tax policies of the 1920s with the Revenue Act of 1932. That law sharply increased individual tax rates at all income levels, with the top rate rising from 25 percent to 63 percent and also increased corporate tax levels. Quite predictably total revenue from taxes increased but so did the size of the deficit. The answer to this was more tax increases during the following Roosevelt years. A key problem with trying to balance the budget with tax increases is that higher taxes fuel more government spending. The second effect is that resentment by the high income group sets in and more effort is expended in tax avoidance or simply in income reduction, due to most additional income reverting into taxes.

This attitude to taxation and other anti-growth policies certainly killed incentives for work, investment, and entrepreneurship. As a result, while the U.S. unemployment rate fell sharply during the tax-cutting 1920s, it soared to 25.2 percent in 1933, and remained very high through to 1940 when it was still 14.6 percent.

All through the years of the Roosevelt administration ever increasing funds were spent on his 'New Deal', and government bureaucracy doubled between 1932 and 1940. One of the first mistaken directions of the new administration was to reduce competition. The reasoning was that too many products in the market lowered prices and prevented businesses from earning money to pay their staff, in particular where farming was concerned. The centerpieces of the New Deal were the Agricultural Adjustment Act (AAA) and the National Recovery Administration (NRA), both of which were aimed at reducing production and raising wages and prices. Reduced production was already happening in the downturn, and it never made sense to try to get the country out of depression by reducing production further. Under the AAA animal husbandry was greatly reduced by slaughtering breeding herds and plantations were reduced by ploughing the plants under in vast areas of the mid-west and south. The NRA was an attempt to control the whole of the manufacturing industry by controlling the output and raising the prices of goods. This of course had exactly the desired effect in that the manufacturing industry went into a slump and required more and more government interference to control and maintain the acceptable quantities of goods allowed. Thus the depression was extended by simply reducing economic activity. The whole thing was deemed unconstitutional by the Supreme Court in 1935 (NRA) and 1936 (AAA) and the economy picked up immediately.

Since at the time a large proportion of the work force was uninterested in joining unions the government interfered once again, and in the summer of 1935 the National Labor Relations Act arrived to ensure that union members could force other workers to join their unions with a simple majority vote, thus effectively monopolizing the labor force. By 1937 the new contracts had raised hourly wage rates and created overtime wage rates as real hourly labor costs surged. There were many more attempts to control the economy, including banking regulations which forced banks to hold greater reserves and again removed funds from the market. In its totality it can be said that the uncertainty of so much government intervention and unpredictable introduction of regulations brought about such a feeling on insecurity by the business community that investment, especially long term programs, was sufficiently reduced to prolong what might have been a brief recession interlude into a decade long depression. Ultimately it was the war effort for the Second World War which pulled everyone out of their stasis and raised the enthusiasm for production once again. Also during the war millions of service personnel aided in reducing the unemployment rate in the general population. Even during the war, however, price controls, rationing and government control of production held back the recovery until the end of the war when everything once again became freely available.

An aside from 1921

There was also a serious depression in 1920 to 1921 which conveniently no one remembers any more. After the end of WW1 the US government found itself in an unenviable position, as the war debt had grown hugely and inflation was rampant at almost 20%. To counter this development federal spending was greatly reduced by about 65% and interest rates were raised from 4% to 7% to slow down the economy. The result was wildly successful and the country went into a deflationary period, unemployment increased to 11% and the consumer price index fell by 15%. Importantly the wage index also was allowed to fall, reducing income in conjunction with prices, and this was not allowed to happen in the 1929 original downturn. But even though this created quite a shock in the financial system, one year later unemployment had dropped to 6% and consumer confidence had increased due to the fact that federal spending was reined in, setting resources free in the economy. The result was, as has been described 'purged the rottenness out of the system', and set off the high confidence period of the 1920s by settling in a period of sustainable growth. This sequence of events shows that harsh measures to correct imbalances work quickly, although painfully, and the market, if left to its own devices, will adjust and recover just as swiftly.

One of the most blatant and defining examples of government mismanagement lies in the Japanese economy. All the way through the 60s and 70s Japan was a paragon of economic development admired by all. The Japanese displayed a rigorous and disciplined approach to business and enterprises, and the economy grew at a steady pace and thus became the envy of the world. What happened next is entirely predictable, except for the timing and the severity, as we have seen from the normal business cycles. In the mid-eighties there was a slowing down of the economy and growth fell from a high 4.5% to below 3%. In response the Bank of Japan reduced interest rates to 2.5% and instantly set off a borrowing and building boom over the next 3 years, which of course led into an investment bubble of enormous proportions and the Nikkei stock index rose to dizzying heights – reminiscent of 1929 – which were unsustainable. A "bubble" was being created through cheap and easy credit which led to massive borrowing for dubious investments. Speculation created real estate prices that were extremely over-valued. Starting in

January 1990 the market started falling as quickly as it had risen, and 2 years later it had halved again. Now the government of the Bank of Japan had nowhere to turn to alleviate the situation and economic stagnation set in. Interest rates were already low and banks had taken on more risky loans and were now unwilling to take on new business. This led to a banking crisis with the result of the whole economy standing still. GDP remained level for over 10 years and the general population was unwilling to spend and invest. Japan then tried more fiscal stimulus programs and kept interest rates low, but this only led to increasing deficits, which stand now at over 200% of GDP. Looking at the current situation in the West, the outlook seems about the same.

To quote from an article by Donald J. Boudreaux of Mason University in Virginia:

Government is power. Government is not to be trusted. Ever. Even if you believe that some government is and will always be necessary, that 'necessary' piece of government should always be regarded as a prudent lion tamer regards the big carnivorous cats that are 'necessary' for him to make a living. To imagine that seemingly subdued purring lions can be trusted to be dealt with in any ways that do not include the use of strong cages, leashes, ceaseless and deep suspicion, and escape hatches is the height of romantic absurdity – wishful thinking of the most extreme and inexcusable sort. Government is by its very nature a dangerous, untrustworthy, dishonest, arrogant, slippery entity – characteristics that are by no means reduced anywhere near to insignificance by a wide franchise, regular elections, and sturdy ink-on-parchment documents called "constitutions."

Unless you are a high-ranking government official, government – no government is ever "Us." It is always "Them." And They are not to be trusted. Ever.

An Economics Tragedy

Near the beginning it was pointed out that a most important aspect of a free economy is the guarantee of private ownership. People in a society will behave differently if they are certain that what they seem to own is really theirs and cannot be impounded at random. There is, unfortunately, a corollary to this and we need to go back to the Magna Carta for this divergence. The Magna Carta, sealed by King John on 15 June 1215, is arguably the most important document ever created and it set the tone for all of Western Society. Some of the clauses resonate through the ages and are the basis of our laws, such as for example:

30. No sheriff nor bailiff of ours, nor anyone else, shall take the horses or carts of any freeman for transport, unless by the will of that freeman.

31. Neither we nor our bailiffs shall take another's wood for castles or for other private uses, unless by the will of him to whom the wood belongs.

39. No freeman shall be taken, or imprisoned, or disseized, or outlawed, or exiled, or in any way harmed - nor will we go upon or send upon him - save by the lawful judgment of his peers or by the law of the land.

40. To none will we sell, to none deny or delay, right or justice.

Here we have defined the protection from property seizure and the guarantee of a lawful process for all subjects. Although, it must be added that the Magna Carta did not set the tone for total freedom of abuse by all people, only the barons and their cronies, actually. But it did serve over the ages to concentrate minds on achieving more freedom for all, and the interpretation and the impact of the charter became more important than the original wording. Interestingly, a second less well known document was issued along with the Magna Carta and this dealt with forests and land ownership, the Charter of the Forest. This of course dealt with the landed gentry maintaining their rights, but provided for access to the common folk and led to the establishment of The Commons (Common Land). This was an area where the common farmers could graze their herds and plant crops and it ultimately is again an example of unintended consequences from actions by a government.

No doubt there was an awful lot of good will behind this idea and surely all affected parties fully believed that the idea of a Commons was to the benefit of all, and it probably worked quite well – for a short time. The farmers grazed their cattle in the area and all was well until of course each farmer had some births and then there were more cattle to feed. Since no one in particular was responsible for looking after the Commons land, eventually all the feed disappeared and any initial benefit was destroyed. This has become known as The Tragedy of the Commons.

The main problem with the Commons arrangement is not at all unusual. Each herdsman has to look after his flock in the short term and wants to maximize his support from the Commons ahead of anyone else – this is simply human nature. If additions to his flock appear they will also go to the Commons since this incurs no costs. The modern proof of this lies in any socialist system or the communal system as promoted by hippies. It assumes that every member will do their bit and contribute equally which is simply made impossible by human nature. Some people want to work early, some later some not at all, and if there is no authority to manage these people, everyone simply does what he/she wants and in the end nothing is done at all.

The tragedy of the commons may not be current any more in the village square but it has not gone away. Most prominent is its presence in the fishing industry. All fish outside of countries' ocean exclusion zone of 200 nautical miles falls into the grouping of common property. Early on there was not a serious problem since fishing vessels were relatively small and the industry fell directly into market conditions. Where there was a large catch available fishing boats would catch as much as they could and took it to market where the price was determined by the quantity available. Where stocks began depleting not as many fishers could make a living and the number vessels were reduced, and a sort of balance was maintained. To even out the cycle and to promote political positions fisheries subsidies began in the 1960s and distorted the market for fish totally. Fishing boats could now be maintained not only with inefficient practices, but also regardless of the amount of fish brought to market, leading to a vast expansion of the fishing fleets and increasing the sizes of the vessels deployed. The outcome is again foreseeable for all but the government bureaucracies: Fish stocks took a dramatic decline over the next decade and in typical vertical thinking governments then started to introduce fishing quotas. Subsidies still amount to about US$ 35 billion per year and the largest contributors are now China and Japan, closely followed by the EU. Subsidies are applied to fuel, management and ports and harbours and these subsidies distort the market and therefore trade. Fisheries that receive subsidies get an undue advantage in the market place over those who do not, and generally large fishing companies capture most of the subsidies to the disadvantage of small scale fishermen. Fishers in developing countries are also disadvantaged since their governments do not have the means to compete with those of developed countries.

The introduction of fishing quotas then proceeded to distort and pervert the market endlessly and led to situations where a catch of desirable fish, or even just a by-catch, had to be discarded (usually killing the fish anyway) at sea because the quota of that fish would be exceeded, or the wrong type of fish was caught, and large fines applied on landing. The quota system was now changed in 2014 and we have a 'discard ban' or a Landing Obligation, which requires that any fish subject to catch limits is retained on board the fishing vessel and counted against quotas except where specific derogations apply.

The best solution to date has been to give ownership right to the fishers. This is done by either assigning certain areas to fishers for their use or by giving out Individual Transferable Quotas (ITQ). This allows ownership of the resource, and it will be in the interest of these owners to preserve their fish stock at sustainable levels.

Nature also had an input into the fishing fracas in that a number of species were now being selectively bred for smallness. Since nets were designed to let through young and smaller fish, those from a large species that were below normal size adults managed to breed much better than large fish being caught and entered into a cycle of selective breeding for reduced size.

There are still many more commons issues to be resolved such as ocean floor mining, the Antarctic Territory and Arctic exploration.

Now the Government some more

What governments do is different from private business. A government will collect money from the population and use it as it sees fit without any input from reality – speak market forces. This is how we have ended up with noisy bird-shredding windmills all over the planet. It is something nobody really wanted but the governments in many countries saw fit to impose on the population, because the politicians know better. An odd thing happens here: politicians who run for office are just people like you and I and anyone can stand for office and be elected. Suddenly now they become elevated to a higher level of knowledge on almost anything, right up to how to go about running a whole society. Up to this point this person may have known a lot about accounting, Unions, the law or farming only, and now suddenly can contradict and manipulate all types of specialists, academics and journalists who have spent their careers focusing on a specific range of knowledge. The ministers in government have the choice of listening to specialist at will, using those who agree and denigrate others who are not in tune with the government. This is not radical news and most people will understand it.

The problem with the economic aspect lies elsewhere. When a government spends money on almost anything it can never do so as efficiently as the individual or a company in business. First of all that money has to also support a governmental bureaucracy and in addition all the consultants and specialists that need to be involved as well. Next, when a contract is given out, only those who are acceptable to the government are invited or considered, and above all, only those who are playing by the unwritten rules of the game. The outcome has to be that the money needs to seem to have been well-spent in the public eye and produce positive publicity. All this means that of course there is no control over costs or accountability in the process – it just has to look good. A personal anecdote may expand this a little: A long, long time ago in another universe I worked briefly for a company who had a federal contract for the development of a lot of new electronic equipment and I accepted a job to lay out electronic printed circuit boards simply because I could do it and the money was really good. I was given several layouts to do and set about drawing. After about a day and a bit they were complete and I went to hand them in, happy to have finished so quickly. Much to my surprise I was told to wait until 2 days later before handing them in, since each drawing had an allocated number of hours attached and these had to be used up. The outcome was that most of the time all the draftsmen sat around reading, playing chess or listening to the radio on headphones. The reason was that the quote had been accepted as it stood and any improvement on the contract was forbidden, since it would mean less money for the next one. My friend and I lasted six weeks there and could not stand it any longer, good money or not.

The point of this is going back to the increase in wealth of society: when competition is removed from a process it will stagnate and become unproductive. Surely the electronics were all designed and built and a product developed. But the amount of wasted money could have been used to produce some additional other developments which would now demand additional funding. Just because the employees were well paid and surely also spent their own money well does not detract from the fact that this project was essentially a form of government welfare.

There seems to be a universal rule that it is almost impossible for a government to spend money wisely, based on the condition that government activity is totally removed from the open market place. Can one really believe that tenured bureaucrats could spend such vast borrowed sums as efficiently as millions of private individuals responsible for their own success or failure? Governmental expenditure often becomes a reaction to the market conditions rather than a lead for the market, and it is usually much too late. Thus we get programs like the idea of 'cash for clunkers', attempted in several countries. This proposed that the government will pay you a sum of money to take your old car if you buy a new, more efficient car instead. The first thing that strikes is the law of unintended consequences, because of the lack of thought and planning behind it. The immediate effect is that thousands of used cars are removed from the market and this drives up the price of the remaining used cars. Secondly, since these cars are physically destroyed, it also removes used spare parts from circulation, making it more difficult to keep other older cars going. The people that suffer are of course the lower income families who have lost access to older, but still useable vehicles. Thirdly, there will be a purchasing shift distorting the market. This offer will be mainly taken up by people who had already planned to change cars and are now purchasing a new car earlier, taking advantage of the offer. This introduces a time shift where more cars are sold immediately and fewer later on. Even the government cannot fight market forces.

During the past few years solar energy has become one of those government promoted excesses in order to please 'green' sensibilities. Now we need to remember that power grids all over the world are constructed to create electricity as the demand requires, and with the availability of a lot of statistical data about human behaviour, has become quite predictable; i.e. when people get up and make toast, when they come home and turn on the lights, when it's hot and air conditioning runs, and so on. The electricity flows from the power generator to the houses and is used up. Solar cells on individual houses have been promoted by subsidising the electricity they create very heavily, and thus enticing many people to finance an installation. What has been totally ignored by the powers to be is that now electricity will flow in the opposite direction, where it has nowhere to go except that it could only be used by other houses on the way and, additionally, the sun being capricious will shine at will and not to the government's decree, and on all houses at once. The outcome is totally predictable in that the power supply companies have no way of controlling the whole mess since their system was not designed for such a set up. Eventually the subsidies have to be cut and a lot of unhappy voters will vote out the administration at the next opportunity (one hopes).

As a side effect, all so-called 'sustainable energy' carries with it another burden no mentioned in the media. Due to the fact that all the power plants that supply electricity when the sun isn't out are now running at reduced capacity for some of the time, but were costed for full capacity usage, the price of electricity has to increase to make up for the lost sales displaced by the solar panels. Therefore the use of the sustainable energy has a negative economic bearing on the consumers.

Electricity generating wind turbines are also on the favourites list of wastage. Apart from the noise and appearance affecting surrounding pristine landscapes, the improbable attraction to birds committing suicide and just the sheer ugliness of the whole thing, they don't work all the time. So to a government body it seems perfectly logical to install the windmills – at consumer expense – and then install a full size back-up plant as well. We have now successfully doubled the capital cost of power generation without one word of dissent and for the most part the liberal press does not object, because it is a feel good situation. Nobody considers what the wasted money could have been spent on to improve every ones lives: roads, hospitals, rail etc. It also needs mentioning that the generators used in the windmills use large magnets that require the mining of rare earths, most all of which takes place in China under unsupervised conditions, producing toxic fumes and radioactive waste. Additionally inordinate amounts of concrete are required for the base and tower, which produces carbon dioxide at a rate of about 700kg of CO_2 for every ton of concrete manufactured. But an assessment of the effect of the construction of windmills is subservient to the feel good factor of using *free* wind. At a future time this will probably be seen as an age of economic insanity where good solutions were ignored, bad solutions subsidised and the preservation of the environment turned into ideological issues that in the end went against the environment.

From this we learn that interference by the government distorts a society's economy. Under normal circumstances people trade amongst themselves at appropriate market values and these are distorted when governments get into business. Quite often this results in government monopolies, especially in what are considered essential services such as water, electricity and communications where the outcome is inevitably that these services then charge above market value because of a lack of competition. Invariably, when these are privatised the costs for the service will reduce because a competitive market demands efficiency.

One of the best examples of a proper competitive market is to be found in the automotive industry. For most people in employment a good ratio of income to car price is around one third to one half of one year's income. So a person earning $80 000 per annum will normally buy a car between $25 000 to $40 000, depending on what a car represents in their life – they may just want transport or they may want to impress others with an expensive car. About 30 years ago this ratio would have been the same except all the numbers would be half of what they are now. What you need to consider is how much more a car offers now compared to 1980. A lot has been invested in making cars safer and this includes body structural design, many air bags, a superior safety belt system, ABS and so on. We now have a touch screen even in lower priced cars, the seats are better and more comfortable, the whole of the interior has a much higher quality and execution and engines are far more efficient and cleaner, although this last one is in part due to government regulations. Yet car manufacturers still make profits. The main process in the industry is called 'continuous improvement', a process that maintains constant surveillance on how your car is received by the market, what the competitors are doing, what problems the current model is experiencing and ideas how you can get ahead of the competition. So, all cars are now safer, better equipped and easier to look after and all this for the same portion of your income.

Contrast this with the Trabant made in the former East Germany: There was a 7-year waiting list, its body was made from paper with epoxy and remained unchanged for 30 years. Powering it was an old two-stroke oil burning motorcycle engine with 18 hp and this was worth over half a year's income. A typical example of total government planning.

Another favourite activity of governments is so-called 'stimulus spending', or 'Quantitative Easing', of which we have experience plenty of late, all around the world. The intended purpose of this expenditure would be to stimulate the population into spending more money when the economy has slowed down noticeably. The thinking man will consider why this is and come to the conclusion that a section of the population has lost confidence in the current economic situation and is pulling in their horns. Less money is expended and more is saved or used to pay off some debt. Under Maynard Keynes influenced thinking (more about him later) the government must now step in and spend extraordinary amounts of money to stimulate the economy and drive people back to buying more stuff. There are a number of flaws in this line of thought. From what we have learned above the government does not really know what is causing the problem and thus takes a shotgun approach to the situation. That is, money is wildly flung about in rescuing companies who have just proven not to be viable, money is spent on projects that have not undergone a proper cost-benefit analysis and mostly on programs that are entirely unnecessary or unwanted. The unintended consequence here is that of course nobody believes this manic activity will accomplish anything. People and companies will take the money and run, and the economy will remain depressed since no confidence has been restored. Here the government ignores the situation where its own interference in the market through uncertainty about taxes, regulations and policy is causing the disquiet among the population in the first place.

A good example of this in Australia was the thought of introducing an additional surcharge tax on mining companies. It came along as a spurious and not fully analysed plan where the consequences again were predictable for all except the government. First, mineral rights taxation was a state right, not a federal prerogative. The outcome was that only a small fraction of the revenue was collected and mainly by companies almost volunteering to pay some amount of tax. Secondly, since the tax proposal was published without any consultation with the industry, and since many mining companies are large multinational firms, an issue called '*sovereign risk*' comes into play. This term refers to the conditions under which companies operate in a particular country. Where there is stable government over a long period of time the investors can be assured that their efforts will have a reward. If you are building a large manufacturing facility for cars or establishing a huge mining project with the surrounding transport and shipping facilities, the investor needs to be certain that financial conditions are stable and predictable. Large projects have been put through financial analysis and have developed a cost/benefit analysis, and follow a prescribed project development over many years before coming on stream. If a government introduces sudden financial conditions that are unexpected and lack industry consultation, investors and financiers are easily spooked and will hold back on further work until confidence has been restored.

There is one other way the government interferes with the economy which has an extreme effect, and that is borrowing. In normal life an individual or a company will borrow a set amount of money to achieve a particular goal. This may be a house, a business expansion or equipment replacement, or a car or a luxury item. In all these cases the loan has a purpose and in most cases there is an economic rationale supporting the borrowing. The loan has a payback period and usually a fixed interest rate for the duration (except for houses). A business will have done an analysis of how these funds will increase income or allow an increase in efficiency. Once again what governments do is totally different and mostly without economic rationale.

Even for a government it makes sense to do targeted borrowing. Business in the country may require support for infrastructure such as roads, rail lines and harbour facilities. This is all very well if there is a plan. For example bonds are issued for a very large infrastructure project that would be difficult to handle through a single company's financing. Let's say it involves a newly established mining area which needs roads, a rail line, a harbor and support for the community that will be established around the project. All the facilities will be shared by a number of companies and it is a good investment for the country, since many people will be employed, the companies involved are allowed to expand and all this will be repaid in company and individual taxes over the years. Once again note here that such a project ultimately increases the wealth of the whole community. There may also be a reason to borrow to upgrade military equipment and even government facilities.

Borrowing in this case is similar to that of business loans: There is a fixed amount, a known interest rate and an expectancy of a reasonable payback period. However, the mechanism is quite different. A government will issue bonds which are purchased by the general population or large funds. They have a fixed life span and a nominal interest rate. When kept in check this is a good and acceptable method of borrowing. They are secured by the government and considered completely safe as an investment. The problem with governments, as always, is that things get out of hand or get perverted in their use.

One of the major drawbacks of democracy is that the government needs to be elected by the population and for that reason they want to look good and be electable. To achieve this, the usual approach is to promise lots of stuff, promise to run the economy well and to not raise taxes. What – you've heard this before?? Also, during its allotted administrative period a government will need to pander to the population through offerings of goodies. These include, but are not limited to, unemployment insurance, pensions, welfare payments, health subsidies, housing subsidies and so on. A 'good' government balances all this out and maintains its right to borrow for specific events. A 'bad' government will start borrowing on a regular basis to support regular running costs of the country and this tends to become a bit of an addiction which becomes more and more difficult to retreat from. Essentially, the government is 'buying' the goodwill of the population with their taxes. Governments have no source of income other than your taxes. How bad this can become is currently being experience by the world: Here are some indicative figures of government debt around the world collected from the web for 2014. The important column is the per capita debt, which will need to be collected through taxes. The total world debt can be seen on the nationaldebtclocks.org.

Country	Debt in US $	per capita	% of GDP
United States	18,540,448,667,000	58,437	106
Japan	10,348,930,000,000	81,487	230
Italy	2,651,413,000,000	43,621	124
United Kingdom	2,554,770,000,000	39,550	90
France	2,329,397,000,000	35,223	99
Germany	2,219,133,000,000	27,481	69
Brazil	1,462,083,000,000	7,211	58
Spain	1,177,200,000,000	25,205	87
Canada	809,271,000,000	22,683	52
Australia	414,502,000,000	17,646	26
Austria	332,508,000,000	39,383	77
Portugal	309,582,000,000	29,520	134

Singapore	290,886,000,000	53,873	102
Ireland	239,672,886,310	52,227	103
Sweden	161,910,000,000	16,611	28
Denmark	157,455,000,000	28,104	47

The magazine *The Economist* also keeps a wonderfully frightening global debt clock at *economist.com/content/global_debt_clock.*

The net effect of large scale borrowing by governments is that they inevitably need to compete in the open market for funds. This means interest rates are put under pressure and are likely to rise if the demand becomes too large. The government of course doesn't care about that since it will pay whatever is required using your taxes.

Having borrowed so heavily, an exit strategy is needed. For individuals and companies this means a way has to be found to repay the loan and this has usually been planned into the contract. For a government there is no higher authority to go to, only the population in the form of more taxes. Since most of the borrowing will be in bonds, the easiest is to simply roll them over at maturity and gain more time. There is limited capacity within the country for large amounts and other countries that have a positive balance of trade will usually buy these bonds and collect the interest. This is the situation between the USA and China, which holds over three trillion Dollars of American funds (end 2011). Quite often a government will also sell its assets to improve the fiscal situation and the above mentioned utilities are a favourite, as well as government land and infrastructure. These can only be sold once and the situation will repeat itself in a short time.

Another portion of debt will accrue from so-called intra-governmental borrowing, or robbing Peter to pay Paul. Where another department of the government such as social security or unemployment insurance has a surplus budget the fisc will issue that department with a form of IOU, while expecting there will be a surplus again the following year. Then this money flows back into consolidated revenue and is spent. Gone.

When all else fails the system has to resort to a certain amount of inflation. Inflation is a dangerous genie to let out of the bottle: a little is not necessarily a bad thing, and if you are old enough to look back 40 or so years you'll find that the western currencies in economically stable countries have changed their value by a factor of about 10. That is a car in 1971 cost about $3000 and now costs $30 000. A cart of groceries would have been $20 and now costs $200. This change has been gradual and steady, with a few hiccups in the middle (early 90's). It means that what you earn covers what you need to spend, with a little discretionary spending on the side, and as costs have gone up so have your earnings. For long term borrowing the effect is somewhat different. If you take a 30-year bond the original amount receives interest each year, but the payback amount after a long time has vastly decreased through inflation, as we've seen it could be just one tenth of the original value, which makes it much easier to pay back at the end. Unfortunately for the government concerned, the payment of the interest for these bonds becomes an ongoing yearly expense and depresses budgetary freedom. In 2011 interest expenses for the USA were in excess of $434 billion and this compares to $549 billion for the total defense budget. The difference here is that most of the defense spending employs people and follows the requirement of circulating currency to make the economy function. The interest payments mostly stay in a savings environment or go overseas.

For governments that are not overly concerned with the stability of their currency inflation becomes a positive thing, but only if kept under some kind of check. With inflation the value of the currency will decline and affect exports from the country by making them cheaper while reducing imports by making them more expensive. Then tourism becomes a major factor where travelers from wealthier countries will be tempted to take holidays there since more can be obtained for less of their own currency.

If we say that inflation is fueled by more money being available to spend, we then need to look at another concept and that is what is called money supply.

Whose money is it?

Loosely speaking money supply concerns the entire quantity of bills, coins, loans, credit and all other liquid instruments in a country's economy. If a government wants to control the money supply in such a fashion that the economy is not impeded by a shortage of funds on the one hand, and doesn't rush into the realm of inflation at the other extreme, means must be put into place to do so. But once again as always in economic considerations it is not that easy since all the aspects of all the liquid assets in the economy are constantly fluctuating. This also includes temporary increases and decreases in the amount of money in circulation. Bureaucracy always finds a way of obfuscating, and thus the money supply was divided into several groupings with the thought it would make it easier to analyse and control. Thus the terms M0, M1, M2 and M3 were invented, each representing a different mix of money. For example M0 is all currency in circulation (coins and notes) plus all currency in bank vaults, and M3 is the widest definition of money also including things such as demand deposits, savings deposits and long and short term deposits. The M3 is normally used to determine and control inflation. If you look into the details and question economists more closely, it becomes a very fluid science and a lot of waffling explanations are offered.

In the year 2000, during a House of Representatives Committee on Financial Services hearing, then Federal Reserve Board Chairman, Alan Greenspan, answered a question by commencing with the statement "Let me suggest to you that the monetary aggregates as we measure them are getting increasingly complex and difficult to integrate into a set of forecasts." This was followed by a lengthy explanation of the fact that the Reserve Bank was unable to define what the money supply was and subsequently admitted that the money supply could not really be controlled reliably – or not at all.

Thus here we have possibly the most influential and powerful banker in the world, who is in charge of managing the most widely used money in the world - the U.S. dollar - telling us not only that he doesn't know what money is, or how to measure how much of it there is, but admitting that it's impossible to manage the money supply precisely because they have not yet figured out what it is or how to measure how much of it there is. Quite astounding. As we know that money supply is almost always increasing (inflation), and therefore decreasing the value of money, it means that our standard of living is eroded over time if our income is fixed or not rising as fast as the inflation rate.

Where does Money come from?

But how, the reader asks, does the money circulate and how does it create wealth. Once again, always go back to the basics and check where the money comes from. The first start of the money was a means of transferring earnings between various producers. At the most basic level all trade balances out, and so the tomato grower grows enough produce to trade for other food stuffs to balance his diet and has enough to cover clothing and shelter. This is a hand-to-mouth arrangement: What you produce covers your life, but no more. At this point the 'economy' is static and all the people involved look after themselves day by day. A bit unpredictable, but it works.

As an aside, this is why any communistic 'command' economy is bound to fail. The state is in control of all production and orders from the suppliers what is needed to keep everyone supplied. However, the state is not an entrepreneur and so does not generate any new products or inventions. These can only be obtained by individuals who spend their own time and money looking for something new to occupy themselves with. The state may set up a research laboratory, but the employees of such will have very little incentive to stretch their minds and efforts just for a medal. Furthermore the objective becomes to determine what to deliver in order to obtain more funding, and invariably this comes down to ever more complex and extensive reports that no one understands.

Ultimately, however, it will be the surplus that matters. Once any of the producers involved generate more income than they need for day-to-day living we enter the realm of an economy, but only if these people cooperate. Just stashing any extra income under your mattress for a rainy day will not spur on the economy. The surplus money needs to be engaged and used to generate more income. And effectively, it is the non-essentials that will make the difference, and it explains why some societies fare better than others and some countries are richer than others.

The producer now has a choice of how to use the additional income and let's say he would like a new wardrobe rather than throwing his clothes on the floor. Assuming there is one, he engages a cabinet maker to build a nice large wardrobe with hinged doors and some glass panels and a beautiful finish. The cabinet maker needs to buy wood from a lumber supplier, hinges and nails from a hardware supplier, paint and varnish from a paint maker and glass from a glazier. All these suppliers in turn have again suppliers of their raw materials and so on. Notice that none of these are essential supplies for the day-to-day life. When the wardrobe is made the producer has increased his wealth by the value of the finished wardrobe and has supported all the other suppliers in part from his excess income. In the end our personal wealth consists of 'stuff' we have accumulated to make us feel good or better off. All of these secondary suppliers will need to buy essentials for their sustenance again and some of the money by and by flows back to the original producers. If you now cascade this through the society we can see how the wealth of that group slowly increases. It is, to use a now outdated and vilified phrase: Consumerism. This is not consumerism in the sense that people are given money (by the government) to spend on things. Rather it is a 'productionism' that places new and desirable products on the market which are then bought by the people who are involved in production. We observe this from the barrage of new mobile phones, digital cameras and fancy cars. Every lowly worker who spends his time producing goods for remuneration is part of the supply cycle placing goods on the market. If he were to receive money for not producing anything the shelves would be bare. On the other hand the money he receives must be spent.

Once the producer from above has whatever else he wanted in his life, he has the choice to deposit his money in the bank and a different cycle begins. The bank uses the money to generate more income to pay its employees, and, to achieve this, the money that has accumulated is lent out against interest payments. Part of the interest is paid back to the producer and part of it is used to maintain the bank's business. The money that is lent out is used by an entrepreneur to build up another business or enlarge an existing one, with the prospect of recovering the money he borrowed and then producing more goods to generate more income. Once again the money is now used to construct buildings and manufacture machinery and so on. You begin to see how the money actually circulates: The amount of money circulating is determined by the amount of income the producer has realised beyond the supply of his essentials. That amount is nothing more than the value of his time and effort put into generating this surplus.

The difference in the wealth of the society comes directly from that additional labour. The producer could very well simply stop every day after he has covered his day-to-day expenses and the society would not have any further additional value added.

The same analogy can be applied to the government. There is a certain amount of revenue needed to maintain the running of the administration of the country and to fulfil obligations such as salaries, unemployment insurance, defence spending, pension payments and so on. An additional amount needs to be included in the budget to enhance the infrastructure of the country leading to the building of roads, harbours, airports, rail lines etc. as these items are also good vote-getters for the next election. But more than that, this harks back to what an asset is: an asset produces revenue rather than liability. The additional infrastructure allows more businesses to operate and existing ones to increase their income. This in turn leads to more tax revenue and thus passes the test as an asset.

As a contrasting example compare the case of building large numbers of wind turbines to generate electricity. First of all, it is more of an indulgence since we have sufficient power at the ready to supply our society. Secondly, this new installation will need to be subsidised not only on the capital cost, but also on the product. The outcome is that no new revenue is produced and the running operation is now a liability in the sense that it will cost money to run, it makes competing power sources less efficient. Thirdly it ignores the alternatives available, such as natural gas which is competitive with coal. This falls into line with the building of desalination plants instead of storage dams, and of building cars with an electric plus a conventional combustion drive train. I can hardly imagine that this can be considered progress – except of false idolatry.

Back to the topic of wealth. All that is considered revenue – whether personal or public – is used up in some way to enhance our lives and it could be considered to fall into three categories of expenditure. At the first level is the necessary cost of daily living such as food, petrol, electricity and laundry detergent. This money comes and goes and does nothing to enhance wealth, except that it may allow some to consume more expensive wine or to eat lobster. The second level are items that will be in use for some time but still limited within a life span such as the refrigerator, your vehicle, furniture and lawnmowers. These will last a while but eventually are replaced or become redundant and subsequently we can consider these to be a component of wealth, since most are there to free your time up for other things (which could be revenue producing), or simply for your enjoyment. The third level is the actual wealth accumulation and now we have houses, jewellery, maybe some art investment and also the cost of higher education. Here we have funds expended for the purpose of increasing your wealth as these items don't wear out, break or become redundant. Note that these things don't produce revenue, so they are not an asset in the economic sense, but they do not deteriorate or disappear. However, most incur an ongoing cost: maintenance and repair for the house or additional insurance costs for your art and jewellery. Note the difference if a business buys equipment or machinery: these are destined for a limited life span and are written off over a fixed time period against the company income and thus do not represent an increase in wealth of the company. Their value accrues to zero.

The same analogy can be applied to the government of a society. There is a large amount of daily expenditure for salaries and consumable materials to keep the country running just like you have at home. Included are expenditures for buildings, vehicles and all sorts of machinery such as garbage trucks, since they should be rented to present a fixed amount of regular costs and thus avoid any unpredictable capital expenditures for maintenance or replacement. The only items in the middle category of investments would be military equipment. This is mostly produced in the country to be defended, where possible, and paid for by the government and thus must represent a type of wealth, since these items are in use for many years and permit the defence of the country and also can help in emergency cases of natural disasters. The last category is vast and includes ports, roads, airports and rail lines plus other items such as national parks and marine reserves. Just like the individual, the country as a whole now accumulates wealth through these investments, but the use is there for all of the citizens, as opposed to individual ownership, which is only for the investor.

Once again we need to be very careful how the government utilises the tax revenue in their spending. Applying it to capital assets is a good thing, but simply increasing bureaucracy and the civil service becomes counterproductive. As the government employment grows, it does so in a non-productive way. There is no increase in assets. Worse, more personnel is withdrawn from the open market and money removed from utilisation by businesses and spent in unproductive ways. The economy actually shrinks, even though employment figures look good because more people are in government employ.

Now the question finally arises: Where does the (printed) money actually come from? It was all very well when the box of tomatoes paper was traded for a chicken paper and both together bought a shovel. So next time a shovel was made the manufacturer could issue a piece of shovel paper with it. This is where the metal bits came into their own and three pieces of silver plus five of copper were the equivalent of a shovel. That is, relatively speaking. The shovel does not have an absolute value, only that which someone who needs one is willing to pay. But free market negotiation solves all that.

Once the government took away the right to issue bits of metal and paper, things began to look different. When the shovel was made and put on the market it actually existed and quite rightly a new piece of shovel paper could be created with it. When some miners dug up more silver and made tradable bits out of this, it also existed and the currency in circulation could thus increase. Where the government takes over the issuing of the currency it now needs to establish a correlation to whatever has actually been produced and the amount of new money printed. This is obviously a pretty difficult task, but allows the intrusion into our lives in that everyone has to report what they have produced and subsequently this is collated and we then pay taxes on that as well. At a certain point this collecting of data becomes more like guesswork and dissociates itself from reality. The government now more or less invents, via the use of statistics, what it imagines the country is producing in additional value. It is important to get this right, because, if you recall, money is just another commodity. If there is too much printed it loses value and we have inflation. If too little is available its relative value increases and people will be reluctant to spend it leading to a reduction in economic activity. The creation of new money and the allocation of purchasing power are a vital economic function and highly profitable. This is therefore a matter of significant public interest and needs to be examined closely.

The government, that is the Central or Reserve Bank, looks after the printing and distributing of money. This is, however, only a small portion of the total currency that exists in the country. When money is printed it is not given to the people directly, but is passed on through the banking system.

New money is created by commercial banks when they extend or create credit, either through making loans or buying existing assets. In creating credit, banks simultaneously create deposits in our bank accounts and this becomes new money when the depositor spends it. Even though the banks' main business is meant to be taking deposits from its customers and lending this money for other uses, the amount available through deposits is insufficient to finance the economy. Thus the Central Bank, or Reserve Bank, issues funds to the banks and charges interest for that. This is known as the Prime Rate and is discussed endlessly in the news media and the political arena. Now the bank has at its disposal seemingly endless amounts of funds to disperse. Obviously this isn't so and there is usually a ratio stipulated by the government as to how much money a bank can lend compared to what it has in deposited reserves and even this can be varied according to the economic circumstances. This is termed the *Fractional Reserve*. During the last financial crisis the ratio was generally lowered, sometimes substantially, to allow more money to flow into the economy.

Ultimately the banks create money by depositing it in someone's account as a loan or payment for an asset, and this is then spent in the economy to purchase other things. Banks are also very careful where they apply this money and want to maintain security through asset backing and most money flows into mortgages and financial investments rather than financing small businesses and manufacturing enterprises. The bank needs confidence that the loan can be repaid and that sufficient assets are available in case of a default.

The difference between rich and poor countries ultimately is determined by the attitude of the inhabitants and the sort of government they are 'blessed' with.

The basic analysis of *Where Does Money Come From?* is neither radical nor new. In fact, central banks around the world support the same description of where new money comes from. And yet many naturally resist the notion that private banks can really create money by simply making an entry in a ledger. Economist J. K. Galbraith suggested why this might be:

The process by which banks create money is so simple that the mind is repelled. When something so important is involved, a deeper mystery seems only decent.

This covers a lot ground so needs to be summarised one more time.

The government receives money from taxes, but usually this is not enough. To fulfill their promises it must borrow from someone. To do so, it creates government bonds via the Treasury, which are simply credit notes that promise the holder to get their money back after a long time with interest. Underlying this, it is often neglected that this money needs to be paid back through future taxation, usually under another administration that will be unlucky enough to have been voted in sometime in the future. These bonds are auctioned off to the largest banks who are interested in investing in the country. In turn the banks get to sell some of these bonds to the Federal Reserve through a process called Open Market Operations. This is a method by which the government can increase or decrease the money supply by buying or selling bonds. When the Reserve Bank buys these bonds they have to pay for them and essentially write a cheque as payment. Except that this cheque does not have any bank account to be drawn from and this is the point where money is created. The banks now take this newly created money and purchase more bonds and the circuit begins again. This is what is simply added to the national debt to be paid off at some unspecified future point. In between all this sit the banks and take a cut from every transaction, still ultimately your tax money. The Federal Reserve is also a private entity owned by shareholders totally unknown, and these shareholders, presumably more financial institutions, receive a 6% dividend as well.

What About Inflation

Everyone who has experienced inflation found they didn't like it. More money is required to obtain the same goods and everyone else seems to be getting the wage raises. Thus inflation is off-handedly declared as being too much money chasing too few goods and in turn the money is devalued to match the amount of money being thrown around to the goods that are available. Seems a bit simplistic and where does all this extra money come from. You guessed it – the government!

To define *inflation* we need to say that it is an increase in the quantity of money, that is not offset by a corresponding increase in the demand for money, with the outcome being a fall in the purchasing power of money. *Deflation* is the opposite, namely a reduction in the quantity of money that is not offset by a fall in the demand for it, such that prices (and incomes) tend to fall. Whether a society is faced with these prospects is determined by the government's *monetary policy*. Thus monetary policy refers to the actions of a central bank, currency board or other regulatory committee, that determine the size and rate of growth of the money supply, which in turn affects interest rates. Monetary policy is maintained through actions such as increasing the interest rate, or changing the amount of money banks need to keep in the vault (bank reserves). The term *fiscal policy* then refers to the way the government receives and spends funds by raising or lowering tax rates and by increasing or (rarely) decreasing money supply. Fiscal policy aims to stabilise economic growth, avoiding a boom and bust economic cycle. Under a loose fiscal policy spending by the government would increase and the budget would be in deficit while interest rates would be lower, while under a tight policy interest rates would rise and the government would curb spending, so as a result the economy should slow down and inflation would lower.

Going back to the original explanation of the creation of wealth, it would say that, as people are busy making and growing things, our wealth increases. Next, to be able to trade these items amongst one another, an according amount of equivalent specie can be generated. That is, the amount of additional money going into circulation must match the value of all the new goods created. Under these circumstances all the goods should maintain their original price. Since an economy is not static, things aren't quite as simple as all that. There are forces that can move prices both ways, up or down. The most common effect is for one of the inputs to the product to change. This is what happens when the price of a barrel of oil increases or some particular raw material becomes very popular and its use increases beyond the current supply. It also happens under adverse weather conditions in area of critical food supplies, which then need to be transported over great distances adding to the input costs. The opposite can happen when there is a sudden improvement in production methods, making these goods less expensive to manufacture. It also happens where some item falls out of favour with the buying public and the demand decreases. Sometimes new technology completely obviates the necessity for an item which is then replaced by a completely new item achieving the same effect for a much lower price. Television screens and solid state storage come to mind. New LED screens have replaced the old cathode ray tubes offering more convenience, lower operating costs and much improved customer satisfaction all at a lower price; and the screens are bigger as well. Almost anything in the computer world is constantly becoming less expensive while offering increased capabilities.

None of these individual events usually are of sufficient magnitude to affect the whole of the economy, so serious inflation must come from somewhere else. In fact, the real outcome should be, as our technology and management techniques are constantly improving, the quantity of goods available should increase and the prices decrease by the laws of supply and demand. So the statement, which can be found in the popular press sometimes, that economic growth fuels inflation is just not true.

What can and has happened in the past is that an economy that is doing well, with a high rate of employment, produces high incomes for businesses, and at that point unions will clamour for getting a better share of this revenue. Through strikes and industrial actions they will enforce wage increases, which in turn will be passed on to the consumer through higher prices and thus pushing inflation. The higher prices in turn will prompt unions to again demand increases to compensate, ultimately for their own indulgences in the first place. Next, this turns into a vicious cycle of inflation, which can unfortunately only be broken by an increase in interest rates to reduce economic activity. This is exactly what happened during the 1970s where this cycle drove inflation to extremes. The start was a typical situation where the USA was in deficit and needed to generate more funds. Going into the election year of 1972 both the President and Congress wanted the economy to look good and thus expanded the money supply and pressured the Federal Reserve to lower interest rates in order to increase business activity. Included in this activity was a freeze on prices and wages – unthinkable nowadays. This all worked right through the election period but the price to be paid was enormous. Once the freeze was off both the businesses and the wage earners needed to make up lost ground and wages and prices took off. At the same time with the increased money supply all went out of control. In 1973 the oil crisis joined into the fracas and was used to a large extent as blame for the crisis. Yet solely the loose money policy of the US government caused inflation to soar first to double digits and to reach 14% by the end of the decade. As a consequence the unions demanded so called COLA (cost of living allowance) which then automatically kept raising wages in accord with inflation and it became a self-fulfilling inflationary cycle.

The general answer about inflation is traditionally described in the *quantity theory of money*. This simply proposes a positive relationship between changes in the money supply and the long-term price of goods. It states that increasing the amount of money in the economy will eventually lead to an equal percentage rise in the prices of products and services. It implies that the amount of money in an economy determines the value of the money in that economy.

105

There is one aspect the astute reader will have observed in the news media. It is stated that even though some countries have been infusing the economy with huge amounts of newly issued funds, in particular the USA, there has not been an according increase in inflation and pundits will say that the economic theory of tying inflation to money printing is wrong. Unfortunately, this is not so. The effect is delayed for several reasons, the first of which is that a large proportion of the funds have gone offshore to earn interest, and also to hold a strong currency against local weak money. The second influence is that a lot of the money will be 'hoarded' in savings or investments, but not to increase spending to purchase goods. Immense amounts of 'theoretical' money is used up in big international funds such as for example the Berkshire Hathaway. Most of the money is represented in share values of international companies such as Apple, Exxon, Google and Petro China. The top 10 corporations alone have a worth of 3.6 Trillion Dollars in 2015. It seems that even as the governments are printing money these new funds are not used in the purchase of goods but are absorbed in the expansion of the probably exaggerated worth of a lot of corporations offering more overpriced products and accordingly increasing the total value of those companies. Along with money tied up in Pension funds plus some of it disappearing in the shadow economy it seems that the issuance of more and more debt is not resulting in increasing inflation. As long as the public has the confidence to expect prices to remain the same, they do not increase their spending even when the money supply expands. Eventually, though, the public will come to the realisation that the money supply will keep increasing and that prices will not return to some previous golden age. To avoid facing higher prices in the future people will begin to spend more of the money that had been stored up to now. If this is combined with the return of large amounts of money from overseas the market will be flooded with money and inflation will finally catch up.

Foreign Trade

The other factor influencing how an economy works is an external one and concerns how we trade with another foreign economy. Since trade, as we have seen, does well when it is free and people can exchange goods and services amongst each other in the group. It then makes sense to extend this to other areas outside the local economic grouping. Trading outside your country has distinct advantages: It extends the palette of products available to in the market, it allows an increase in production and sales of your existing products, and it presents an opportunity to obtain the same products at a lower cost, freeing up funds for other items. This last point is of great contention and will be addressed a little later.

First of all a misconception needs to be cleared up at the outset and that is the argument that money leaves the country and can't be used by the inhabitants any more. In Australia large amounts of income are generated by the mining industry which consists of very large international companies. Recently a politician obviously unaware of the economics of trade stated that these companies should pay much higher taxes since "80% of the profits are leaving the country anyway". He must think that these funds simply disappear down a black or green hole never to be seen again. So picture yourself in another country, you own shares in a large Australian mining company and you have received a satisfying dividend which presumably you deposit in your bank. Being in a different country you have no use for the Australian Dollars and the funds are exchanged into the local currency. Now the bank has Australian Dollars bought from you and in turn needs to get rid of them. A number of things can happen now: another customer will need the $AU to purchase something there or they are simply sold on the currency market. Interest rates may be favourable for $AU and the money is invested in bonds or certificates of deposit with an Australian Bank. In any case the money is somehow repatriated to Australia since it cannot be used in any other country. In a macro sense this complies very neatly with the necessity of circulating money. Imbalances in this arrangement are generally adjusted by the trade in the currency. If a currency is very popular, maybe because that country's economy is doing well or their interest rates are higher than others, then more money will flow into that economy and the value of its currency will increase because of its desirability.

The Concept of Comparative Advantage

This concept, first articulated by Daniel Ricardo, merits its own section because of its immense importance today. The concept simply states that each entity should concentrate on products which it is most capable of supplying at a lower cost, while at the same time trading with other entities which are not as efficient. It is a little confusing but an example will illustrate quickly what the implications are for world trade (and for individual interactions as well).

At first it is defined that anyone who is better at something than anyone else has an *absolute advantage*. Say you are an architect and the very best in the land. At the same time you are also the best draughtsman for architecture. Since the more valuable activity is that of architecture you would engage someone who is slightly less of a draughtsman to do your drawings at a lower cost than your time as an architect is worth. Thus the lower cost draughtsman has a comparative advantage, because your opportunity cost for drawing alone is too high when you could be earning more in the architects function. To establish someone's comparative advantage one needs to compare the opportunity cost. It is more efficient to sublet an activity to someone else if you can achieve a higher income from another activity.

The more important aspect of this lies in international trade where there are constant complaints about protecting a country's industries through trade tariffs and import duties, in order to maintain employment and preserve those industries. A simple example puts this attitude to rest most emphatically. Take two countries, both of which produce tires for cars and TV sets for the home. Country A can produce 200 tires or 100 TV sets in a day, so assuming half the time is spent on each they can manage 100 tires plus 50 TV sets a day. Then there is country B who can only manage to produce 50 of either in a day resulting in 25 of each every day. Although country A is vastly superior in all manufacturing, trading with country B will give both an advantage. Looked at in total both countries can produce 125 tires and 75 TV sets a day.

Examining the opportunity costs in country A, 1 TV set is equivalent to 2 tires while in country B 1 TV is equal to 1 tire. Thus country A can produce tires cheaper (in terms of TVs) by a ratio of 2 to 1. In country B there is no difference: producing 1 TV has the same cost as 1 tire. Therefore country B can produce TVs cheaper – in terms of tires – than country A and here lies the advantage. Country B should now produce only TV sets which is where their advantage lies. If country A imports TVs from country B they are setting free their advantage and for 25 TVs imported from B they can make now an additional 50 tires plus only 25 TV sets. Since country B has produced no tires they will have to import tires from country A to make up the 25 required, but the total of production is now 150 tires and still 75 TVs which is better than before trading. If country B is willing to trade 1 tire or more for each TV it produces and country A is willing to trade 2 tires or less for each of country B's TV's, then they will settle at a price between 1 and 2 tires for each TV. They now have the same number of TVs as before but have an excess of tires to export. Magic!

There will be a lot of people contradicting this theory on the grounds that externalities, such as the cost of pollution in the second country, are not captured, or that the workers freed up from one type of production cannot readily be employed in a higher quality industry. Also an objection may be that in the long run these conditions will change and by that time one has lost the ability to manufacture the higher cost good at home. These sorts of diatribes are spurious in that the original theory is just that – it is up to the participants to negotiate the conditions and for the countries to anticipate future outcomes and act accordingly. It is lazy to say that what applies today does not work anymore tomorrow – that is the way of the world.

Reserve Currency

The observant amateur economist will have noticed that the US Dollar tends to be prominent in international transactions and in the valuation of various processes generally. The reason for this lies in the position that the Dollar occupies as that of a *Reserve Currency*. This term is used when there is a common use of one currency between other currency countries. If France buys oil from Iraq then the transaction takes place in US Dollars. This is more of a convenience rather than a hard rule and other countries have sufficiently strong and reliable currencies that they can be used in international trade. The US Dollar is just the one that is most wide spread and the most held foreign currency up to now. Originally the first reserve currency was the British Pound when it was backed by gold, since for many countries it was more convenient to hold the Pound rather than physical gold. Trading was usually done in gold, but using the Pound had the confidence that the Bank of England would hand over gold at a fixed rate upon presentation of the bank notes.

After the Second World War through the Bretton Woods Agreement this function was passed to the US Dollar while it could be traded for gold at the fixed rate of $35 per ounce. At the same time the International Monetary Fund (IMF) was formed to maintain the Federal Reserve's commitment to keep the gold value fixed. However, being banks, this agreement was not held, and the US did not hold enough gold to honour all outstanding currency as promised. When called for by France and later other countries gold reserves depleted, and in 1971 the gold link to the Dollar was broken. The Dollar was then kept as a reserve currency because there was so much of it floating in the world that it was still more practical to use.

A currency that is used universally in international trade requires that the issuing country has to be a large trading country and that the currency holds its value in respect to valuable commodities. Other countries may have steadier currencies such as the Deutsche Mark and the Swiss Franc, but trade with these countries was dwarfed by the enormous US economy. All foreign monies have to return to their country of origin eventually and this can only be done by investment in the country or by purchase of her goods; and there were always more of these available in the US economy.

Of late, however, the Dollar has suffered from inflation, and, through the growth of other country's economies like the European Union and the rise of the Chinese economy, it has lost a little of its shine. There have been indications that the Chinese government has amassed a large store of gold and prevented external trading in gold, which could lead to the demand for the Chinese Yuan to increase dramatically which in turn would lead to a drastic reduction in the value of the US Dollar. Many holders of US Dollars throughout the world would seek to return these back to the US leading to a flood of currency into the US, causing prices to increase. Keeping in mind that approximately half of the issued US Dollars reside outside the country, the risk to the Dollar is rather high. As long as the US government insists on issuing more money through its policy of quantitative easing, the Dollar will be inflating. Only a change in direction of this policy can prevent an ultimate serious devaluation of the US Dollar.

The Trouble with Banks

The trouble with banks is the same as with the government and with businesses: they are all run by people. This may sound mundane, but you have to think about it. In government what happens is that representatives get elected and before you know it they are the specialists at everything, they now need to show the world that they can do all this better than everyone else and believe they have a mandate to introduce all manner of extreme reforms just to satisfy their egos. This does not necessarily apply all the time but we can be sure it will show up sooner or later. And the same applies to a bank.

Keeping firmly in mind that the bank has a board of directors and innumerable shareholders, it is unsurprising that they all want to benefit from being involved with a bank. You, too, are involved in a bank, but at the other end. Remember that the bank takes your money and uses it to earn money for itself. Only then can the bank expend any thoughts on how to give you a share. Whenever this does not work in the bank's favour, the rules will be changed. Fees will go up, returns on investments will go down, and interest rates on loans will go up – as long as this is favourable for the bank.

Initially the bank's purpose was to take your money and lend it in turn to those that required funds for other business purposes; whether to build a new building or to expand an existing business, the purpose was always to increase the wealth of the community. You could lend directly to an entity and receive interest, but the bank exists to absorb the risk contained therein by spreading it among many clients, and having the backing of lawyers that an individual could ill afford.

There are, not unexpectedly, a number of complications that appear at this point. Since the bank has your money and generally lends it out to others it must make sure you have access to your funds should you suddenly desire to spend them. If the money is not actually there the bank has a problem and must round up your money elsewhere. The result of this is that banks all borrow and lend money amongst each other, borrow from the government Reserve Bank or search for money in the big wide world. Government regulations have also intruded and created rules that govern banks behaviour. The first is that of course a bank must maintain a percentage of their deposits in cash and liquid reserves for that very reason and this called *liquidity*. In Western democracies that percentage can be anywhere from 5% to 20% and varies if markets experience difficulties such as in the financial crisis of 2008. The term for this is *fractional reserve banking*. It merely means that anyone taking in someone else's money can safely lend only a portion of it, a fraction having to be retained as a reserve against likely withdrawals. Credit Unions and Building Societies have different rules and are restricted to loan out only exactly what there is on deposit.

Now considering how banks borrow and lend money brings on a new concern. The funds banks lend to individuals and enterprises for a large part tend to be long term commitments – 10, 15, 20 year long term debt to give the borrower predictable outlays and to allow financial planning for the business. However, when someone deposits money with financial institutions he wants to hedge his bets by not wanting to predict the future, and so most investments of this type will be short term in nature – 3, 6, 12 months and less frequently 2 or 5-year terms. This leads back to the situation where banks are constantly on the look-out for funds to help them balance these two opposing directions.

What happened next is why many blame banks for perverting the whole system. Since banks have immense amounts of money available and need some return on this money, what started as a simple system of depositing money and having it available for withdrawal or other wealth creating measures eventually turned into a system of gambling. The same people mentioned above, who are looking for a return on their investment now said, well, all this money is not doing a lot, let's trade shares, deal in currencies and buy corporate bonds. This way, what was a deposit bank turned into an investment bank, and some say that this is in fact an illegitimate use of your money. Of course, all is well as long as the depositor's money is still there for withdrawal, but soon greed sets in, especially when things have been going well for a while. Thus more and more funds are diverted and invested ultimately not only in the stock market, but also in inter-bank gambling.

Consider this in the USA: It seems that the Carter administration's Community Reinvestment Act of 1977 was the first step down the road of banks being compromised. This act forced financial institutions to lend mortgages to individuals who were previously thought to be an unacceptable risk for lending. These were later referred to as *subprime* lending. Whether this involves any social overtones we should leave to other literature to discuss. An awful lot of the poor credit then was bought up by the federal agencies of Fanny Mae (Federal National Mortgage Association) and Freddie

Mac (Federal Home Loan Mortgage Corporation) which only represent more tax dollars wasted. These two agencies, even though they are independent from the government, were once again a very bad idea. They are meant to purchase mortgages from the banks, thereby freeing up funds for more mortgages to be sold. Of course all the riskiest mortgages wound up in their portfolio. Some of these were bundled into packages, called *Mortgage Backed Securities*. The original act was amended several times to increase scrutiny of the banks and enforce compliance. Later it was amended to include student loans through the Higher Education Opportunity Act of 2008, which is currently building up for the next crisis.

The outcome was that the default rate on mortgages increased but essentially the banks had no immediate recourse against non-payment. Additionally, since no bank wanted to carry all this risk on their own these 'products' were bundled: high risk and low risk loans were assembled into multi-billion dollar packages and resold to other banks. These were CDOs – Collateralized Debt Obligations. CDOs are simply collections of various interest bearing debts such as bonds and mortgages divided into several 'tranches' which are established by the risk involved. Senior tranches are very solid and involve little risk and subsequent lesser tranches carry higher risk and higher interest rates. But all arrive together in a package.

Another bundle was called Credit Default Swaps and here we get more into the gambling realm. A CDS is essentially an insurance policy on an investment. The buyer of the CDS pays the seller a premium similar to an insurance premium. If the protected investment defaults the seller must pay the buyer the nominal value of the investment. If the investment is relatively safe such as municipal bonds there is little risk. As time went by more and more dubious investments were included in CDSs and the outcome was that, just like an investment in shares of a company, the original seller of the CDS can go bankrupt and the insurance is then worthless. So the whole thing is based on the solidity and confidence in the seller but not true market values.

Since some loans in the CDOs had a higher interest rate, it made the 'bundle' look very attractive and the borrowings were secured by actual investment value. This became a game of inverse musical chairs: Whoever was left holding the larges bundles, once defaults set in, would be the loser in this gambling game between the banks. Eventually defaults became large enough to be noticeable and prices fell due to an oversupply of properties and banks became owners of a lot of relatively valueless real estate. Once the domino effect set in it became the global financial crisis of 2008 and the actual problem now was that no entity trusted any other and the normal supply of money circulating between the banks dried up. No bank was going to lend money to another bank if it was not sure of repayment, and since all the trading of 'bundles' involved a lot of deception as to their true value – in fact it is certain that no bank knew any longer what was contained in these packages and what the implications were – financial institutions simply hung onto their funds until the situation became more settled. As a consequence, a lot of companies that had long or short term debt to be rolled over during this period became unable to find new funds, or were forced to pay exorbitant interest rates and thus could no longer manage their finances and consequently were bankrupted through no fault of their own! This in turn affected large investment funds especially retirement funds that were heavily weighted to shares which now lost value or disappeared altogether.

So let no one say that the banks are poor little innocent lambs.

A lovely unattributed parable found on the Internet illustrates the situation:

Helga is the proprietor of a bar. She realizes that virtually all of her customers are unemployed alcoholics and, as such, can no longer afford to patronize her bar.

To solve this problem, she comes up with a new marketing plan that allows her customers to drink now, but pay later. Helga keeps track of the drinks consumed on a ledger (thereby granting the customers' loans).

Word gets around about Helga's "drink now, pay later" marketing strategy and, as a result, increasing numbers of customers flood into Helga's bar. Soon she has the largest sales volume for any bar in town.

By providing her customers freedom from immediate payment demands, Helga gets no resistance when, at regular intervals, she substantially increases her prices for wine and beer, the most consumed beverages. Consequently, Helga's gross sales volume increases massively.

A young and dynamic vice-president at the local bank recognizes that these customer debts constitute valuable future assets and increases Helga's borrowing limit. He sees no reason for any undue concern, since he has the debts of the unemployed alcoholics as collateral!

At the bank's corporate headquarters, expert traders figure a way to make huge commissions, and transform these customer loans into DRINKBONDS. These "securities" then are bundled and traded on international securities markets.

Naive investors don't really understand that the securities being sold to them as "AA" "Secured Bonds" really are debts of unemployed alcoholics. Nevertheless, the bond prices continuously climb, and the securities soon become the hottest-selling items for some of the nation's leading brokerage houses.

One day, even though the bond prices still are climbing, a risk manager at the original local bank decides that the time has come to demand payment on the debts incurred by the drinkers at Helga's bar. He so informs Helga.

Helga then demands payment from her alcoholic patrons, but being unemployed alcoholics they cannot pay back their drinking debts. Since Helga cannot fulfill her loan obligations she is forced into bankruptcy. The bar closes and Helga's 11 employees lose their jobs.

116

Overnight, DRINKBOND prices drop by 90%. The collapsed bond asset value destroys the bank's liquidity and prevents it from issuing new loans, thus freezing credit and economic activity in the community.

The suppliers of Helga's bar had granted her generous payment extensions and had invested their firms' pension funds in the BOND securities. They find they are now faced with having to write off her bad debt and with losing over 90% of the presumed value of the bonds.

Her wine supplier also claims bankruptcy, closing the doors on a family business that had endured for three generations, her beer supplier is taken over by a competitor, who immediately closes the local plant and lays off 150 workers. Fortunately though, the bank, the brokerage houses and their respective executives are saved and bailed out by a multibillion dollar no-strings attached cash infusion from the government.

The funds required for this bailout are obtained by new taxes levied on employed, middle-class, non-drinkers who've never been in Helga's bar.

Now do you understand?

Here is a follow up on the 2008 crisis, starting again in 2001. The situation was further compounded, after the so-called dot-com bubble burst in 2001, and with the 9/11 disaster combined to lead the Federal Reserve under Alan Greenspan to lower interest rates dramatically. This may have been well-intentioned, but the outcome was the opposite of the intention. A bubble in home ownership began as lower interest rates drove more people to purchase homes or refinance their homes at lower rates. It was then inevitable that house prices rose dramatically due to higher demand and many owners now had houses that were worth much more than they thought. The market once again confused price with value – the price may go up but the value is still one house, depending on location. Owners now refinanced their more highly rated houses with new higher loans and spent the extra money. This all looked good in the economy but was not sustainable. By and by half of all this mortgage money flowed to Fannie Mae and Freddie Mac whose portfolios now became immense. Without going into the details of the following crash, it turned out that the two agencies also misled the public about the extent of the insecure securities that were parked in their portfolios. It seems to have taken about $200 billion to enable them to continue in business after 2008. The US government, however, states that all the money for their bail out has since been paid back and additional funds have also flowed into general revenue.

Shadow Finances

But things are actually much worse than this example. As mentioned earlier almost all countries are in debt in one way or another and their only revenue is your taxes. During the 2008 financial crisis governments promised support for the banks, that is, financial backing in case of need. Governments also promised to back other governments, basically to save the appearance that all is under control. But it was not, as the European situation showed. With all this to-ing and fro-ing between governments, banks and more governments, the total value of all this money involved in bailing each other out is assumed to be 100 times the size of the real world economy. Think about that – 100 times. This is referred to as the Shadow Financial System. Sounds like the sort of bubble we were talking about earlier is at the root of this situation. And bubbles burst – as the South Seas Bubble did. Where this shadow bubble is heading we need look no further than Europe again. As more and more money is required by the defaulted economies, the European Union demands more and more integration. The establishment of a larger overriding monetary institution, for example a European Rescue Bank, allows the governments to 'invent' more funds for this institution and for a while more invisible money is shuffled around the table behind everyone's back. When the crunch comes next time there will be calls for a worldwide financial institution – and heaven protect us if this leads to the ultimate institution - a UN level bank!

There is another layer to the Shadow System and that concerns private institutions. This is the network of non-depository financial institutions such as investment banks, hedge funds, so-called structured investment vehicles, money market funds and all sorts of non-bank money institutions. In other words any institution where money collects out of reach of regulations, which includes unregulated activities carried out by regulated institutions. Remember that the basic bank consists of two components: deposit and lending. The bank takes money in from depositors and pays an interest on that (or not) and the same bank lends money out to commercial customers for mortgages, consumer loans and other business loans. In this business the bank faces two problems: a liquidity risk, should depositors suddenly decide to take out their money and a solvency risk if all the outstanding loans suddenly go bad. These are known problems and are well dealt with through backstops in the system to protect the banks and the depositors. To make money available for a sudden withdrawal crisis there is usually the federally run Reserve Bank to make funds available to the bank. Where the bank runs the risk of insolvency through bad loans or investments a Federal Deposit Insurance system is in place to protect the depositors up to a certain point. The regulatory support structure of a government is provided to take care of these known and conventional risks.

However, a lot of investment institutions will take on corporate bonds to earn interest at a better rate and fully well understanding that the risk is higher. What was now invented behind the scene was a splitting of the risks for these investments. There is a risk on the interest rate which may become unproductive as interest rates change, and there is a risk of credit default where the issuing company is bankrupt. All these investments were split into the three components: the original money for the bond, an interest rate risk and a default risk. The latter two became known as interest rate swaps and credit default swaps, where another institution sold a sort of insurance via a premium to carry the risk for the original investor.

119

The problems began when these packages came up for renewal and the lending institution was a little more worried than before, and therefore changed the conditions by a few percentage points. The borrowers were now left with a gap of a few percentage points and needed to fill this with other funds.

Looking at the market would not help because we are operating in the shadows here. There are no market guidelines or listed values available and this inevitably led to a write down of the original asset. What we don't know at this point, and the market out there still doesn't know, is where it stops. As long as every player can convince the other players to play along the system struggles on, but from our bubble section earlier we have learnt that this is also just a bubble, although an immense one, that is still growing, and a small crisis can make it burst. It is a game of confidence once again and probably the only way out is to adjust the insurance premiums to match the risk – if that risk can be defined more closely.

Just to give an indication of the size of the problem, here is an excerpt from an article in November 2012:

"The shadow banking industry has grown to about US$71 trillion, US$6 trillion bigger than thought, leading global regulators to seek more oversight of financial transactions that fall outside traditional oversight. The size of the shadow banking system, which includes the activities of money market funds, monoline insurers and off-balance sheet investment vehicles, "can create systemic risks" and "amplify market reactions when market liquidity is scarce", said the Financial Stability Board, an international body that monitors the global financial system. "appropriate monitoring and regulatory frameworks for the shadow banking system needs to be in place to mitigate the build-up of risks," the FSB said in a report. (Bloomberg)"

The FSB was established via the G20 forum in April 2009 to monitor and try to control finances worldwide. It is unclear how it will find all the money and then convince the institutions to let the FSB control the investments, or even just set down guidelines to be followed by all the participants and non-participants. No institution will be ready to disclose all their shenanigans on an international stage, so good luck to them. The shadow financial system will probably lead to the biggest crash of all when someone calls for the payment of real money and it will not be there.

Capitalism

Capitalism! There is that word again. All the nasty connotations drop from the heavens. All our problems can be easily laid at the doors of greed, selfishness and love of money. Where does the word come from – and how does it relate to business?

The words 'capital' and 'capitalist' appeared first in the middle of the 18th century. There was some use of these words in France previously, but this seemed to refer simply to individuals who had capital available to invest in farming or factories. David Ricardo gives the following definition of capital:

"Capital is that part of the wealth of a country which is employed in production, and consists of food, clothing, tools, raw materials, machinery, etc. necessary to give effect to labour." [1817, David Ricardo, Chapter V, On Wages]

More generally the term capital referred not necessarily to money but to all the components available to be utilised in a business, including human capital, that is, a workforce of skilled and unskilled labour that could be employed to create goods. Capital would thus also be land for agriculture or buildings and machinery.

In all cases of the early usage of these terms they are describing an availability of capital to achieve ends, i.e. employing people to produce goods by using the capital to invest in the business and to pay the employees. Never was there any indication that this was at all systematic. Even Karl Marx never used the term capitalism directly, he always circumscribed it as 'capitalist form of production' or similar wording. It was not until the early 20th century the term was more widely applied. The only people who needed to coin a usable term were of course our old friends the socialists/communists. No one ever who followed free market and free trade principles has claimed that capitalism is a 'movement' or that capitalism is a 'system', and there are no Capitalist Parties. There are, however, socialist and communist movements, systems and parties. It is evident the term was thrust into the public domain simply to create a target and to provide a counterpoint to socialist and union activities.

Capitalism can be described but not defined. It has no program of purpose or ideological objectives. It is a resultant condition of human interactions brought into existence by the same factors that form a social order, where it provides the operating formats for what are called economic activities. Capitalism carries within it the guarantee of private ownership, including the means of production and ensures that all interactions between human beings are conducted on a voluntary basis.

A capitalist as defined would only want to be free to carry on business and trade and to remove restrictions of status, so that individuals can follow their own wishes and inclinations and not have these imposed upon by conventions of church, state or unionism. The result of this freedom is the liberation of the spirit and inventiveness of the human and liberates untapped energies for the pursuit of happiness. In no way must we equate self-interest with selfishness since the latter is simply an inward-turned extreme with no particular point. Self-interest on the other hand, is compatible with the interest of others and fosters it. Following ones inclinations and attending to ones occupations results in finding the best possible allocation of limited resources, with the result of improving not only his but everybody's circumstances.

Furthermore, a combination of competition within sectors of production and cooperation amongst different sectors of production leads to a partition of labour between different specialties and provides increases in productivity in order to satisfy an increasing consumer market. This is particularly important when considered in the realm of free international trade. We've already seen that money of one currency cannot actually 'disappear' overseas, it has to return by some economic means. And a similar fallacy persists in the world of free trade amongst nations whereby some highly educated entities believe that cheap overseas labour destroys the local economy and undercuts established pricing, thus forcing workers from the labour force. Nothing could be further from the truth.

A typical current example is being constantly used by the economically illiterate, and that is that the Chinese currency is vastly undervalued and thus affects the output of countries importing from China at prices local manufacturers cannot match by reducing internal demand for local goods. What is forgotten in this argument is that first of all the Chinese products are to a large extent an input into the local economy thus making even local products less expensive, and allowing local manufacturers to expand their output while still making a profit. Secondly, the money saved by buying the lower priced imports can be spent on other things, some of which will be made locally, and some of which will be services, once again conforming to the requirement of currency circulating. So, if indeed the Chinese government is keeping the value of the renminbi artificially low, the result will be inflation in China as their own imports will be priced too high. This will in turn eventually result in price rises in the importing countries as well. Importantly, this effect of importing low cost goods is no different from an event of technological breakthroughs, which lowers production costs of some items, and is this not what all producers are looking for constantly?

And yet, books and movies invariably present the capitalist as the enemy, as the perpetrator of unspeakable human suffering. The businessman is invariably presented as lying and deceptive, as an agent for social and human harm, as greedy and manipulative and only concerned with the exploitation of the defenseless worker to squeeze the last possible bit of earnings out of everything. The only way to save humanity from such evil is for the 'hero' to step in who refuses to 'take any more of this', or for the government to regulate the behaviour of these individuals and companies to protect society from such malevolence.

Sometimes it seems that only Ayn Rand's work *Atlas Shrugged* in particular stands alone as a bulwark against the relentless onslaught of the educated elites against capitalism. Here is her take on the evil of money:

"So you think that money is the root of all evil?" said Francisco d'Anconia. "Have you ever asked what is the root of money? Money is a tool of exchange, which can't exist unless there are goods produced and men able to produce them. Money is the material shape of the principle that men who wish to deal with one another must deal by trade and give value for value. Money is not the tool of the moochers, who claim your product by tears, or of the looters, who take it from you by force. Money is made possible only by the men who produce. Is this what you consider evil?

The educated elite, the intelligentsia, of course, only resents the success of the lesser class because the entrepreneur has managed to be successful by sheer work and cleverness, rather than by elite education and top level connections. Following capitalist principles evens out the playing field, so to speak. It appears that you have businesspeople, who don't seem to be very intelligent or well-educated but have lots of money, acquire political power through their wealth, and then rise in the social hierarchy, whereas the really intelligent people, the intellectuals, are less important. The reaction to this situation is the forcing of more regulations and prohibitions to bring the business community back under control of the intellectuals. The idea of a free market does not sit well with the elite as they don't really understand its dynamics and fluidity of markets, which appears uncontrolled at all times. The outcome is that the business community is legislated in such ways as minimum wage laws, medical care systems, pension deductions and a number of freebies such as maternity/paternity leave and carer's leave. All these ultimately have to be paid for by the customer in higher prices for goods.

124

Foreign Trade Again

People trade because they want to; trading makes it possible for them to satisfy their desires with less exertion. When a nation imports more than it exports during a given period, its consumers are better off — or at least they can be: much depends on who controls the increased amount of wealth. And yet, we always hear about 'balance of trade', which must be positive under all circumstances: the media, the government, the opposition - all want a trade surplus. Why this should be so is difficult to explain.

In the imagination of people who haven't thought this through properly there exists an exploited class of workers in other countries, who are slaving for little pay to supply the first world countries with luxury goods at low prices, while at the same time destroying jobs in these first world countries. When you look a little closer you would find that the exploited workers in developing economies are mainly in agriculture, mining, services to the elite and manufacturing for local consumption. Generally workers involved in export trade are in particular 'economic zones' or operate under special economic conditions. Every country's administration strives to minimize unemployment to pacify and occupy the population, and export in a lot of less developed counties is an ideal way to support this endeavor. Usually the factories or work places are set up and paid for by foreign investment, and the managerial structure – which would not be available locally – is also imposed from outside. As a result the government is made to look good, supporting the development of the country's industry and helping the population to be employed and most likely also become better educated. All this is achieved with just a few tax concessions on revenue that would not have been there anyway without outside support. The outcome is a situation where the local population sees an increase in wealth because individuals are employed and spend money received from exporting goods. In the countries where these goods arrive the population also benefits from an increase in wealth, since a lot of the goods imported now cost less than when produced locally and the individual has more money available for other items.

Government Again

Before examining some economic theories over the ages we once again have to look at the selfishness aspect. If there were to be proper economic theories that could be verified, who would they serve best? The shovel maker just does his thing and the farmer just produces vegetables to trade for other stuff, and they do not need nor are they interested in financial theories. They are interested in how to grow things better and how to make things more efficiently and then more money will come to them.

There is once again only one entity interested in theories and control and that is the government, this time in conjunction with vested interests, speak banks and other financial institutions. The reason for the government is very simple: to exert control. If all participants in the economy are left to their own devices the government cannot control the individual or better yet the masses. All theories that have been invented by so-called economists are in support of government – see the case of Napoleon above. Originally the amount of money in circulation was directly related to all the products that had physically been produced by someone. The shovel maker received a note for 5kg of tomatoes for one shovel he delivered. He can take this to the wood mill and receive 10m of round wood for his handles and now the tomato note is in the hands of the wood mill owner. He can pay one of his men for a day's work who takes the note and collects the tomatoes. The note is now back with the original issuer. He will hang onto it and pass it onto another customer for some other product. So far there is a direct relationship between the products and the notes in circulation. If the tomato grower has a good year he can issue more tomato notes, BUT he has to keep in mind that eventually he will need to deliver the according amount of tomatoes for his notes. It thus behooves him to keep precise track of all the notes he has issued to be sure he can still deliver. The interjection of a generalised note of some overriding value, such as the invention of money provided does not invalidate this system. He now receives money for his product and spends it to obtain supplies and food etc. If he wants to have more money he will need to grow more tomatoes. Ultimately this implies that all the notes in circulation represent all that the society has produced or is producing - at that moment in time. Now some will say that this is a good reason for something like the gold standard to be introduced, but of course there is not enough gold in the world to support this any more.

This was only possible for a government who wanted to take over the system of money circulation and ultimately introduced gold as a promissory note, you know: ...promises to pay the bearer on demand. All nonsense of course, no government would actually pay you out in gold – or any other commodity for that matter. You can still buy gold from a bank, but at inflated prices and treated as just another commodity.

Once government has a hold of the money in circulation there will be only one aim and that is to make itself popular for re-election – where these elections are held. If the money supply is controlled by the government all relationship to the original bartering system has been broken. It becomes irrelevant if the shovel maker has made 100 shovels for which he expects to trade enough food for the same time period that he spent making shovels. The government imposes an artificial value to the bartering chip - minus their taxes – and you are simply left with the hope that you can still buy enough food. The actual value of the currency is determined by the vagaries of government thinking.

Since now the actual value of the money has become dissociated from the goods it represents, the government has to start inventing reasons for its actions, and why things aren't working as expected, should it all collapse. The money a government spends does not actually produce goods for the market and by and by the value of the money in circulation is diluted, which in simple terms means inflation. To offer reasonable sounding explanations in order to hide sheer incompetence, theories have been produced to explain all manner of things. The first persons looking at some form of economic theory did this out of curiosity and usually in conjunction with other lines of investigation going at that time, but these theories soon were perverted in order to feed some self-centred and selfish purposes of the next theoretician. Since then there has been a constant conflict between those who want to leave people alone to do their business as in *laissez-faire* and those who want to control society by the economy, the *dirigistes*. Along the way, a government will try to extend control over other endeavors like communications, water, transport and bank regulations for example. The outcome is as usual: the government will support those directions of thinking that support their own ideas of how best to exert control, and actively fight people who oppose this direction of thinking. The current idiocy of climate change is a very good example of this type of support – no one who questions the alarmist theories and predictions has ever received a single penny of support, but gets vilified and smeared at every opportunity.

So the direction of economic thought begins innocently with people contemplating what makes the world and society work, and later having these thoughts attacked and twisted into more self-serving or government serving directions. As we will see next, economies tend to run in a cyclical fashion and it is exactly this cycle of growth and regression that the government wants and needs to control.

Economic Cycles

When we look at the history of science and engineering there is a definite path visible how theories were put forward, tested and either discarded or built upon. The reason for this is simply that all scientific theory can be repeatedly tested and verified by anyone and its ultimate acceptance rests on a step called falsification. This means that whenever a single fact appears that does not fit the proposed theory and cannot support it, the theory has to be changed or abandoned. This doesn't mean that all scientists are all that honest - history abounds with examples where a scientist has simply skewed the results of his tests to fit his pet theory. He may have invested years in a program only to find it led nowhere or was entirely unsupportable. Human nature does not like to admit failure, and with even a small amount of self-deception this person might alter the results of his investigations to suit his pet theory, and perhaps also maintain research funding. The outcome is usually inevitable in that no other scientist can replicate these results and the theory then collapses.

With economic theory the situation is quite different. There can only be theories and observations. We cannot try an economic theory on a society and then go back and say that didn't work, so let's try a different approach. Once a governing body has applied an approach to influence an economy they are stuck with it, and, much like the scientist above, do not like to admit failure and instead constantly change the interpretation of the activity to suit the current situation. Thus there can never be an ultimate verifiable theory of economics simply because we cannot have a control situation alongside an experiment in economic manipulation. Or in the words of Ben Bernanke:

"Economics is a highly sophisticated field of thought that is superb at explaining to policymakers precisely why the choices they made in the past were wrong. About the future, not so much. However, careful economic analysis does have one important benefit, which is that it can help kill ideas that are completely logically inconsistent or wildly at variance with the data. This insight covers at least 90 percent of proposed economic policies."

We have on the other hand some examples available where after the ravages of the Second World War side by side economies were established with different principles. So we have East/West Germany and North/South Korea. Taiwan against mainland China is a good comparison showing how a free market system immediately produced a higher living standard in Taiwan, while China served as an abysmal example of totalitarian socialism. The outcome proved to be that ultimately China had to accede to allowing more and more economic freedom, although individual or politic freedom is still not to be expected under current plans. The economies of Hong Kong and Singapore provide a different type of comparison. Both started as free economies but whereas Hong Kong under British rule was left to its own devices, Singapore became more and more controlled by a dirigiste government. The outcome is that both entities have a high standard of living, but (at least until 1989) Hong Kong has actually a 20% better economic position and Singapore has instead accumulated a mountain of debt (300 billion $US in 2015 or 110 % of GDP) while Hong Kong in 1989 had no debt.

There are luckily some facts that are very basic and observable and can be used to develop theories in abundance. First of all there is the economic cycle. We have no details on it but it does exist and goes like this: at some point where we start everybody is confident and does their business and all is going well. This is called *expansion*. As the expansion takes its course there are always some pessimists in the crowd and since a little inflation is inevitable, the negativity can spread and business slows down to what then becomes a *recession*. This is followed by a *contraction*, where people tend to pull in their horns, spend less, pay off debts instead, and there is a general reduction in business activity. This also cannot last because others now see opportunities arising out of these ashes and jump in with new schemes, and utilising cheap financing start up new enterprises. This in turn inspires confidence in others who don't want to miss out on the upturn and we head into a *revival*. Much as the other stages it is self-perpetuating as more and more participants join in to make a buck and we go back to expansion.

What we don't know anything about is the length of time these cycles take. An expansion can last 2 years or 12 years. No more can we say how strong or weak each stage will be and even though each cycle is recurring it is not cyclical, that is, each section can be of different length and amplitude to each other and to each new recurrence. Needless to say governments obviously hate this sort of thing and want to control it. There is nothing worse in life for an administration to have an election coming up, just when the economy is slowing down and unemployment increasing. Normally they try to throw more money at it. Your money again.

Let's look a little closer at the cycles. In an *expansion* the whole world is full of confidence and positiveness. There are no wars or only small skirmishes, there is lots of international trade and the cost of living is manageable or even considered cheap. People will spend more and, if interest rates are low at this time, will also borrow more readily. There is labour mobility, rising commodity prices, an abundance of work availability and even longer working hours to satisfy an increasing demand. The expansion in demand allows prices to rise and companies to invest in expanding facilities and companies are likely to have good bottom lines and offer increased dividends, which in turn leads to a rise in the stock market as well. All this propels the economy into a paradisiacal situation and the happiness index is high.

Nothing lasts forever and the demise of this situation is already planned in – we just don't know when. Some companies will stretch too far in expansion, some unions will demand too much in wage increases and ultimately some companies will be in strife. Unit costs of products have risen but now profits are squeezed and the financial results no longer look so great. Banks have issued all the loans they can within their liquidity limits and borrowing rates begin to creep upwards everywhere. Central banks will try to fight inflation by raising rates and making access to money more difficult. Consumers decide they no longer will accept price increases and become more discerning in their purchases and begin to pay down debt or just save a little more. Slowly profits begin to decrease and company reports become slightly more pessimistic. Journalists, ever sensationalistic, pick out a few cases of bad news or the demise of some sectors or companies and predict dire consequences. As sales slow down, inventories have to reduce, more special sales are announced and a general trend of reducing all the optimism sets in. As with the expansion period, the signals feed on themselves and a snowballing effect sets in. If now a few banks get into trouble as well, having been too careless with their investments or too generous with their lending, the front page news becomes more and more pessimistic and cataclysmic and we are now in full *recession*.

A *recession* can be defined as some period (usually 2 or 3 quarters) of no growth or regression, or what is illiterately referred to as 'negative growth' (conjuring up Dot Wordsworth's fabulous expression 'negative precipitation' in the Spectator, describing a drought where the evaporation rate exceeds the rainfall), and finally leads to *contraction* where all of business operates at much lower levels than during the expansion. Companies are loath to hire more staff, and many actually need to reduce staffing levels, which leads to reduction in the volume of production and trade, and an increase in unemployment as job opportunities disappear. Prices of raw materials begin to fall and subsequently prices of products fall as well as competition for market share intensifies. Now everything is snowballing in the opposite direction: confidence is gone, new projects and expansions are put on hold, inventories are at a minimum and banks are in competition to offer lending at better rates.

Since companies have poor balance sheets and reduced dividends due to lowered income, share market prices fall and equities in general become generally more attractive. After all, not everyone has gone broke – some have just laid back waiting for the upturn which inevitably comes. The lower prices stimulate investor interest and a few start picking up bargains. Soon more and more participants in the market realise the worst may be over and start loosening their purse strings, re-stimulating the market. No one wants to be left out of the possible upturn and markets begin to heat up again. In the meantime companies have had an opportunity to reduce waste, to improve productivity and streamline their operations. It is said the best time to invest in new capacity is during a downturn and so it proves again: Those who are ready for the newly increased demand can service the improving market best and begin to make early profits as the contraction ends and we are heading for the next expansion cycle.

A more pernicious and troublesome condition will occur where the confidence for business to regroup and kick start a new cycle has waned, and everyone is just sitting on their hands waiting for a signal. Interest rates may already be low, but unemployment is not coming down and instead prices are slowly rising, This is called a period of *stagflation*, which is a contraction of the terms inflation and (economic) stagnation. It is probably not a proper economic term and has more to do with journalism; nevertheless, you know it when you see it. The first time stagflation made newspapers was in the 1970s when, due to the sudden rise in oil prices (from $3 to $12) caused initially by OPEC countries being upset about the Yom Kippur war, prices of some products necessarily rose, driving some inflation which then seemed to feed on itself. People next began to expect continuously rising prices of goods, so they bought more. This rise in demand pushed up prices, leading to demands for higher wages, which pushed prices higher still in a continuing upward spiral. Union contracts increasingly introduced cost-of-living allowance clauses (COLA), and the government began to peg some payments, such as those for Social Security, to the consumer price index. In turn the government required increasing funds to run the country and increased borrowing which led to increases in interest rates slowing the economy further. There was also an increase in the money supply to combat the deficits which made money cheaper and drove inflation. This was only stopped when the new chairman of the Reserve Bank Paul Volcker dramatically reduced money supply, which did stop inflation, but increased interest rates and led to a recession lasting several years.

A rather more predictable and disconcerting situation can arise in between all this economic activity and that is the formation of a *bubble*. A bubble will be started by hysterical investors, and, as many occasions prove, is not historically recognised as a problem, as they re-occur periodically even though it is obvious there will be no difference from last time. The most famous one was over Dutch tulip bulbs. Yes. All started quite harmlessly: During the late 16th century wealthy business owners in Holland developed a liking for recently imported tulip bulbs to grow for their own pleasure, or to show off their wealth. These bulbs were exclusive and cost far more than an ordinary workers yearly wages. This continued over many years and, as bulbs became more prolific and more varieties and colours were bred, a larger market developed. There was no guarantee that the promised fabulous version would always bloom as expected, but the very rich could afford to take that risk. Many bulbs were only sold in bloom for that reason. By 1634 sales became more widespread and took place throughout the year making room for speculators to enter the fray. The previous group of buyers usually were aficionados of the plant and knew much about tulip growing and the different characteristics of the plants. The speculators only entered because they saw money to be made from a commodity, be it one of which they knew nothing. Soon a futures market developed and bulb contracts were being sold and resold without bulbs being there as yet, and anyone with a bit of sense could have foreseen the tears to come. Additionally, Dutch trade was flourishing and the economy was in an expansionary mood, giving these new investors a sense of euphoria. Whereas the market previously traded in specific single bulb products, it now became a mass market selling these by weight and quantity and the connection to the beautiful flower was lost. The outcome, as stated, was predictable, and a lot of people lost interest as even the lesser varieties started to fetch enormous prices. Someone has to be left holding the bag and by February 1637 sales collapsed.

The next famous bubble occurred in the South Seas. This was purely a share market bubble and set the tone for the future. With the founding of the South Sea Company in 1711, whose aim it was to convert £10 million of government war debt into shares, which in turn, through annual interest payments from the government, and a monopoly for all South Seas trade would generate an income principally out of nothing. Then in 1720 the company proceeded to take over the entire government debt and gained support by making secret deals allocating additional shares to government officials to gain support. The Initial Offering was at £300 a share and sold out immediately. Several more successful offerings followed, which propelled all manner of companies to be founded by others latching onto this development, and all promising unlikely or impossible products. The typical market hysteria set in and prices for stocks soared, while their founders deployed themselves overseas. Not long later in 1720, overseas investors and wealthy individuals started to pull out of these schemes and by September the bubble had burst and the government was holding the debt again. Parliament conducted an investigation, corrupt politicians and businessmen were imprisoned, and over £2 million was confiscated from South Sea Company directors.

There was a French Mississippi Bubble in 1716, a British Railway bubble in the 1840s a US bubble in Florida real estate in the 1920s.

The bull market of the 1920s repeated this pattern once again with the usual outcome, followed by the Japanese market crash of the 80s and we all remember the dot com bubble of 2000. The main point here is that this happens when investors confuse price with value, so that rising prices imply greater value, justifying even higher prices until they no longer do. It also helps if cheap credit is available at the same time.

The famous crash of 1929 was particularly devastating, and hit the economy extremely quickly. From 1921 until 1929 the American economy was growing consistently and positive feelings prevailed throughout the economy, which led to an unwarranted exuberance on the part of inexperienced investors who firmly believed the market would just keep climbing. This led to unprecedented borrowing and borrowing on margin which is of course fool's gold. In 1929 the government started to raise interest rates to try to cool the economy and by October of that year all the speculators were beginning to realize that once again we had a bubble which was about to burst. When investors tried to get out of the market it was too late and the stocks they had purchased were falling fast. Margin calls destroyed these investors and also many banks who could not retrieve funds lent against the margins. The outcome was that a lot of people who had nothing to do with the market also lost their wealth through defaults of the banks they were deposited with.

Finally, the stock market crash of 1987 was the single largest one-day crash in history. Once again investors were far too optimistic, and the Dow Jones almost doubled from 1982 to 1987, but, as an inevitable correction set in, another crash became a certainty. On 19th October 1987 a large number of very aggressive sell orders hit the market and the Dow lost 23% in one day.

The existence of these cycles and booms and busts drove the early thinkers to develop rational economic explanations of the market and the behaviour of the participants. A later chapter will examine what is called *History of Economic Thought* (HET).

Thinking Large

When we look at the development of economic theories it seems that some confusion enters as to what may be described as 'accounting mathematics' and what relationships and laws can be generated concerning all of economic 'behaviour' in a society. The former is very precise and predictable and allows accountants and individuals to deal with the particular idiosyncrasies of their particular society. The latter would want to establish rules and relationships on a far grander scale, concerning almost all of human behaviour where monetary matters are concerned. You can see right away the conflict arising in this endeavour – human behaviour per se varies very little: people will want to look out for themselves and those around them who matter. This is of course greatly influenced by what society around them and the state above them decrees at any one time.

Out of this desire to analyse and deal with the economy in general has arisen the term *macroeconomics*, which seems to want to pretend that there is actually an overriding set of rules that can be used to predict economic outcomes. A search for definitions of macroeconomics yields some very interesting answers that need to be considered very carefully and critically. At a most basic level it states: Macroeconomics examines the economy as a whole and deals with topics such as 'growth of an economy', 'short-run fluctuations in the economy', 'What are economic indicators and what influence do they have' 'What are the effects of interest rate changes' and so on.

A higher level definition will state: "Macroeconomics is the branch of economics concerned with aggregates, such as national income, consumption, and investment". Or: "The study of whole economic systems aggregating over the functioning of individual economic units." Underlying all these studies must be at the beginning the behaviour of individuals or small entities on a microeconomic level, asking what would the individual do when presented with a new economic situation. And now, in a way, we have already dipped into pretty deep waters of philosophy. First and foremost this can be no more reliable than an opinion poll. How individuals or corporations (still run by individuals) will react to a novel situation is at best a minor statistical exercise, and probably not a very rational one. Some outcomes are quite predictable such as the Treasury lowering interest rates to near zero will definitely force investors to look for other means of accruing an income from their investments. What they will then look for becomes more obscure. The first reaction may be to seek out blue chip shares with a good return or to go to government bonds followed closely by corporate funds in shares or metals or currencies. All of these head in the direction of introducing progressively more risk. You will, however, never hear a Treasury say that they want to lower interest rates so people will take more risks.

A free market economy rests on the principle of participants being free to pursue their endeavor within the law, and this is the greatest asset of that freedom. Millions of individuals using their own initiative decide on their own what activity would give them a measure of success, but with the full understanding of possible failure. Yet no other system can come close to allowing so many people to discover of what they may be capable.

Profits?

Now let's just recap what companies are all about. Usually an individual or a group of individuals put together their resources and labour to begin an enterprise to make or produce something or offer a service to the world. This is called seed capital and enables a new company to operate for a time until sufficient revenue is produced to enable that company to continue existing. Notice that once again, these are the entrepreneurs who risk their money and their time and effort to establish a new entity. If all goes to plan they will eventually make a profit and the usual sequence then is to reinvest most of these profits over the years back into the business to let it grow. At some point comes a time when the funds from the participants no longer suffice to reach the next stage of expansion and the company will need to look elsewhere. This is when a firm goes public via an Initial Public Offering (IPO), that is, a prospectus is issued extolling the virtues of the company and the wonderful road that lies ahead with a little injection of cash. If the prospects look good the company will be allowed to sell shares on the open market and individuals or companies, who believe there is a viable and promising business, may buy these shares with the prospect of eventually earning a dividend from the company. In the case where the company becomes hugely successful there is the added allure of an increase in the share price, a capital appreciation. In theory the share price is determined by the size of the dividend which has to be slightly above the lending rate of cash in the open market. For a company that represents very little risk the dividend rate will be near or at the lending rate – for riskier undertakings the dividend rate will need to be higher to compensate for the possibility of not having a dividend (or share value) at some time in the future if things go sour.

This was eloquently pointed out by John Stuart Mill in his *Principles of Political Economy* where he outlines the investment required for a good to become available:

If a person has a store of food, he has it in his power to consume it himself in idleness, or in feeding others to attend on him, or to fight for him, or to sing or dance for him. If, instead of these things, he gives it to productive labourers to support them during their work, he can, and naturally will, claim a remuneration from the produce. He will not be content with simple repayment; if he receives merely that, he is only in the same situation as at first, and has derived no advantage from delaying to apply his savings to his own benefit or

138

pleasure. He will look for some equivalent for this forbearance: he will expect his advance of food to come back to him with an increase, called in the language of business, a profit; and the hope of this profit will generally have been a part of the inducement which made him accumulate a stock, by economizing in his own consumption; or, at any rate, which made him forego the application of it, when accumulated, to his personal ease or satisfaction. The food also which maintained other workmen while producing the tools or materials, must have been provided in advance by someone, and he, too, must have his profit from the ultimate product; but there is this difference, that here the ultimate product has to supply not only the profit, but also the remuneration of the labour. The tool-maker (say, for instance, the plough-maker) does not indeed usually wait for his payment until the harvest is reaped; the farmer advances it to him, and steps into his place by becoming the owner of the plough.

One is constantly exposed to this term of 'profit' and yet, there is another side to that coin and it is called 'loss'! Profit is never guaranteed just because there is a good product, and loss is the market's way of telling the manufacturer to stop making this particular product.

Circulation Again

As mentioned at the beginning, any economy only works if the money is used to be passed on to others for more goods or services. This makes sense and can be easily envisioned by the neophyte in that the circulating funds present the income for all those in the loop. How then is it that there is unemployment well beyond the numbers of those who may just not see any point in working? A question many would like answered and none more so than the sections of government concerned with employment and those who need propaganda for the next election.

Recapping, it is the entrepreneur who kicks off things. The first step is for an entity to think of some item needed or desired in the market and then to produce this and offer it. The one proviso is that the price is right. Can this entrepreneur produce an item that the public wants in the quantity he can supply at the price the market accepts? In itself the process should be simple: Use some raw materials the price of which is known, establish a facility and the costs and overheads of which are also known and now match all this with a work force willing to work for a price that will allow the product to be marketed at the acceptable price. This last step is the critical one since the labour cost is also a marketable item and thus can vary considerably. The entrepreneur needs to go to this market and request a labour supply at a certain pay offer and in free market those seeking an income must decide on their own if they are willing to accept this offer. They are acting as their own entrepreneur, selling their labour at a value the market can live with.

You can see where this is going. When there is an oversupply of labour the price will reduce to a new level, that is, a lot of workers will have to accept a lower income. If this is left as is, a lot of people with a somewhat lower income will keep the economy rolling. Now of course the bleeding hearts will proclaim that this is not a living wage and the big bad companies must pay more to the labour force, regardless of the real value of the product being supplied. So was invented the concept of a *minimum wage*. The next step is that the additional cost of labour has to be paid by someone, and this can only be the consumer whose purchase price increases. Also notice that this is the early stage of redistribution so beloved by the socialist mentality. The so-called oppressed receive more than their worth and the so-called rich can pay for them, regardless of realistic values. The outcome is inevitably the same: The increased price of the item reduces its appeal and sales are lower. This in turn leads to lower employment and shows the failure of the socialist interference. The redistribution idea has now produced some people earning more than they should, and others, who were willing to work for a lower price, are actually out of work. Some workers who already receive wages well above the legal minimum will benefit—because they will face less competition from the unskilled. That is why many unions are strong supporters of higher minimum-wage rates. Some employers and employees in places where wages are already high will benefit because they will face less competition from businessmen who might otherwise invest capital in areas that have large pools of unskilled labor. Inevitably before imposing concepts such as minimum wages, overtime penalties and weekend work rates, no one has consulted the workers affected by these laws. Many are not adult family men or women who require that living wage for their lives and the appropriate time to spend with their children. These penalties disregard students who just have to work odd hours to enable their studies to continue. Some are of a religious bent that does not require the Saturday or Sunday to be a special day for rest and reflection and there is nothing wrong with letting workers individually decide if they prefer day or evening shift work.

The same result comes about where unions are involved. The purpose of a union is to make its management popular with the members and this is easily accomplished by pushing constantly for higher wages and introducing what are called penalty rates. The privileged few who are included in the union benefit from excessive incomes in relation to their worth, and are additionally rewarded for the arbitrary definition of evening work or weekend rates. There are plenty of individuals for whom an evening shift is preferable or who do not care what day of the week it is when they work. The outcome is the same in that many people who could be employed are now out of work because the market will only accept a certain price for that particular item. In any case, many employees are absolutely essential on weekends, holidays or late at night, and all we are addressing here is how many more would be willing to trade these off-times for time off during weekdays and in the daytime.

A little more analysis on redistribution leads to the conclusion that this is happening in any case without any imposition by government decrees. There are those who would have us believe that it is imperative to redistribute wealth to those who don't seem to have any. For that purpose our taxes are taken and given to these have-nots with the purpose of improving their life with free money. As we know this doesn't usually work simply because these ungrateful people then demand more and more just because it is available.

However if we spare a thought for the wealthy we will find that here too this redistribution is actually taking place all the time. You may ask yourself for example what use is the service industry: It doesn't fit the picture of manufacturing and increasing wealth of society. But what is happening is that the wealthy are using their funds for the benefit of themselves while at the same time benefiting those with lesser expectations. If you consider going out for a meal and a drink, you would probably have just as much fun if you were to pick up your meal at the counter and drew your beer or poured your wine yourself. Thus we don't need waiters and bartenders. But since you want to indulge yourself with the money you have earned, you are quite willing to pay someone for bringing food to your table and mixing your drinks for you. Similarly we have cleaning services, delivery services, child care etc. All of these types of service are not essential but make life easier and are worth the expenditure.

What's more, these employees really appreciate the capitalist way of redistribution which gives them a purpose in life and a feeling of accomplishment. Those on receiving end of the socialist way of redistribution invariably become resentful and bitter when spending their life on hand-outs and becoming dependent on them. There is a secondary effect that takes place in the background, in that people spending their money on services also have an interest in getting the best for their expenditure. This raises the standards all around and results in better food and drink and better services for your convenience. Restaurateurs will go and find the best products to better compete with other venues through the simple fact of competition. Thus all our lives are improved and standards are raised all around.

Once again this proves that the money the individual spends for their own good is much more wisely dispensed than a bureaucratic distribution which is without purpose or judgment.

People who Made Theories

"..by itself Economics affords no solution to any of the important problems of life. I agree that for this reason an education which consists of Economics alone is a very imperfect education."

Lionel Robbins

Before starting into what are called theories we must firmly keep in mind that economies cannot be predicted, that economic theories cannot be proven like scientific facts and that all else is speculation. Since originally people only wanted to be left alone and governments of all persuasions would not leave them be, all theory about economics is simply centered on the effect of government! Imagine if every day you got up, did your bit of labour or thinking or inventing and knew already who would want your product and a fairly constant reward, there would be no need for anyone to spend time developing theories of what is to be, because it is known. Once a government introduces taxes, trading restrictions, minimum wages, pension plans, import tariffs, export restrictions and an endless list of ways to control our life, this all provides the most fertile ground for speculation and theorizing. Notably it is still utterly useless, because we cannot predict sudden behavioural changes in government or any changes to the economy any better than in society in general. And thus were spawned whole Universities, myriads of books and magazines and endless arguments – all founded on sand, shifting that is. No sage has yet been able to predict a market crash, a recession or a sudden bubble burst. They can talk about what might happen, since there are endless scenarios, and someone will always be able to say they predicted this or the other crash, but never exactly to be on July 17 or any other day. At the time of writing the biggest issue in the world was the future of the Eurozone and, depending on when you are reading this tome, you may look back and say "well that outcome must have been pretty predictable", but not now, before the happening.

At times it seems that all economic theory is simply there to refute previous or competing theories, or to expand endlessly on other pet conjectures of the various authors. This is not to denigrate any of the work of the great authors, but to point out that all analysis still does not allow us either to predict, let alone control the economy in the future. Most of the early economic theories were started by observation of the behaviour of people, and being grounded in reality were quite appropriate and still stand strongly today, except that some later theories became the flavor of the month instead and misled participants into dead ends of thinking or entirely misdirected interpretations.

One problem that arises immediately is what the definition of 'Economic Studies' or 'Economic Science' should be. One claims it to be "the general causes on which the material welfare of human beings depends" (Cannan), another "the science which treats phenomena from the standpoint of price" (Davenport); or perhaps closest: "the study of the general methods by which men co-operate to meet their material needs" (Beveridge). A dictionary definition usually will read: "The branch of social science that deals with the production and distribution and consumption of goods and services and their management" – and so we have again brought the social aspect into the discussion. Ultimately economics is not a mechanism or a machine – it is people using their property to engage in transactions.

This section will briefly touch on a vast pile of accumulated knowledge – not necessarily wisdom – which is referred to as HET, or History of Economic Thought. Every student of economics will be exposed to years of study of the history of what has been proposed in the past to explain how people behave under varying economic conditions and for the most part fails to do so. The basic concepts of the early thinkers were good and simple and recorded human behavior quite well. Later, when new writers tried to influence human behavior, the study of economics seems to go off the rails and the outcome we have is the turmoil that represents the 20th century.

No matter how much we want to believe in the goodness of man and the freedom of a free enterprise system, reality is always different. From the earliest days on, forces inimical to free enterprise have imposed themselves on the scene. So before economics was even considered a field of study these powers controlled national economies to their advantage, or better what they thought would give them advantage. Up until the 20th century economic theory was concentrated on observing people, how they interacted economically and describing what went on. Some extremely brilliant economists observed how markets worked through the old principles of barter and free trade, and those who became too greedy or careless rightly suffered the consequences. Above all, as we saw earlier, somebody has to do something useful for others to start an economic cycle. This is called *value adding* and refers to the fact that the entrepreneur starts with materials and labour and creates something of value to others, which is then sold to produce revenue and in turn create more value. This was first elucidated in an observation which is referred to as *Say's Law* and simply proposes that when there is a supply of a good there will appear a market for it as it is purchased by its users. All the early economists up to the beginning of the 20th century are generally noted as classical thought and the capitalist base of this was proven through the immense wealth that was accumulated by free societies through the 19th and into the 20th century. Then, in 1936, a man by the name of John Maynard Keynes wrote a book which in one fell swoop was meant to throw out all of this previous thought and substitute his own. Unfortunately he was somewhat ideologically biased and interpreted the classical direction to mean that, through the value added process and the free market, there should never be any unemployment, because everyone who is employed is also a spender and it all should even out. This cannot be true since not all people spend evenly or wisely and thus the market has to include some ups and downs and there will be periods of economic downturns producing some unemployment for some short time. Keynes interpreted this as a failure of the free market system and imposed his theory of government interference in way of government spending to replace the spending that was lacking in the population.

This turned out to be a very bad idea since there was no value adding involved, and subsequently the economy was bound to be diminished as money was circulating but producing lower value. Now, where in the past the market was determined by the supply of goods for sale, Keynes invented a term called *aggregate demand,* and he used this to impose the thought that a government, using statistics, could determine when this demand had fallen and have it replaced by government spending. In line with this reasoning he had another thought bubble, which stipulated that there could be a glut of goods in the market due to lack of buyers and thus manufacturers had to lay off workers due to this lack of demand – same line of thinking, just to support his socialist idea of the government controlling the economy. Unfortunately for society in general this was accepted in almost all quarters and we are still living with the consequences of this horrible direction. But now let's look at the history.

From the 15th to the 19th century economies were nation based and underpinned by a system of Mercantilism. The main objective of Mercantilism was to increase the power of the nation-state. One of the important aspects of national power or strength was wealth that was equated with specie. The states that followed a policy of mercantilism tended to see trade, colonialism and conquest as the primary ways of increasing wealth. There was no systematic, comprehensive, consistent treatise, no leader, common method, or theory. Each "mercantilist" sought advantage for a specific trade, a merchant, joint-stock company or social group. Protectionism is often seen as a primary characteristic of Mercantilism. Gold and silver was seen as wealth and to be acquired and hoarded by creating a favourable balance of trade or exploitation of colonies. This led to huge expenditure on militarism, conquest of colonies and warfare against enemies to gain economic advantage. Commerce was to be conducted in a war-like manner to gain advantage over other nations, where one nation's gains could only be achieved at the expense of another. Through this direction thinkers became aware of inflation for the first time: since more wealth contained in the country produced more money in circulation, prices invariably had to rise to absorb the additional funds.

Additionally, during the original medieval feudal period there existed a system of power in the hands of the landed gentry who rented out plots of land for subsistence farming and also established the system of guilds. The guilds were composed of skilled artisans and merchants who were granted letters of patent from the monarch. They restricted innovation, trade and entry to any other artisans who were not members of the guild. Through what is known as *rent-seeking* today, the guilds imposed a dead-weight loss on their respective economies by receiving financial support from the feudal lords. There were good and bad effects through the existence of guilds: They would assess the size of the market and allow a corresponding number of artisans to work and the quality of the products was tightly controlled. Guilds were also a monopoly and controlled output, prices and were against any changes to products that might upset the existing order. Work from other cities was prohibited from sale and price discounting was not allowed. Within the guild there was support for one another and some forms of charity for poorer members were also in place. Guilds lost their power by and by and by the beginning of the 19th century the first signs of capitalism appeared, that is, the products required by the people were no longer made within a guild but by the entrepreneurs running businesses.

A new group of thinkers appeared in the 19th century and were designated as Physiocrats. They had analysed the prevailing economic conditions and advocated more of a laissez-faire direction, where state taxes and royal excesses should be reduced. They held in common the idea that all things are part of an interconnected system that is rational and comprehensible to the human mind and believed that a natural system, free from the intrusions of an improper man made law, would result in an improvement of the human condition. This group was not large and lasted only a short time, but their ideas were powerful and influenced the development of economic thought in the following generation.

147

There were some thinkers who concerned themselves also with economics early on who tried to establish proper theories such as Richard Cantillon (1680 – 1734) who was the first to put together an extremely detailed and interesting publication on economics in the *Essay on the Nature of Trade in General*, published posthumously in 1755. In this he addressed all general topics of wealth, trade, life in a human society, application of labour and the circulation of money. He was also the first address the importance and critical role of entrepreneurship and presented the theory that money enters the market in a slow step-by-step fashion. A chapter is devoted to the analysis of the circulation of money and the influence on money by the 'Undertakers'. Interestingly, Cantillon also realised that there is 'rapidity' to the circulation of money, which can be slow or fast depending on the frequency of payments such as land rent are made. This shows up in modern times as the velocity of money. In his *Essay* many more issues were addressed than can be described here and the interested reader should follow up on Cantillon's amazing insight into economics.

A writer as important and influential to publish work on economics was Jean-Baptiste Say (1767-1832). Say was influenced by Adam Smith and Richard Cantillon and produced treatises about economics based on a free *laissez-faire* approach, which in fact was what described the economic world at that time. However in his endeavour he seems to have fallen afoul most unexpectedly of Napoleon who sat him down and told him he had to adjust his theories to serve the state and a war economy based on regulations and protectionism. Say did refuse and was consequently removed from his position in the French *Tribunate* and thus we have an early indication how almost any government will attempt to influence and subjugate an economy to its own ends.

What prompted Say to begin his work was his disagreement with the then held belief that a downturn in business activity was caused by either a scarcity of money or a general overproduction of goods: in other words a lack of demand. These two go hand in hand and are mostly misrepresented. Every business produces goods according to what the prediction of the market is thought to require. When the goods are made according to a price that is acceptable to the market, then these will sell at what is a 'market clearing price'. Thus, since all the people involved in the making of these goods have already been paid for their work, the funds are in the market to purchase these and other goods. A scarcity of money can only occur at the point where the entrepreneur wants to start producing a good and requires the start-up funds, so he needs credit if he does not have the funds already, but a lack of funds cannot occur in the market when the goods are available. As to overproduction, it is the corollary in that the production has to match the money paid out to produce the goods. There may be a plethora of one good or another but this implies that another good will be scarce, all based on the preferences of the consuming worker.

For completeness we need to address Say's Law which is often quoted but does not really convey a lot. Say described markets as having a *natural harmony*. This he described thus: any product placed on the market creates its own demand and thus every demand in the market creates its own supply. These statements relate to the interdependence of an economy where an exchange of goods is associated with the according specialised labour of each product. He wrote:

It is not the abundance of money but the abundance of other products in general that facilitates sales... Money performs no more than the role of a conduit in this double exchange. When the exchanges have been completed, it will be found that one has paid for products with products.

Essentially this meant that anyone who makes a new product markets it as quickly as possible to avoid losses of that product's value, and as soon as the income for these goods has been received, those funds are to be spent again to avoid a loss in monetary value through inflation. This of course describes exactly the situation we began with: money must circulate to be of any use at all, and this circulation once again results in the demand for more goods expanding the economy. The implication of all this is that only the production of actual tangible items can stimulate the economy but the creation of money itself cannot. Prosperity should be increased by stimulating production, not consumption. In Say's view, creation of more money simply results in inflation; more money demanding the same quantity of goods does not represent an increase in real demand.

It takes us back to the shovel maker who must make shovels to the demand in the market: if he makes too many his prices would have to come down and he would run into losses. This happens all the time in the modern world where a product is dominant in the market and then loses market share as other products become more popular. Business must be aware of this sequence and adjust production accordingly.

Notably, what Say is describing as supply and demand, includes the workforce as labour, implying that for the correct price the supply of workers will match the demand from the goods producing entities. There may be temporary imbalances leading to unemployment, but this would equal out as demand for labour increases due to new production. Minimum wage laws, however, would succeed in destroying this relationship. It is also important to note that Say himself did not create a 'law' as such and did not refer to his writings in that way. Only later did other interpreters extend his ideas into the shape of a rule or law. Nevertheless, his observations and realisations are probably the most important of all in the history of economic thinking and are sadly lost currently to the modern demand thinking by the so sadly lacking in intelligence 'intelligentsia' residing in government and major educational and news organisations.

A contemporary of Say, Thomas Robert Malthus (1766 – 1834), also addressed the issue of supply and demand, but from a radically different direction. Malthus' great interest was population studies. He compared population growth with increases in food supply and noted that the latter occurred far more slowly than the former. In the process it seems that poor Malthus has been misrepresented and maligned ever since. His publication of *An Essay on the Principle of*

Population in 1798 caused an uproar among the wider educated population, while at the same time being greatly admired by other economists. His conclusion was that even though population was increasing and food supply was growing at a lesser rate, people in general were not starving en masse, and therefore economic choices were being made to alleviate the situation, and these forces must be studied. Unfortunately today his writings and the term "Malthusian" are used to describe a pessimistic prediction of the communal demise of a humanity doomed to starvation via overpopulation.

Adam Smith (1723 – 1790) wrote such an easily read contribution that he is probably the best known and most quoted and referred economic writer of all time so far. His book _An Inquiry into the Nature and Causes of the Wealth of Nations_ published in 1776 is actually an analysis of what people do to make society function. Here we find the first description of the division of labour, an analysis of how prices come to be and what constitutes natural price. He points out that a price consists of the three components of rent (for the land) or what we may now call overhead costs, the cost of labour and the realised profit. In this case the profit is really the labour earnings of the entrepreneur who owns and runs the business.

The 'natural price' is described thus:

"When the price of any commodity is neither more nor less than what is sufficient to pay the rent of the land, the wages of the labour, and the profits of the stock employed in raising, preparing, and bringing it to market, according to their natural rates, the commodity is then sold for what may be called its natural price."

Here we also find the first description of what we may call supply side economics. The first step in any economic action is for someone to supply the market with the commodity and then the demand determines the price. If the good is sold at the 'natural price' from above, it allows the entrepreneur to supply a certain amount of this good to the market. If the demand now increases but no more goods can be supplied the price goes up, since there are more customers than items of the good. If the demand does not reach the quantity of supply the price will fall until purchasers are willing to pay this price. He now points out that, if the price is higher than the market accepts, either labour costs and/or rent costs have to be reduced by reducing the amount of land rented and reducing the amount of labour supplied, until the price and quantity matches the market demand. The point here is, quite rightly, that market forces determine sales and values, and that they adjust accordingly to always come near the 'natural price'.

Next he looks at the fact that, where products are produced for the market, someone must finance these: materials have to be purchased and labour paid before the product is ready to be sold. Thus we have again the entrepreneur, or in this case the 'capitalist' – he who supplies the capital to have goods made.

Adam Smith was also the first to point out that under no circumstances can the government be entrusted with any sort of influence over decisions made by private businesses of the people, and furthermore that governments are 'the greatest spendthrifts in society'. His most famous realisation was that of leaving the market to itself to supply all goods and materials required for the running of the society was as if guided by an *invisible hand*:

As every individual, therefore, endeavours as much as he can both to employ his capital in the support of domestic industry, and so to direct that industry that its produce may be of the greatest value; every individual necessarily labours to render the annual revenue of the society as great as he can. He generally, indeed, neither intends to promote the public interest, nor knows how much he is promoting it. By preferring the support of domestic to that of foreign industry, he intends only his own security; and by directing that industry in such a manner as its produce may be of the greatest value, he intends only his own gain, and he is in this, as in many other cases, led by an invisible hand to promote an end which was no part of his intention.

Nor is it always the worse for the society that it was no part of it. By pursuing his own interest he frequently promotes that of the society more effectually than when he really intends to promote it.

Above all he concluded that the wealth of a nation is not based on the accumulation of bullion, but on the accumulated total of labour, products and services in the country – that is what we now call Gross Domestic Product. Along with this, he opposed restrictions on free trade amongst nations and the imposition of tariffs or prohibitions of import/export:

If a foreign country can supply us with a commodity cheaper than we ourselves can make it, better buy it of them with some part of the produce of our own industry employed in a way in which we have some advantage. The general industry of the country, being always in proportion to the capital which employs it, will not thereby be diminished, no more than that of the above-mentioned artificers; but only left to find out the way in which it can be employed with the greatest advantage. It is certainly not employed to the greatest advantage when it is thus directed towards an object which it can buy cheaper than it can make.

This is a lesson which still to this day does not seem to have convinced most of the socialist or union oriented minds in our society, who are forever complaining that cheap imports from countries with lower manufacturing costs are destroying jobs.

For those more interested in what the (economic) world looked like in the 18th century the book is quite fascinating and filled with some astounding attitudes and examples of economic conditions and activities at the time. All in all he has presented an enormous amount of realistic economic analysis and setting the tone for much future work to extend free thinking.

153

Greatly influenced by Adam Smith was David Ricardo (1772 – 1823), who became interested in economics later in his life and made some extremely important propositions which still stand today. His career in economics started when he published a number of articles in 1809 pointing out that England's problems with inflation was the result of the Bank of England's propensity to issue excess unconvertible banknotes, leading to an inquiry into what was then called the *Bullion Controversy*. The situation had come about through the various Napoleonic engagements England had, which required extraordinary sums of money, and this could only be supported by printing money since taxation had reached its limit. Once the war expenses stopped, inflation abated and the gold standard was reintroduced. In short, Ricardo was an early believer in the quantity theory of money, pointing out a relationship between the generation of credit and inflation.

Ricardo also articulated what came to be known as the law of diminishing marginal returns. One of the most famous laws of economics, it holds that, as more and more resources are combined in production with a fixed resource - for example, as more labour and machinery are used on a fixed amount of land - the additional value of the output will diminish. He lastly also formulated the idea of comparative costs, today called *comparative advantage* which is the main basis for allowing free trade today. The idea is this: a country that trades for products it can get at lower cost from another country is better off than if it had made the products at home. This idea is still extremely controversial today, with trade restriction and subsidies hindering trade and wealth all over the world. The topic will be elaborated later in this book. Ricardo's main contribution is to be found in the book *On the Principles of Political Economy and Taxation* (1817). An extension of this thought line was the theory of rents, which is the realisation that where more land is cultivated for food production, eventually far less productive land would also need to be utilised. But as less produce became available from the poorer land, tenants would be willing to pay higher rent on more productive land, thus enriching the landlord but not the farmers. For this reason today farm subsidies, selectively applied, do not support farmers but landholders.

Another writer that needs looking at is Claude Frederic Bastiat (1801 – 1850), an economist and politician in France, who was dissatisfied with the kind of analysis of economics that went before him. He avoided talking about production and financing and productivity, but was instead intrigued by what constitutes 'value'. First and foremost he was for free trade and a *laissez-faire* policy. He fought vigorously to contain socialistic attitudes and to promote freedom of action and for the individual to control his own economic destiny.

Bastiat is a delight to read if for no other reason than to prove that the French proverb *Plus ça change, plus c'est pareil* was coined quite correctly then and is always valid. Judging by some recent elections, this paragraph really shows how people were exactly the same then: Bastiat spent long discourses to explain basic economic situations and the listeners said *"Well this is obvious, why are you explaining this?"* and then proceed to vote the complete opposite to what was explained.

Reading Bastiat's explanations, the one that stands out was his continuous emphasis of the *"full picture"*, or more clearly *"what is seen and what is not seen"*. Very clearly we now live in an age of "seeming" rather than "doing". Governments are elected on the basis that they *"seem to be doing the right thing"*: Governments apologise to past mistreatments and situations; they spend vast sums helping some unfortunate people, who subsequently increase in numbers (thus assuring their vote); even vaster sums are spent on so-called *environmental issues*. These latter were at one time a positive and desirable action to support a clean environment, but have now grown to unmanageable and increasingly expensive but less effective activities. In typical bureaucratic fashion, once invented the department cannot be uninvented and thus spends its time and money on more and more obscure and irrational projects, costing the tax payer ever increasing sums, simply to justify its own existence, but with no remnant of actions that benefit society or increase wealth, all in accordance with Parkinson's law.

Economic truths must be established only by examining not only the immediate consequences of an action, but also by seeking out the hidden consequences that are not instantly obvious and that may only show up in the longer view. Additionally we must examine the effect not only on the directly involved person or group, but also on all the people, and on society as a whole for really large issues. His most poignant example is his *Fallacy of the Broken Window.*

It begins by the naughty son breaking a window and a furious father has to spend 6 francs to replace it. The onlookers claim that unfortunately for the father he has to spend this money, but on the other hand the money supports a glazier and broken windows in general support the glazing industry. This is true and economically correct. What is not seen is that the citizen has spent 6 francs on one thing and not another. He could have bought shoes or a book for example. Being a random act the money doesn't actually benefit the glazing industry or society in general.

What is also not seen is that the father had a window before and now still has only a window, whereas he could have had a pair of shoes as well as the window. If we consider the man as a part of society, we come to the conclusion that society has lost the value of one window. From this Bastiat proposes the maxim that *"Destruction is not profitable".*

The point of the parable is that there are three participants: The father who has lost 6 francs, the glazier who has gained 6 francs and the shoemaker who has missed out on gaining 6 francs, and whose industry is correspondingly discouraged by that amount. The shoemaker's situation is the part that remains *unseen*, that remains in the shadows. This leads to the final conclusion that restrictive trade practices are just as destructive since they prevent industries from earning an income.

Following through this scenario Bastiat points out that of course taxation falls into the same category: Money is taken away from society to be utilised in a way that does not actually increase wealth, it is just there to support all the employees of the government and its activities. Were the money used to drain a swamp for example, the benefit would in the end be much larger than the simple cost of draining the swamp. It would make that land arable and assure income of a far greater magnitude.

A very typical Bastiat thought process is explained in his article from his revolutionary magazine in June 1848, that the policy of "laissez-faire", or "let things be done" was in opposition to the policy of the state, which was to "prevent things being done":

"Laissez-faire! I will begin by saying, in order to avoid any ambiguity, that laissez-faire is used here for honest things, with the state instituted precisely to prevent dishonest things.

This having been said, and with regard to things that are innocent in themselves, such as work, trade, teaching, association, banking, etc., a choice must be made. It is necessary for the state to let things be done or prevent them from being done.

If it lets things be done, we will be free and optimally administered most economically, since nothing costs less than laissez-faire.

If it prevents things from being done, woe to our freedom and our purse. Woe to our freedom, since to prevent things is to tie our hands; woe to our purse, since to prevent things requires agents and to employ agents takes money.

In reply to this, socialists say: "Laissez-faire! What a disaster!" Why, if you please? "Because, when you leave men to act, they do wrong and act against their interests. It is right for the state to direct them."

This is simply absurd. Do you seriously have such faith in human wisdom that you want universal suffrage and government of all by all and then you proclaim these very men whom you consider fit to govern others unfit to govern themselves?"

This early group of economic sages basically observed society and recorded what they noticed. There were no grand theories of altering the make-up of society, or to direct an economy in new and utopian ways, but it was realised early on that socialism forced on the population was simply authoritarianism in a new guise. During the period of this analysis of economics some concepts developed that need explaining here. We saw that a good has three components of material, labour and land, but there are other components called *externalities*. From Bastiat we learnt about the unseen, and from these three components the seen product is created and marketed. What is not seen are the externalities, as for example in pollution created by the production process. This pollution affects a third party, namely residents of the society, who have nothing to do with the product, but who nevertheless have a price to pay in health costs or maybe just quality of life. Another unseen would be the havoc that is wreaked upon the landscape by mining or logging activities. Not all of these are negative - achieving a higher education produces the effect of contributing more value to society and paying more tax. A fruit or flower grower attracts bees for pollination, and at the same time provides the beekeeper with free honey. We need to note that installations such as roads and bridges, rubbish pick-up and street cleaning are not in this category, since they constitute part of a contract between citizens and the particular level of government.

Finally we need to appreciate the great thinker John Stuart Mill who published *Principles of Political Economy* in 1848, and his approach to the importance of capital is most important to understand today, as most of the world has gone off in different and destructive directions. Mill outlined the importance of capital in the sense of machinery and equipment to produce goods as well as the capital available in human labour. He describes this as "*...a requisite without which no* *productive operations . . . are possible: a stock, previously accumulated, of the products of former labour. This accumulated stock of the produce of labour is termed Capital."* This means that the fruits of previous labour is reinvested in the business and accumulates the capital for future endeavours. This does not imply that capital is synonymous with money, since money cannot supply the means of production unless it is exchanged for other things that do so. This accumulated money from the past is then also invested in the payment for future labour. Out of this Mill derived some extremely important axioms concerning capital. The first states that *Industry is limited by capital.* This goes back to where earlier it was shown that it was a surplus of product from one entrepreneur that allowed the future production to be financed. In this case the limit is that the accumulated capital can only be applied to future production until more goods can be marketed. What Mill was referring to here was the condition where a government of the day would impose import restrictions or other government chicane and then proclaim that thus it had created a new industry or business to replace the forbidden imports. But in fact no previously available funds were involved – it was claiming to produce goods out of a simple government directive, disregarding the fact that previously obtained capital is necessary to do so. Judging by some of the world's governing bodies actions today, not many understand this axiom at all.

His next theorem states that the source of capital is the result of savings. If all the income from all sources were continually spent, there would not be any funds available to invest in future machinery, materials and buildings etc. and production would cease. This leads to the next statement that even though we are talking about saving, the money is nevertheless consumed, just by waiting until a future consumption is needed or by someone else who borrows it for investment. And finally the most important insight of all, stating that the economy runs on the investment into goods and not by the demand of the market: *"What supports and employs productive labour, is the capital expended in setting it to work, and not the*

159

demand of purchasers for the produce of the labour when completed. Demand for commodities is not demand for labour. The demand for commodities determines in what particular branch of production the labour and capital shall be employed; it determines the direction of the labour; but not the more or less of the labour itself, or of the maintenance or payment of the labour. These depend on the amount of the capital, or other funds directly devoted to the sustenance and remuneration of labour. " This harks back to the supply side/demand side of arguments where the recent decades of government expenditure has been wasted on giving away money or printing money with the hope of improving the economy without actually adding value or generating any goods. It is also interesting to see that even 200 years ago the same misconception prevailed in certain quarters where it was proponed that the demand existing for goods resulting from the production is creating demand for labour, even though the labour has already been paid for during production.

As we can see these early thinkers all fully well understood the destructive economic force that governments represent, and yet as we look into the 20th century it will get worse. We have already seen that money spent via taxes by the government can never be as effectively utilised as in the private industry. The reason is very simple in that a government agency is never required to justify and explain and account correctly for expenditures made. In the private field the company proposing an investment will need to have all its ducks in a row, there needs to be a business case, due diligence, a proper accounting of the expenditure and all the back-up material of quotes, business plans and solid contracts before anything gets approved by the Board of Directors or the shareholders or just simply private investors. Ultimately these managers of public companies are also accountable and if shown to be incompetent will be removed from their position and if acting illegally in the management of the entity will have to face a court. Have there ever been a politician being sacked for incompetence or jailed for lying?

There are many more worthy economists from this era, but we need to move on. The most critically intrusive event leading into the 20th century was of course the First World War. In the period before the war politicians already drove the direction of increasing income taxes (individual and corporate) and at the same time promoting welfare services such as pensions, increased health care and health spending. During the period from the early 1900s into the 1920s income taxes in most westerns countries moved from the 6% range to over 30%. Corporate taxes were also targeted but more in a way of imposing 'excessive profits tax'. This applied to income a company generated let's say over 8% profit for example, which was deemed a reasonable return on the investment.

At first these taxes were highly successful and produced large revenue streams. But tinkering with the rates and constant adjustments up and down and removal and introduction of other forms of taxes produced an unpredictable mish-mash of tax regulation, and accordingly larger government departments for administering these. The whole thing ran into the brick wall of 1929. Enough has been written about the causes and effects and the reader is welcome to follow these up on their own, keeping in mind that everybody blames everybody else for the event and what follows, but we can be pretty sure that government interference through interest rates, building projects and protectionist policies didn't help.

There is one effect that seriously influenced world economies, and that is a dramatic reduction in government revenue due to a fall in business activities and thus a reduction in GDP. There was only one way of overcoming this shortfall, and that led to deficit spending – and the great proponent of this was John Maynard Keynes.

At first sight Keynes seemed an intelligent, reasonable and well educated person. In 1919 Keynes published a book (*The Economic Consequences of Peace*) outlining his objections to the punitive reparations payments imposed on Germany by the Allied countries after World War I. The amounts demanded by the Allies were so large, he wrote, that a Germany that tried to pay them would stay perpetually poor and, therefore, politically unstable, and here he was entirely correct. Later, during the 1920s he published more books concerning monetary policy and monetary reform, where he outlined his initial promotion of the central bank's control of interest rates to control inflation. Thus, when prices tended to rise, the interest rates should go up and when prices fell interest rates should be lowered. This is fairly uncontroversial stuff and falls in nicely with government ideas of how to control the economy.

What is forgotten in most reviews of Keynes' writings is that he was essentially a socialist. He studied at Cambridge and belonged to the Fabian Society and in his earlier writings was working up to a critique of laissez-faire and a build-up of government powers. In his booklet *The End of Laissez-Faire* (1926) he wrote as follows:

Many of the greatest economic evils of our time are the fruits of risk, uncertainty, and ignorance. It is because particular individuals, fortunate in situation or in abilities, are able to take advantage of uncertainty and ignorance, and also because for the same reason big business is often a lottery, that great inequalities of wealth come about; and these same factors are also the cause of the unemployment of labour, or the disappointment of reasonable business expectations, and of the impairment of efficiency and production. Yet the cure lies outside the operations of individuals; it may even be to the interest of individuals to aggravate the disease. I believe that the cure for these things is partly to be sought in the deliberate control of the currency and of credit by a central institution, and partly in the collection and dissemination on a great scale of data relating to the business situation, including the full publicity, by law if necessary, of all business facts which it is useful to know. These measures would involve society in exercising directive intelligence through some appropriate organ of action over many of the inner intricacies of private business, yet it would leave private initiative and enterprise unhindered. Even if these measures

162

prove insufficient, nevertheless, they will furnish us with better knowledge than we have now for taking the next step.

My second example relates to savings and investment. I believe that some coordinated act of intelligent judgement is required as to the scale on which it is desirable that the community as a whole should save, the scale on which these savings should go abroad in the form of foreign investments, and whether the present organisation of the investment market distributes savings along the most nationally productive channels. I do not think that these matters should be left entirely to the chances of private judgement and private profits, as they are at present.

And more extremely yet:

My third example concerns population. The time has already come when each country needs a considered national policy about what size of population, whether larger or smaller than at present or the same, is most expedient. And having settled this policy, we must take steps to carry it into operation. The time may arrive a little later when the community as a whole must pay attention to the innate quality as well as to the mere numbers of its future members.

Remarkably, Keynes and many of his cohorts managed to amass fortunes through capitalist ways of investment, speculation and trading in money markets while at the same time calling for tighter controls over capitalism.

However, after 1929 and into the thirties nobody really knew what to do to bring the economies back up to full steam, unemployment remained stubbornly high and there was a lack of confidence in trying to restart businesses. Keynes then thought long and hard about these matters and came up with a book, *The General Theory of Employment, Interest and Money.* In the General Theory he proposed firstly that to reduce unemployment the government should hire these people for government works projects, and to afford this the government should borrow or print money to pay for the works. After a slow start of course a government would love this thought because so many unemployed would be so grateful and vote to support this activity. Oddly enough, Keynes was all for a free market, and once near full employment was achieved the market should again operate freely. But once the cat was out of the bag it was too late. All the economists following this publication interpreted whatever they wanted into the Theory and any semblance of a free market was lost as more universities, think tanks and news organisations endlessly put forth more strange ideas based on Keynes' thinking without recalling Bastiat's warnings of hidden effects.

The main thrust of Keynes' thinking was in the direction of inventing the term *Aggregate Demand* (A). This he described as the sum of consumption (C), investment (I) (in the sense of investing capital to produce goods to produce other goods) plus government spending (G) (on publicly provided goods and services). This created the (in)famous term $A = C + I + G$ where the aggregate demand A is to be the demand for the Gross Domestic Product (GDP). Some analysts throw in the difference between import and export as well.

If you are not a recently trained economist there is a lot of fun to be had in tearing this apart. First and foremost a demand does not represent a good, so the consumer can demand all they want – if the goods are not on the shelf he gets nothing. Let investment stand for now and proceed to the G. Once again this is the money the government has received through taxes from the previously mentioned consumers. So it is first not a separate entity at all, just diverted funds. Secondly, most of this money is dispersed to social welfare needs and thus unproductive. Does it get counted again under the letter C when the recipients spend this largesse? This would imply that the more money the government throws at the population the better the economy looks. And, of course, that is exactly what a socialist government wants to demonstrate to their loyal voters.

Next, the equation implies that, when the consumer starts spending less, the government needs to increase spending to maintain GDP, leading to more 'stimulus spending', which is really only forced redistributive spending, since it takes taxes from the population and spends the money in turn. In reality the government is actually removing money from the economy by not letting the individual spend as he sees fit. One cannot take money from one section of society, apply it elsewhere and claim an increase in wealth or GDP. One cannot make up for a lack of production by spending more money

A lack of demand does not necessarily imply a lack of funds. Many people may have plenty of funds available but prefer not to spend them for a variety of reasons. They may want to put away more money for their retirement, they may want to simply invest the money or use it to pay down debt, fearing a future increase in interest rates. The government also has no control over the spending of the stimulus money by the individual. Again the money may be just put away into savings or it may be spent on imported goods, thus adding nothing to the GDP. These economic manipulators always seem to think they can second guess the individual and they always fail.

Keynes' main direction of thought centres around the 'aggregate'. He wants to analyse the totality of an economy: aggregate income, aggregate consumption, employment, investment and so on. Thus he called his theory a *general* theory and he relegates all previous accumulated *classic* knowledge to *special* theories that do not address the economy as a whole. In particular, he discards the writings of Say and disputes the assumption that supply creates demand, which in his interpretation also implies there should never be any unemployment, since it was implicitly assumed that the economy was always working at full capacity. His new theory focuses solely on the assumption that we can permanently assure full employment by maintaining total expenditure at an appropriate level. As a theory it is too simple and totally ignores first the function of the government interference and secondly the behaviour of the

165

individual. Ultimately there must be ups and downs in an economic cycle, since there is no other way of correcting any upsets in the market and no matter what the theory says, there will always be some disturbances in a free market.

Unfortunately Keynes major thrust of argument was centred on the way employment and unemployment was treated in the classic theories of economics. In particular he seemed to have taken exception to a publication by Professor A.C. Pigou titled *The Theory of Unemployment* of 1933. Pigou was facing a monumental task for his work and was also involved in government committees reviewing opportunities to reduce unemployment. His cerebral but somewhat flawed and probably unhelpful book required later amendments, and can't be considered to be greatly influential in the scheme of things. Keynes re-examined the problem of unemployment and chose to divide unemployment into three classes: one group of workers who are essentially between jobs or who are briefly not in work due to a change in production quantities, and these he calls 'frictional' unemployed. The second group are people who are 'voluntarily' unemployed', comprising of workers who, for various reasons of social change or legislation or refusal of available payments, stay out of the work force. The third and new classification is that of the 'involuntarily' unemployed which he defines very obliquely as:

Men are involuntarily unemployed if, in the event of a small rise in the price of wage-goods relatively to the money-wage, both the aggregate supply of labour willing to work for the current money-wage and the aggregate demand for it at that wage would be greater than the existing volume of employment.

This definition is of course meant to lead to the proposition that the market is driven by demand. It implies even if there are enough workers and enough companies willing to employ these, if the market does not demand sufficient products the workers are left unemployed. The preface to his work gives a clue of what we are looking at. Keynes outlines that the book is aimed at his fellow economists, of which there could not have been many with the same direction. He then beseeches them to examine their theories and adopt his new one. In fact his theory is aimed at a new lot of economists who will follow this new direction and apply it in government.

Keynes then spends a lot of verbiage trying to explain how the government can more readily combat unemployment through its spending and here we encounter an argument that surely brings down Keynes' whole discussion in one paragraph. In Book 3, Section 10, he compares gold mining against government spending as a preferential approach to unemployment:

For example, unemployment relief financed by loans is more readily accepted than the financing of improvements at a charge below the current rate of interest; whilst the form of digging holes in the ground known as gold-mining, which not only adds nothing whatever to the real wealth of the world but involves the disutility of labour, is the most acceptable of all solutions.

If the Treasury were to fill old bottles with banknotes, bury them at suitable depths in disused coalmines which are then filled up to the surface with town rubbish, and leave it to private enterprise on well-tried principles of laissez-faire to dig the notes up again (the right to do so being obtained, of course, by tendering for leases of the note-bearing territory), there need be no more unemployment and, with the help of the repercussions, the real income of the community, and its capital wealth also, would probably become a good deal greater than it actually is.

What is neglected here once again is the fact that the gold miner, of whatever caliber, is the entrepreneur who invests his own time and money in the belief that the sale of the gold (provided free in the ground) is a good business idea, if he can sell the product on the market. Keynes' approach is almost unbelievably inappropriate since the money buried in the ground is your tax money and doesn't come for free. It would be better to have people do nothing and collect money, at least it would save the cost of the burying of the money bottles; neither the burying nor the digging up adds any sort of value to the world. As an aside, 'unemployment relief financed by loans' is of course synonymous with deficit spending.

If looked upon charitably, Keynes' theories may have been well-meaning but were essentially based on a flawed premise. He maintained that the free market economy of laissez-faire was to blame for the economic disturbances of the 1920s and 1930s, while neglecting completely that large scale government interference had already poisoned the free market, and that his resolution was simply to add more government controls and interference. His original statement that this book was not meant for ordinary public consumption was entirely correct in that all his analysis and advice was only of use to governments and those advising governments while being paid by the government. There was no useful data to be gained for private business or the individual since the direction was to control the economy.

Insofar as Keynes' socialist pedigree is concerned, many misinterpret some of his writings to point to a total socialist economy, but this is far from the truth. One paragraph often cited reads:

The State will have to exercise a guiding influence on the propensity to consume partly through its scheme of taxation, partly by fixing the rate of interest, and partly, perhaps, in other ways. Furthermore, it seems unlikely that the influence of banking policy on the rate of interest will be sufficient by itself to determine an optimum rate of investment. I conceive, therefore, that a somewhat comprehensive socialisation of investment will prove the only means of securing an approximation to full employment...

With this statement he did not imply nationalization or even control over businesses, but simply control over running of the economy. In this way he ignored the fact that there would be no reason to believe that the state could run an economy better than would the individuals running the companies.

168

But beyond this no obvious case is made out for a system of State Socialism which would embrace most of the economic life of the community. It is not the ownership of the instruments of production which it is important for the State to assume. If the State is able to determine the aggregate amount of resources devoted to augmenting the instruments and the basic rate of reward to those who own them, it will have accomplished all that is necessary. (CH.24)

There is another line of reasoning promoted by Keynes which is completely fallacious and based on his own circular thinking. He invented the term of an economic multiplier which was supposedly meant to strengthen economic growth by a multiple of initial spending. This was meant to kill two economic birds with one stone by proving that more demand will stimulate the economy and that saving was inhibiting economic activity. He starts by saying that if one person spends $100 at a tailor that tailor now has $100 to spend in turn. When the tailor now saves 10% of that which is $10 and spends $90 for new shoes, the shoemaker will have $90 to spend and now goes to a grocer and spends $81 and also saves $9 the effect multiplies all along with each successive recipient. The outcome Keynes claims is a multiplier effect of several times the original spending and if the government supplies the original $100 this will be magically turned into over $600 and the economy will boom. Moreover, if the participants only save 5% then the total will be over $1200 and thus savings must be avoided to stimulate the economy. The fault here is that we are not trading money but we are exchanging goods, and each item in the chain has already been paid for, there is no new activity. Each contributor has invested his own funds to place an item on the market. And finally, if the government collects taxes on the transactions profits – to pay for the original $100 - more money is removed from the chain and growth is actually inhibited.

And lastly, Keynes' theory was not even new since the same discussion between supply and demand took place a hundred years earlier, when Malthus in his book *Principles of Political Economics* was the proponent of 'effectual demand' deficiency due to increased withdrawal of funds from the market. After many years of argumentation this point was finally laid to rest by Mills in his eponymous work.

To conclude we can use words of Ludwig von Mises in 1950:

"... the "new economics" of Lord Keynes. The policies he advocated were precisely those which almost all governments, including the British, had already adopted many years before his "General Theory" was published. Keynes was not an innovator and champion of new methods of managing economic affairs. His contribution consisted rather in providing an apparent justification for the policies which were popular with those in power in spite of the fact that all economists viewed them as disastrous. His achievement was a rationalization of the policies already practiced. He was not a "revolutionary," as some of his adepts called him. The "Keynesian revolution" took place long before Keynes approved of it and fabricated a pseudo-scientific justification for it. What he really did was to write an apology for the prevailing policies of governments.

The unprecedented success of Keynesianism is due to the fact that it provides an apparent justification for the "deficit spending" policies of contemporary governments. It is the pseudo-philosophy of those who can think of nothing else than to dissipate the capital accumulated by previous generations.

It is worth noting at this point that whenever in the 20th century a government decided to reduce debt and decrease government size and spending, the economy took a turn for the better. Examples are Australia in 1931, the UK in 1933 and the USA under Truman in 1946.

All about the free market is outlined in great detail and with great conviction in the excellent book *Free Market Economics* by Steven Kates.

The outcome is that the economic world divides into two distinct camps: One side and by far the larger group, is the Keynesians who want to continually have the government interfere in the economy, mainly by throwing money at the population; and on the other side are the traditional supporters of a free market where more of the market is left to its own devices, and the interference is minimal (or absent). These latter are sometimes called The Austrians, because the Austrian school of economics around Friedrich Hayek and Ludwig von Mises is the main proponent of this approach.

We can safely say that the adherents of Keynesianism have not done us any favours over the years and this is summed up nicely in a quote from Deirdre McCloskey:

How do I know that my narrative is better than yours? The experiments of the 20th century told me so. It would have been hard to know the wisdom of Friedrich Hayek or Milton Friedman or Matt Ridley or Deirdre McCloskey in August of 1914, before the experiments in large government were well begun. But anyone who after the 20th century still thinks that thoroughgoing socialism, nationalism, imperialism, mobilization, central planning, regulation, zoning, price controls, tax policy, labor unions, business cartels, government spending, intrusive policing, adventurism in foreign policy, faith in entangling religion and politics, or most of the other thoroughgoing 19th-century proposals for governmental action are still neat, harmless ideas for improving our lives is not paying attention.

The Austrian school of economics was first designated as such in 1871 with the publication of Carl Menger's *Principles of Economics*. Menger introduced some principles which are still accepted today and lay the foundation for free market economics. First he showed that the value of a good is not determined by the amount of labour put into the product, but by the ability to satisfy the buyer's wants. This then led him to the statement that both sides gain from an exchange. Buyer and seller will exchange something they value less for something they value more, and both sides of the interaction gain. This led to the appreciation of the middleman, such as shopkeepers, who facilitate the transactions between the buyer and seller. Without a middleman the transactions would have been more costly and time consuming, or not taken place at all if buyer and seller did not happen to meet.

Menger also pointed out that economic analysis is universally applicable and is based on an individual's subjective preferences to make decisions about choices. It must be emphasized here that all of the Austrian thinking is not based on wild theories about the market and possible human behavior, but on the realistic observations of the past actions and consequences. Individual persons, as mentioned earlier, face a constant stream of choices in their daily life, which are based on their preferences, opportunity cost decisions and what is called the *marginal cost*. Marginalism refers to the usefulness of an item in opposition to its abundance – at a particular point. The most frequently used example compares water to diamonds: water is immensely useful but has a low cost because of universal abundance; diamonds on the other hand have no usefulness at all (apart from the industrial type) and yet fetch enormous prices due to individual choice (which, as an aside, is also controlled by a large diamond cartel to maintain high prices). Your first bucket of water at home would have huge value if that was all you had, but since it flows freely, its value diminishes as you have more available. If you were in the desert and facing dehydration you would gladly trade a diamond for that bucket of water, and thus the usefulness is reversed. This is an immensely important principle and affects much more esoteric decisions concerning health care, the environment, sport and entertainment or tax as compared to the incentive to work. *Marginal value* is defined as the incremental value achieved from additional output. In the bucket of water example the first bucket is of large value while each subsequent bucket has less value. This means, if you valued the next one by more than its price, you'd buy another one. Alongside this concept is that of *marginal utility* and, as an example, if you have no shovels and need one the first one you purchase has great utility, the second one has far less utility and may only be valuable if the first one breaks and you need to continue shoveling. A third shovel would have no utility at all, since you would probably prefer to spend your money on something more necessary. For business, marginal value represents the value of producing one more item of a good than what is being produced now. If goods were not produced at the margin, then all goods that are necessary and useful would be expensive and only useless ones would be cheap.

What the Austrian thinkers were trying to accomplish was to inject a modicum of science into their analyses by making observations and then setting out theories. The basic position was that everything centered on the individual and choices, focusing on exchange relationships, and the application of all this to the social sciences, concerning what people think and believe in their daily transactions. Further, the price of goods determines the actions of individuals, and price is considered a signal conveying to the participants the relevant information in order to make decisions. If the price of an item changes, all concerned must make quick decisions as to the effect this has on their behavior or their next decision. Then the entrepreneur is at the centre of activity, since he is the focus of changes and exploiting new opportunities, thus maximizing use of scarce resources and constantly providing improvements in products. The foundation of a market system relies on individuals making choices for their own good – it is not an ideologically imposed system, but still creates a complex system of pricing and exchange signals that make up a working market. The bottom line is always the same in that the market needs to be free and unfettered to bring about the best economic outcome for all involved.

Ludwig von Mises was one of the last members of the original Austrian School of Economics, which later moved to North America. His most popular work, *The Theory of Money and Credit,* was published in 1912 and served as a standard textbook for a long time. Von Mises concerned himself mainly with the investigation of business cycles and the analysis of credit transactions and approached all his reasoning from a classical economic point of view. Later he fought hard to counter socialism and the influence of Keynesian thinking. Several theorems von Mises presented were extremely important to modern thinking, and some actually supplanted classical thoughts. One of these was the definition of money simply as a medium of exchange, which led to the direction that, what used to be the objective value of goods, became a subjective value. This means that previously the value of an item to be traded was considered to be based on the amount of labour and material that had been invested, and should be priced accordingly. Von Mises overturned this approach by attaching a subjective value to an item, meaning that it was worth what a buyer saw as value for himself and was willing to expend, such as for an expensive motor car or an oil painting.

Von Mises also addressed and resolved another issue that had confounded economists in the past: the difference between goods and money when applied to the supply-and-demand determination of value of commodities. Whereas an increase in the supply of tangible consumer goods confers a social benefit by raising living standards, an increase in the quantity of money only serves to dilute the exchange effectiveness of its currency and derives no social benefit at all. In fact where an increase in goods enriches society, an increase in money supply impoverishes the community by raising the value of goods and driving inflation. This realisation transformed the dissociated thinking of the past between individual behavior and economy wide thinking into a connected and single relationship between micro- and macroeconomics encompassing individual choice with the effects of monetary policy. Out of this realisation arose his most brilliant contribution, the Regression Theorem. The readers is invited to study the details of this at their own leisure, but summarizing, the theorem states that all money has arisen out the demand for goods in the past where the money was introduced to deal with these. The result of this is to say that no currency can be established by some outside force such as a government decree, social contract or artificial schemes, such as had been proposed by other economists. Money, so to speak, arises organically in a society and only if it is based on a market. Recapping from the beginning of the book, it was the manufacture of the shovel and the growing of tomatoes which enabled the entrepreneur to issue credit bits for these values. If you have nothing to offer to the world there can be no money representing products.

There is a lot more to Mises' work than can be discussed here, but an extensive presentation can be found at the Mises Institute under the title *Ludwig von Mises: Scholar, Creator, Hero* by Murray N. Rothbard.

One of von Mises' best known students was Friedrich A. Hayek, who not only dealt with economic issues but also pursued many social issues, in particular dealing with authoritarian government and its application in the perversion of a free democratic society. His major economic work was *Monetary Theory and the Trade Cycle* (1929) and much later his famous work *The Road to Serfdom* which appeared in 1944. Later in 1947 he founded along with many other luminaries, such as von Mises, Milton Friedman, Ludwig Erhard, Karl Popper and Henry Hazlitt, the Mont Pèlerin Society, which to this day presents a platform for advocates of a free market society. The group is not aligned with any ideological or political forces, and its sole objective is to facilitate an exchange of ideas between like-minded scholars in the hope of strengthening the principles and practice of a free society and to study the workings, virtues, and defects of market-oriented economic systems.

A Word About Marx

A lot has been made of the theories of how to implement a communistic system, and obviously several of these have been tried out over the last century and generally failed miserably. Karl Marx did spend a lot of verbiage on economic theories, but what he was predicting and expecting has never come about. First and foremost

175

the reader must appreciate that during the early stages of the industrial revolution people flowed from the countryside into the cities to do all sorts of exceptionally menial work and were stretched to their limits for the most part. The real reason for this is not exploitation by factory owners but the fact that whatever life they were facing in the city was far better than subsistence living on the land. What Marx saw in this was only the exploitative part and he fully expected that the 'capitalists' would grow ever wealthier at the expense of the subjugated workers, until these would bring about a revolution to dispose of the capitalist classes. Next he claimed that all added value of a good was only achieved through labour and only by the workers, that is, the factory owners contributed nothing to the value of an item. The unavoidable upheaval would not happen through violent revolution but through the collapse of the capitalist system. The reasons for this collapse would come from a situation where, due to endless competition, profit margins would shrink until they were zero and, at the same time, the workers would constantly become poorer, until the system collapsed and the workers took over. Marx used an awful lot more words and sophistry for this conclusion, but that is what it came down to.

In all this analysis and theorizing some major flaws are apparent. His whole theory was based on the assumption that there was a basic days' work, a 'labour-day', with a society wide value, but this would produce differing amounts of product in various industries. This led to the conclusion that in some businesses labour could not produce sufficient product to compensate for labour cost, and in others just a half day's labour produced all the product needed, allowing the capitalist owner to have an immodest amount of profit. This is of course unrealistic as every business matches the costs of producing a good to the market value of it, otherwise the business would not be viable.

Out of this arose one of the most risible deductions Marx invented and that is the concept of 'surplus value'. If a business pays an employee sufficient money to be able to cover his living expenses, and this is equivalent to let's say 5 hours of work on a product, but the worker is kept working for 8 hours, then the difference of 3 hours labour will all be profit for the 'capitalist' without any further benefit to the worker. Therefore all capitalists strive to have the workers work as many hours per day as possible to maximize their profits. Admittedly during the middle of the 19th century, in the throes of the industrial revolution, there may have been some truth in this, as workers did not have much power over their conditions of work, and this ultimately led to the founding of unions. The argument still contravenes actual business mathematics. The components of a product of material, land and labour plus a percentage profit lead to the selling price of that item. Should one business collect more profit through this surplus value, their product would soon become uncompetitive and another competing business would sell more of this item as it would be cheaper in the market.

For a truly worker owned industry to function all participants would have to contribute equally, and the theory runs immediately into a variation of the tragedy of the commons. In a normal business workers are paid according to their contribution and good management applies their workers to the tasks they are most suited for. If this cannot be achieved, that worker would need to work elsewhere. In a communist system all workers are equal and are treated equally so there would be no control over individual performance. Since now some workers would perform as required, but are placed next to someone who is not contributing, resentment would set in and the 'good' worker would soon slow down as well, thinking why should I work so hard when the guy next to me doesn't do much at all. Production would consequently slow down and shortages would set in, which is exactly what has been shown in socialist countries. Venezuela being the current best case against socialism, as people have to queue for milk and bread, if it is there at all.

The fact that an entrepreneur could produce anything that came to his mind and then market this item did not sit well at all with Marx, and so he had to invent the term 'socially necessary'. In his interpretation it meant that the product needed to be useful to society, and through his reasoning this would have to be determined by most likely a government bureaucracy directing what is to be produced and in what quantities. The flaw here is that this is exactly what the free market determines without government planning and at maximum efficiency at that. Additionally, this socially necessary labour time would also have to hide the shirker from the previous paragraph in that for every product there would need to be an amount of time allocated to give it a value. If a worker spent more time to make the same item, only the amount of socially necessary time would apply to determine the value of that item.

The next flaw in the thinking is the lack of value. If all products are there for all and produced by a government decree, there is no market price for these goods and thus nothing has a particular value to give a price in the market. This has been shown probably the best in the example of the former East Germany. By and by the government decree developed all products that were available in the free economies, but always in a fixed format and of varying quantities. There was a car, actually two types of cars, but the product never changed or developed and was always in short supply. There was a camera of reasonable quality, and this was used solely to generate income via exports, and again the development could not keep up with the constant improvements as made by the Japanese. With no competing products in the market development simply stood still. The reason the free market works better is due to what was termed as *creative destruction* by the great Austrian economist and Harvard University professor Joseph Schumpeter in his classic 1942 book *Capitalism, Socialism and Democracy*. What this proposes describes is that progress in a capitalist economy requires that the old give way constantly to the new. Production technology in a free economy improves constantly, and new products and services are always on offer. Each business is forever working to replace older less efficient products, equipment and processes with newer and better ones. Electricity replaced oil lamps, automobiles replaced horses and computers replaced typewriters and whole typing pools. Even if each time there may have been a period of painful adjustment in the work force, ultimately more people were later employed in the new businesses than before, as the new is invariably so much more potent than what was replaced, and whole new areas of endeavour are opened up. There are far more people employed in computer programming now than there were typists and secretaries before the advent of the personal computer. It is exactly this process that so inhibits any socialist approach. If you have a totally planned economy the new cannot be let in to replace the old since this would prove the state planners wrong, because everything they start with is already perfect and need not be replaced.

The power of creative destruction also carries its own decline in the form of envy and what is called progressivism by the left. Most universities today are controlled and run by a socialist element based on equality and correctness. The elite academia is envious of people with no higher education – the entrepreneur – becoming immensely successful and rich, while they remain basically bureaucratic employees and the trend is to consider capitalist business as crass and bourgeois. What is forgotten is that the wealth created by capitalism has bankrolled a massive expansion of the educational system, empowering the intellectual class that hates that wealth. As shows up in the anti-globalisation movement, the forces inimical to the acceptance of free markets will not understand the extent to which the whole world has become wealthier through free trade and markets. It is just too hard to accept that a market without state guidance and redistribution systems will improve everyone's lives far better than socialism ever could.

Above all Marx was a communist and all his work was solely guided by the drive to establish a reason to promote and introduce a communistic society. He wanted to see this utopian wonderful society established much like a religious leader. It was to be totally egalitarian and would abolish private property and any individualism – all had to work in the bidding of the state. No population would ever subjugate themselves voluntarily to this abomination, and so it always has to be introduced via a totalitarian system. Marxism expects a change in the nature of humans and removal of incentives and individual thought. Need we say it: USSR, all of Eastern Europe – all gone now. We are still seeing it live in North Korea, Cuba and progressively in Venezuela. China, Vietnam and Laos are officially still communist countries but have had to modify their commercial systems to embrace some free enterprise of the population, although the right to property is still in question. Under the Obama administration in the USA we are beginning to see the first vestiges of a police state being established to protect new and extensive socialist policies. Public prosecutors have wide ranging powers under the US system and are using these to hound conservative participants. Departments which should have no need for enforcement sections are introducing SWAT type military teams to protect their edicts. This has happened for example in the Department of Homeland Security which has morphed from an anti-terror agency into a large military style police force, reaching into all local police departments and distributing military hardware. The impression one gets is that the population is the enemy and needs to be suppressed at all costs. Other departments not in need of police defense, but have developed strong police presence for their operations, would be the Environmental Protection Agency, the Education Department, the National Park Service, the Department of Labor, the Export-Import Bank of the United States, the Tennessee Valley Authority, the Bureau of Land Management and the National Oceanic and Atmospheric Administration, the agency known for its weather forecasts. The upshot from this extremism is that what once were civil offences, such as being in arrears on a payment or not filing all required documentation for some activity, become criminal offences and, instead of being served a warrant, the offender is now arrested and his possessions confiscated through federal edict. Every democracy is subject to this type of development where the elective passes responsibilities to the administrative to make their own life easier, but without the appropriate oversight being installed as well.

If you read something like the following news item one day it should send a shiver down your spine:

Christopher Newport University has authorized the operation of a full-time, professionally trained police department, responsible for the safety and welfare of all members of the University community and their guests. University Police are committed to providing a safe and secure environment.

A University with its own full time 24 hour police department, not just a security force, professionally trained? A university?

Private Equity, Capitalism's Secret Weapon

Created in the United States in 1946, private equity funds are collective investment schemes that didn't become serious economic players until the 1970s in Silicon Valley. Early private equity investors, also known as venture capitalists, would buy shares in promising new industries like high-tech and sell their investments at a considerable profit. Eventually, private equity funds spread beyond Silicon Valley and invested in a wider range of industries. Today, they raise capital from cash-rich investors – pension funds, insurance companies, wealthy individuals – or borrow it from commercial banks and other financial institutions. Then they invest in various companies. The goal of the private equity fund is to sell those investments – often to another private equity fund – and turn a profit.

Smart investors from private equity funds select poorly managed companies whose value can be increased by extending, reducing, or reshuffling their activities. After buying a significant number of shares in such a company, a private equity fund can redirect or replace its management structure. Private equity managers may terminate redundant workers to increase productivity, scale back or eliminate less profitable departments, or use the company's existing business to extend its brand and reach. For instance, Bain Capital, the

181

private equity fund founded by Mitt Romney, turned Staples from a local brand into a national office supplier.

In the simplest sense, private equity investors reallocate capital where it will be most effective – from less productive uses to more profitable ones. Private equity funds propel capitalism's creative destruction and, by promoting innovation and reducing obsolescence, they fuel economic growth.

At the same time, by speeding up processes that might otherwise take a long time – such as the decline of an old industry and the emergence of a new one – private equity funds make the social costs of creative destruction more visible. Those who defend free markets, creative destruction and private equity, must do a better job of explaining their genuine benefits while supporting effective social policies to help workers make smoother transitions from old industries to new ones.

Away with Banks

Or at least central banks or reserve banks. Paper money as we know it today is a currency based on nothing. A constant flow of money is created by central banks at their or the governments will and whim, and economists seem to see nothing wrong with this situation. Such a state money system really presents a cartel situation where the banks' funding conditions and the interest rates are determined by a quasi-state agency. The constant increase of bank reserves is simply a subsidy to banks through specie and credit, and this credit growth is not driven by the amount of savings deposited, but by central bank policy and the expansion of the banks' balance sheets. New investment is supported by money printing and not savings, leading to continued debt accumulation. Today's macroeconomists see nothing wrong with this situation and believe fully that they can accurately anticipate the consequences of their financial manipulations and control the outcomes. They seem to expect stronger growth with a bit of inflation injected and all being created from a void.

The amazing hubris that is displayed by the central bank's pretension of control was displayed by Ben Bernanke: *"...lower mortgage rates will make housing more affordable and allow more homeowners to refinance. Lower corporate bond rates will encourage investment. And higher stock prices will boost consumer wealth and help increase confidence, which can also spur spending. Increased spending will lead to higher incomes and profits that, in a virtuous circle, will further support economic expansion."*

If the government can control to such an extent and with such a wonderful outcome, why do we even need a market at all? The bank will simply control all of the economy and no more worries for us. Unfortunately for us and the market, the saga around Lehman Brothers and the 2008 crash proved otherwise right away: there was no control, the banks cannot be prevented from lying about their status, and the federal government was unable to let market forces correct the situation, and so the crash turned into a full blown recession. Now we have a situation where interest rates are practically zero, or even negative in some countries, causing untold harm. The money supply will need to be constantly increased through more deficit thinking and more and more people are depending on government handouts. Under a free market system all the entities that had no right to continue to exist, due to their abysmal investment strategies, should have vanished and been replaced by fresher and more realistic firms with a better understanding of (classical) economics and more rational approaches to running a company. However, as it turned out, the government interceded and almost all of the original players were forgiven and they carry on as if nothing had happened. Only, a lot of private and smaller investors lost their money and presumably a new lot of money will be invested in the same schemes leading to the next downfall.

Looking back, the original intent of having a reserve bank was to contain 'bank runs', that is times where the confidence of depositors has taken a hit for some reason, and people want to withdraw their cash from a bank in case of a bank's default. The central bank would provide cash to the bank in trouble and thus prevent the default happening. The main reason that this was a problem stems from the regulations at the time in the USA, which prevented banks from operating in other states and placed a large number of other trading restrictions on the banks. The result was that there were thousands of small banks scattered throughout the country and many had dubious management and policies. If a bank was in difficulty the reserve bank could now supply funds to placate the customers who were reassured that their funds at the bank were always available. Originally, this was probably a good concept and stabilized the banking system and gave the consumer confidence, but it also could have been solved by interbank agreements to make funds available temporarily. The Bank of England had already been in existence since 1694 in various guises, but has been officially independent most recently only since 1997. As long as this bank operated as an insurance system to protect the customer from losses due to bank failures, there was some sense to the business.

As with all these sort of good idea projects, by and by it turned into more of a bureaucratic establishment and as such it needed to grow and establish new powers. Nowadays the Reserve Bank acts as a clearing house for all interbank transactions, check processing, electronic transfer services and looks after banking regulation and supervision. Above all it implements monetary policy, as expected by the government and maintains liquidity by releasing funds to banks on a regular or an emergency basis. This happened after the 11 September attacks which stopped all transport and essentially all banking for several days. Finally it controls interest rates and prints - issues - money, supposedly to control market imbalances and to avoid crashes, and here the system has been spectacularly unsuccessful. Since the Second World War there have been 6 major crashes in the US economy and the last one from 2008 with the economy 6 years later still not fully recovered. The problem is that the managers of these monetary controls have no way of predicting how the individuals in the economy will react to the measures, so the outcome is always different than predicted. The worst feature of the central bank system is the printing of money. At any time the Reserve Bank can release more funds simply by buying up Treasury Bonds and giving the money to banks in the community.

So how about getting rid of the central banks? A lot of argument will be presented as to why we cannot possible do this and the world would come to an end. What would take its place? How would the economy run in a controlled manner? Who would be in charge of issuing money? But let's first see what the bank does in detail.

The Reserve Bank was set up by bankers for the benefit of banks. It has been, since its inauguration, an undemocratic institution with appointed managers who are essentially unaccountable. Its main purpose was that it would eliminate the business cycle of the economy going up and down – in which it has failed completely. It would take a most naïve mind to believe that the bank is actually free from all political influence, in particular as it does not need to underlie the Freedom of Information Act. The bank was supposedly in charge of banking regulations and to oversee banking activities, but judging from past performance, especially in the 2008 events, nothing has been achieved on that front. Moreover, the US government is in debt to the tune of something over 18 Trillion Dollars which means that interest rates have to stay low to extremely low, otherwise it would become impossible even to service the debt. But let's not forget that during the Great Depression the Fed allowed hundreds of small and medium-sized banks to fail, and again during the Great Recession the same thing happened, except that all the large Wall Street clients were left unscathed. So much for the original purpose. On the private side the bank distorts the market by continuously and selectively bailing out financial institutions that have come close to collapse. The Government Accountability Office in a report from 2011 listed the Reserve as having made loans in excess of 1 Trillion Dollars to financial institutions during 2008/2009. For this the sum of $660 Million in fees for 103 contracts 'to carry out these emergency activities' was expended, and most of these were placed non-competitively. These sums are simply staggering and do not represent what one might consider control and regulation – it is more like a free for all for free money. It is also quite a long way from the original intent to support private banks against a 'run' on money, as it is no longer the individual investor who is being protected – the protection is now applied to the bank's management, who, in a normal competitive world, would be sacked. It is notable that all the countries that are part of the IMF have central banks – and all these countries are in deficit.

By the way, what happens to those Treasury Bonds sold by the government to the Reserve Bank? They are auctioned off to the world in general, but they carry an interest component, meaning the government has to actually pay back more than the money it created. The debt is greater than the money issued. Where does the money to pay this come from? Guessed correctly: from the taxpayer. Once again the population is liable for a cost that has produced absolutely nothing and enriched all the wrong people.

If we are looking at the system where an authority such as a central bank controls, plans and executes the management of the economy via the currency, it does seem as though we are looking at a system which resembles a communist command economy, rather than a free market. In a free market interest rate would be determined by supply and demand of funds and simple agreements between borrowers and lenders. Somebody has to go and read Adam Smith again. A free market is perfectly capable of controlling the economy in the most effective and efficient way, only the size of the government would have to suffer a little bit. In the words of Thomas Sowell who fully promotes the abolition of the Federal Reserve without replacing it with a new institution: "When someone removes a cancer, what do you replace it with?"

The fact remains that reserve banks or central banks were invented and instituted by banks for banks, not for the better of the economy.

On a world scale things look no better. We have the International

Monetary Fund (IMF) and the World Bank, and both of these are meant for the betterment of humanity in general, that is to help those who, with a little help, would be able to improve their own standards of living, much as a loan to a small business will allow it to expand and engage more workers for the benefit of the local economy. But guess what?: It hasn't worked out that way. The World Bank was set up in the USA in 1944 with the help of J.M. Keynes! to deal with reconstruction in a war ravaged world but has in the meantime, as any good bureaucracy does, grown into a behemoth bank with 5 divisions loaning money throughout to 200 member countries. Over 30 billion Dollars are distributed every year in loans, grant and funding, and about 5 billion Dollars in expenses are required to run the whole thing. Some of the funding comes from some of the wealthier member countries as subscription fees, as comes most of the top management. The rest of the funding is done just like all other central banks, by issuing bonds on the international market and creating mountains of debt. Quite a lot of criticism has come from the countries that are to be supported. Since the direction for the investments in these developing countries comes from the top contributors, it is not always in line with the local requirements according to the people having to live with the creations afterwards. In many cases original inhabitants of areas have been moved forcefully from areas declared as wilderness parks, other have been moved to allow a dam to be constructed and quite often local forms of corruption have diverted funds away from their purpose. As is to be expected the micromanagement of such an immense structure is fraught with danger and misuse. There are some opinions that go as far as saying in the end these programs are still taking needed income away from the poor in developing countries, where repayments have to be made on loans that have been imposed and are partly used by the countries' governments without regard to the population. Usually local investment in health and education, never in armaments, is reduced or halted. There have also been reports of threats and intimidation of persons who would point out any failings in the bank and the projects under its management. The problem here seems to be the same we are already used to: instead of setting up private businesses with ownership of the assets and the products, large agencies are in charge and simply ride roughshod over any locals in the way, while not having an interest in the product as a help to the population, but as a means of paying back the loans. Large scale plantations of export product are not necessarily the answer to help locals.

The second partner is the IMF. Anyone seeking access to World Bank funds must be a member of the IMF. The IMF was established to smooth world commerce by reducing foreign exchange restrictions, and by using its reserve of funds to provide short term loans to countries experiencing temporary balance of payments problems, so they could continue trading without interruption and achieve a balance of payments. Since the debt crisis of the 1980's, the IMF has assumed the role of bailing out countries during financial crises (caused in large part by currency speculation in the global casino economy) with emergency loan packages tied to certain conditions, often referred to as *structural adjustment policies* (SAPs). Unfortunately the IMF structure has at its top an almost immovable board that determines strategies and operates in a totally authoritarian manner. Thus investments are only approved to needy members with typically strict conditions attached. These are to raise interest rates, to cut back government spending and maintain a balanced budget. The problem with this approach is that it is applied universally to all countries, regardless of specific circumstances. Additionally the IMF, in its aims alongside other large international organisations, is deeply supportive of almost any green scheme, obsessed with inequality and in that direction supports any additional form of tax on the wealthy and the wealth creators.

The Asian crisis of 1997/1998 was brought about exactly through this unwavering direction. The governments of Malaysia, Thailand and Indonesia were running good economies and had only a short term problem caused by poor private investment practices and by foreign investment funds, but not by government mismanagement. The term imposed by the IMF now turned this into a full recession by making it harder for small companies to obtain loans leading to many bankruptcies and increasing unemployment. This, in addition to the directive to remove any subsidies on oil or food products, led to social turmoil as well. Joseph Stiglitz, a former senior vice president and chief economist at the World Bank has written many articles of the shortcomings of this approach. Ultimately the world does not need either of these institutions but stronger local partners that can deal more readily with the differing circumstances.

Since bankers always recognize a good thing when they see it, we will now have an Asian Infrastructure Investment Bank for the countries of the far East who are obviously not contributing enough to the IMF or World Bank, not to speak of the Asia Development Bank which has been there since 1966 and has already 67 members throwing money around the region. It will be another large bureaucratic structure full of people who believe they can run things better than private investment, and yet who will consume huge amounts of money without any regard for efficiency or effectiveness.

If you thought that this was the complete story, think again. There is on top of all this the International Bank for Settlements (BIS). Originally, the BIS was created out of the Hague Agreements of 1930 and took over the job of the Agent General for Repatriation in Berlin. When established, the BIS was responsible for the collection, administration and distribution of reparations from Germany – as agreed upon in the Treaty of Versailles. But as things go in the world of bureaucracy, this institution didn't just disappear when the world changed after World War II. It transformed by turning its focus to the defense and implementation of the World Bank's Bretton Woods System. Between the 1970s and 1980s, the BIS monitored cross-border capital flows in the wake of the oil and debt crises, which in turn led to the development of regulatory supervision of internationally active banks. More recently, it has concentrated its efforts on the global financial stability and capital reserve requirement accords. Next BIS became the agent for the European Monetary System, which is the administration that paved the way for a single European currency. And today, the BIS has become the central bank of central banks. The Bank now represents the interests of nearly all of the world's central bank institutions, and manages a significant share of their reserves, including gold holdings. What we have here now is the top dog of the finance world. The BIS is run secretly and autocratically by a collection of the world's top bankers from both private and central banks, and these same interests are also the ultimate owners of the BIS, showing it for the totally self-serving institution it is. Article 3 of the Statutes says: *The objects of the Bank are: to promote the co-operation of central banks and to provide additional facilities for international financial operations; and to act as trustee or agent in regard to international financial settlements entrusted to it under agreements with the parties concerned.*

After the war the BIS was accused of collaboration with the Nazi government and its liquidation was called for. None other than John Maynard Keynes opposed this and used his influence with the British and American governments to scuttle the idea and in 1948 the original dissolution decision was reversed. Since then the BIS has striven to dominate world finances through its supranational position and, as it is not responsible to any other authority (!!), we must assume that the ultimate purpose is for a politically unified world which is then dominated by the banking system. Probably not so far removed from where we are now. The real danger is the next step, which can be discerned through appreciation of the total global indebtedness and control over the derivatives economy around the world. The dry run of this was the unification of the European market with a totally senseless monetary union which is falling apart after not even 15 years of existence. The BIS has the power to issue what are called Special Drawing Rights (SDR), which in effect is the start of a world currency.

Total world debt now stands at close to 300 Trillion Dollars which is entering the realm of fantasy; it can never be repaid at current currency values. Behind this stands the market for derivatives. Derivatives, as described earlier are wads of paper containing fictitious investments that are traded between banks on a roulette

190

basis. The market for derivatives in 2015 is closely estimated at about 1.6 quadrillion Dollars – that is 1600 Trillion Dollars or 1 600 000 Billion Dollars. Faced with these sorts of numbers one must come to the conclusion that essentially money of the fiat type is becoming meaningless, just bits in a computer any more. Imagine if only 10% of these derivatives were called for one day, much as in a poker game, the delivery of an equivalent 160 Trillion Dollars in something real would be necessary – keeping in mind this is more than twice the world's GDP – and there is nothing that can be delivered in turn. In the meantime the game between banks goes on regardless, and bankers are counting their illusory billions in profit every year while ignoring the emperor with no clothes.

The next step is easily imaginable where the system as such is near collapse and the BIS comes forward to deal with the 'financial emergency' by declaring all currencies invalid and only its own SDR will be traded from now on. This can only be done in conjunction with the disappearance of actual cash, which is well under way. It may not be a bad idea to put away some (a lot?) of small gold and silver coins under the floor boards just in case. The reader is invited to look up the multitude of conspiracy theories on the web under derivatives and BIS.

GOLD

In the beginning there was gold. And then there was the gold standard and then we need to know why. The most intriguing aspect of gold is that it has held its prime position as a desirable commodity from time immemorial in all parts of the world where people have found it. There is such an intrinsic beauty and desirability in gold that from the moment someone finds a little speck of glitter in a riverbed it becomes an item of envy and admiration. Almost every society in history has had an appreciation of gold and immediately attached a trading value since all wanted to have such a beautiful adornment. Gold has many desirable advantages bringing about such popularity in ancient times. Gold is (or was) quite easy to find in riverbeds, dry or running, in rubble heaps of collapsed mountainsides or just when digging for other purposes such as agriculture. Gold is bright and shiny and does not corrode; it is malleable and melts at about 1000 deg C and at that can be alloyed with other materials such as copper, zinc and silver to give different hues of gold and also to harden the very soft pure gold and make it more suitable for jewelry. Written mention of the value of gold, as well as silver, dates back as far 3000BC in Egypt; it is mentioned in the Old Testament and played a large part in Greek society and mythology. Initially gold was mainly owned by the powerful and well-connected, or owned by the priesthood to be made into objects of worship, or used to decorate sacred locations. As discussed earlier it provides an extremely compact and portable medium of exchange and accumulation of wealth thus leading directly to coinage. Lydian traders in western Anatolia seem to have been the first to have used gold as coinage about 700BC, and their king, Croesus of Mermnadae, became famous for having quite a lot of it in his possession, which ultimately did him little good when he used it to raise an army, attacked the Persian empire and lost his own Lydian kingdom.

Gold was so desirable that all throughout the ancient empires, Egyptian, Greek and Roman, enormous efforts were expended to mine for gold above and below ground, and a lot of methods of mining such as hydraulic extraction by diverting waters through the gold bearing ores are still in use today. Gold, along with silver, was the common currency throughout the Greek and Roman empires and served as a great enabler of trade and the economy in the region.

The difficulties with gold began when government took it upon itself to hoard gold and silver, and instead fob off the population with bits of paper claiming to be of the same value. People are not stupid and nobody really believed this, and ever since then governments have been trying to make the population believe they can be trusted with the economy and the value of the currency. The discovery of the New World in the 15th century brought about an enormous increase of the gold hoard of European countries and gold dominated the economies until into the 18th century when paper money began to dominate. Thus by the beginning of the 19th century a *gold standard* was introduced. This implied that even though people held pieces of printed paper as currency, the government would promise that all the currency in circulation could be traded back for the equivalent in gold. Trading in gold was restricted, governments began accumulating a stockpile of gold, and gold was then used to alleviate trade imbalances between nations. To this day these stocks of gold still exist and governments around the world currently officially hold about 32,000 tons in reserve gold. All the mined gold in the world is estimated at about 173,000 tons, but is likely higher than that since not everybody is really very willing to admit their holdings and their mining success. If we take gold at $1200 per oz. the official holdings would amount to 1.5 Trillion Dollars and all the known gold would be worth about 8 Trillion Dollars. This is where the problem originates. When the economies of the world were much smaller, the gold being held by governments and traded amongst nations still bore a resemblance of the value of each country's currency, and the line 'promises to pay the bearer on demand' could conceivable still have been delivered. The currency in actual circulation in the USA alone is 1.36 Trillion Dollars, just matching the gold reserve. As an aside, about 40% of this currency is actually held outside the USA. The 2014 GDP of the USA was about 17 Trillion Dollars and of the world 75 Trillion. So the connection of gold value to actual society's total worth was broken a long time ago. Unless of course gold prices rise to maybe $15,000 per ounce and make up for the shortfall in value!

Great Britain was the first to adopt the gold standard in 1821 and it was internationally adopted in 1871, but has had a checkered history since. During the First World War the gold standard was suspended as countries needed to borrow money and tax more to finance the war. Following the war there was a strong desire to continue with the gold standard but the British Pound and the US Dollar by and by became global reserve currencies, that is, smaller countries bought these currencies to back their own economy, and gold began concentrating in the large economies. The turmoil after the war and through the 1929 crash and following depression resulted eventually in the USA revaluing gold from \$20.67/oz to \$35.00/oz in 1934. The effect of this was that the value of the US Dollar dropped sharply and most of the world started selling gold to the USA at this higher price, ending with 75% of the world's gold being in American storage. After the Second World War the Bretton Woods Agreement, which introduced an adjustable pegged foreign exchange rate system based on the gold standard again. The newly founded International Monetary Fund (IMF) was given the power to intervene in the market where an imbalance of payments arose. This only lasted until 1971 when, due to inflationary pressures and a general decline in gold holdings the fixed price of \$35.00/oz was finally abandoned and the price of gold could be determined by a free market.

So why should there have been a gold standard at all, since it only operated for historically brief periods? It was meant to be the first formalised standard to keep up with international exchange rates. It was ultimately unable to do so because large amounts of gold reserves were required by each country to overcome large fluctuations in the exchange rates of currencies, and this ultimately proved too costly. The problem with gold is also that it is just another commodity in line with oil and iron ore. Where the price is fixed, the market is distorted, which in turn is taken out on other things such as currencies. Left to its own devices gold, as recent history has shown, is a very volatile commodity and mining thereof is greatly influenced by its value, constantly changing the rate of new additional gold. Under a gold standard, should the demand for gold suddenly increase perhaps due to some growing industrial demand, the value of currency would have to decrease and all other goods would have to decrease in price – spelled deflation, including wages. Worse yet, any existing debt would actually increase as there would be less money available to pay it back. The best example for a comparison is the state of the Mediterranean countries, especially Greece. These joined in a monetary union with the newly created Euro currency, which is an equivalent to a gold standard, and this removed these countries control over their currency. The outcome is quite predictable since these countries previously had greatly devalued currencies for a reason: Their productivity was lower, their government spending was higher and the lower value of the currency made it easier to trade and brought foreign currency into the country to make up for their loss in value.

This currency equivalent of a gold standard makes central banks impotent to fight inflation or deflation, much less do anything to combat persistent unemployment. Exactly the same effect would happen with a real gold standard – the flexibility to deal with changing economic conditions is removed. In the period after the 1929 crash the countries that gave up the gold standard soonest recovered most quickly.

As an investment gold is purely a speculator's game. Ownership generates no income – in fact there will be costs for storage – and thus it is a liability. What the expectation of the gold investor shows is that he owns a lump of metal that someone else will pay more for in 6 months' time. In the words of Warren Buffet: "Gold gets dug out of the ground in Africa, or someplace. Then we melt it down, dig another hole, bury it again and pay people to stand around guarding it. It has no utility." Certainly some people have made money on a capital gain from gold in the past, but it still is a simple gamble of one investor betting against another. Then, if you sell for a profit, there will be capital gains tax, depending on your place of residence and your honesty. As for jewelry: only if you really love the item as a decoration. Any value from the work input is lost and on sale the item is worth its pure gold weight only and, since there is at least a 100% mark-up on jewelry, this is a losing position (except for some very high value fashion names such as a Fabergé egg).

Bitcoin

The invention of bitcoin needs to be assessed in view of von Mises' Regression Theorem, as it seems to contradict the prohibition of artificial currency schemes.

It is not exactly easy to understand the ascendance of the bitcoin as it was supposedly started by a Japanese, Satoshi Nakamoto, through the publication of a white paper which was released on October 31, 2008. Its original intent was to have a currency for computer technicians, and they can only be obtained by what is called *data mining*. The concept foresaw a finite number of bitcoins being buried in computer code and gradually released until 21 million would be available by the year 2040. Only large computer users or large groups of computer user are able to 'mine' the coins by running lengthy code on powerful computers. This means for its value there would be no point in someone trying to collect a bitcoin from home since it would take in excess of its value in time and effort to obtain one coin. For the same reason would it be unviable for someone to counterfeit coins as the amount of work is too large and only one could be generated at a time, unlike in currency counterfeiting where the work invested in one plate can produce many bank notes. Bitcoins are registered on a decentralized storage and are tracked by 'miners', people who are in charge of tracking and storing bitcoins and the information. For this they are paid, of course, in bitcoins. Each bitcoin is simply a data ledger file called a 'blockchain' and contains information defining its existence and a record of all previous transactions. Bitcoins only exist digitally, so when you receive one you need to store it safely on your computer or memory stick and make sure you don't lose it because then it is gone for good. The .dat file you receive should be copied and stored as a duplicate backup every day you do bitcoin transactions. Every single trade of bitcoin blockchains is tracked and tagged and publicly disclosed, with each participant's digital signature attached to the bitcoin blockchain as a 'confirmation'. These digital signatures, when given several seconds to confirm their transactions across the network, prevent transactions from being duplicated and people from forging bitcoins. While every bitcoin records the digital address of every bitcoin wallet it touches, the bitcoin system does NOT record the names of the individuals who own wallets. In practical terms, this means that every bitcoin transaction is digitally confirmed, but is completely anonymous at the same time. The most appealing aspect of the bitcoin is its anonymity. No bank, no government agency or law enforcement can track or access your bitcoin wallet or transactions. These transactions can be observed live on a web page blockchain.info and it is interesting to see how vast the activity has become. No doubt the various agencies of government, banks or the UN will soon try to grab control over this system, and we will have to wait and see how readily control can be wrested away.

Concerning the Regression Theorem it remains to be seen how the currency develops in the future and what effect the limited supply will have on its value. At the moment it is maybe a quasi-currency, but still it can be used to carry out natural transactions. From the original reasoning money originates from the market—not from the State and not from social contract. It emerges gradually as monetary entrepreneurs seek out an ideal form of commodity for indirect exchange. Instead of merely bartering with each other, people acquire a good not to consume, but to trade. That good becomes money, the most marketable commodity. Thus bitcoin is a payment system for goods and services much like using a bank draft or credit card where no physical currency is exchanged. So there does not seem to be a conflict here with the Regression Theorem. Bitcoin is probably much closer to a real transaction as it has lost – got rid of – the third party of banks and financial institutions – all payments are done peer-to-peer. It is PayPal without banks. In the beginning a bitcoin had no value at all and this value was only determined through use of the system, essentially just an accounting ledger. As people started using bitcoins they attached a value according to demand – this is no different from the old gold coins. The implications of bitcoin are actually quite enormous if time proves it out. No third parties means the currency affects the existence of banks and above all the control of the State as to the value of the currency. We would be right back to page one of this book where the entrepreneurs traded with one another for values they determine.

One of the shortcomings of bitcoin use is beginning to appear now in that traders will need to register with the government as a trading business, and this is once again where the government can get its hooks into the system.

The War on Cash

Still in its infancy, but already in development for many years is the war on cash being instituted by governments and banks. All governments hate cash. Governments, at least modern western governments, have always hated cash transactions. Cash is private, and cash is hard to tax. So politicians trump up phony reasons like drug trafficking and money laundering to win support for bad laws like the US Bank Secrecy Act of 1970, which makes even small cash transactions potentially reportable to the Feds. The second participant in this war is of course the banks. They miss out on transaction fees, physical money is hard to store, transport and protect, and banks are required to keep branches open with actual persons handing out or taking in cash. All the new methods of payment with tap cards and services like PayPal are growing immensely in popularity much to the delight of the organizing companies. Debit card companies don't actually get involved in money stuff, they are just an accounting system between customers and banks via the merchants – an ideal business with no defaults, no risk and endless fees. The next big competition will come from the mobile phone transactions cutting out the debit card middle man and acting directly between the merchant and your bank account. And in fact it is now being proposed to institute direct transfers between mobile phones without using a bank account. The money will be portable and stored in an account on your phone and a transaction takes place phone-to-phone – all traceable of course.

So, what's not to like? The government wants to trace everything you do, just like you've seen in the spy thrillers like Jason Bourne; the banks love the trend as it allows less and less customer contact and more fees for nothing; even public transport everywhere seems to no longer want to deal with cash and has gone to great lengths to establish fare cards topped up elsewhere. Counterfeiting will become a lost art and pickpockets will need to find a new line of endeavour. Of course the downside for the individual is that you *can* be tracked everywhere and all your finances are traceable (which may be good if you ever need an alibi!). Even the war on terror is being exploited by some governments. The amounts of cash one can withdraw from a bank is now being constantly limited more extremely, through the excuse that it will prevent terrorists from purchasing weapons or explosives. If you have ever noticed that, where guns have been outlawed, criminals still have no problem getting their weapons via other means and this will be no different, except your freedom to hold cash is being destroyed. This is France 2015:

The French Finance Minister, Michel Sapin, has announced a drastic tightening of the use of cash in France. As the newspaper Le Parisien reported, citizens will be strictly monitored beginning September 2015 if they make payments in cash. Restrictions will include:

- *A limit on cash payments will be reduced from 3,000 euros to 1,000 euros.*
- *Tourists can only pay up to 10,000 euros in cash, so far there were 15,000 euros.*
- *If a Frenchman wants to change money into another currency, it must still do to 1,000 euros without identification only. So far, French could buy foreign currencies for 8,000 euros.*
- *If a bank customer stands out more than 10,000 euros a month from his account, the bank must report the transaction to the Money Laundering Authority TRACFIN.*
- *Banks must inform the authorities of all cargo transfers within the EU that exceeds 10,000 euros. This regulation impacts checks, pre-paid cards, and even gold.*
- *The control over crypto-currencies like Bitcoin are set to be tightened drastically.*

This is the economic tyranny we are beginning to face. What is rightly yours belongs to them, as they see it. We no longer live in a democratic world as more freedoms are constantly being eroded. This is all about controlling the people to sustain government power. And finally, this is the banks' ultimate solution to runs on banks – it will no longer be possible to withdraw your money as you please, and most likely even to transfer it, if the bank, or the banking system, is in trouble. Our freedom is based on the protection of rights to our property and money is part of our property. Therefore, how we decide to use our own money is part of that freedom and must be protected from interference by the government or others for that matter and we must insist on the freedom to use any form of money as we choose in our own legal dealings.

Luckily there are a multitude of large players trying to muscle into the market for a cashless society and it will take some time before the final solution is arrived at. Nevertheless, the propaganda is out there trying to make the prospect palatable: Set up your phone with the connections to all your favourite shops and restaurants and when you walk in by just saying "pay Michael H", or some code, you automatically have all payments arranged without calling for a bill or even passing by a cash register. That it is very appealing must be admitted and for a generation who grew up with a phone in their hand fully understandable. Thus founder of mobile payments provider Square, Jack Dorsey: "I think there is a general desire in American culture right now to find something that is more *crafted*, more *personal*."

There is another direction that banks need to reinforce and that is the latest insanity of negative interest rates. In order to 'stimulate' investment and spending some European banks now have negative interest rates, that is, there is no interest rate, and there will be a charge on any amount held in a bank account. In this case it is preferable to hold cash under your mattress since there is no charge for that. This has happened before and was called *demurrage* and one form of it showed up in the invention of stamp scrip. Stamp scrip was paper money issued usually in smaller locality and required each user to pay a small fee 2, 3 or 4 cents at each transaction until the nominal value had accrued in stamps on the paper and it was then redeemed at face value. Through all the transactions the scrip had then raised many times its own value to fund local projects and alleviate unemployment, but in effect was just a low value tax. Actual negative interest rates have also occurred before but were confined to specific cases such as US Treasury Bonds in the 1930s, but these included some positive tax implications, as well as an option for the purchase of higher yielding bonds later on. Switzerland imposed negative interest on foreigners in 1970 depositing money there to stem an inflow of foreign currency from countries with high inflation.

It is unlikely that negative interest rates will be around for long since anyone with a cash asset will use it to pay down other outstanding debt rather than see it shrink in the hands of the banks. The result will be that the banks' balance sheets will shrink and their cash assets will grow leading into a sort of dead corner of no business transactions. Only time will tell.

Ultimately there is the darkest and greatest danger lurking underneath all these plans, and that is control over your funds and your life. You have just lost it. As the example of Cyprus shows, and Greece will soon be next, a government can at any time instigate a law to confiscate a portion of your money assets and you will not be able to do anything about it. In March 2013 the Cypriot government passed a law that would confiscate a percentage of bank deposits above 100 000 Euros and freeze withdrawals to stop a banking caused crisis essentially initiated by joining of the Cypriot currency into the Euro. Note the word 'confiscate'! This was caused solely by ill management of the economy by the government and even more foolish investments by the banks. And don't believe it can't happen where you live. With the planned complete automation of transactions the government and the banks will have the power to deal with your money anytime they need to get bailed out. In the extreme, the authorities could remove your freedom to pay or contest any demand such as parking fines, tax on interest paid or simply instigate surcharges.

The next step in this saga is already well under way with the central banks proposing introduction of an E-currency controlled by the banks. An exchange rate will be introduced between the E-currency and cash and this will be constantly eroded by reducing the cash value against the E-currency with the effect of coercing the public into the banks' currencies as paper cash constantly diminishes in value. It is clear that the banks will not rest until all your possessions are essentially under their control. How the population will still buy illegal drugs is not elaborated here.

Forcing the people onto a system of digital fiat currency transactions offers total control via a seamless tracking of all transactions in the economy, and the ability to block payments if an uppity citizen dares get out of line. Once all money exists only in bank accounts – monitored or even directly controlled by the government – the authorities will be able to encourage people to spend more when the economy slows or less when it is overheating.

Once again the real reason for the push against cash currency comes from the banks. The insane direction of generally applied negative interest rates is limited by the amount of this the depositors will accept. At the moment negative rates of about -0.50% seem to be the maximum that can be accommodated; it is really like a service fee: keep your money with us and you pay a fee. At higher rates it becomes beneficial to pay for your own security to keep cash elsewhere. So the more insidious thought that appears to overcome this obstacle is that a negative interest rate is no different from inflation: Over time your money has less worth – it will have less purchasing power. All this of course is still mired in Keynesian thinking which would say that some inflation is absolutely necessary to compensate for growth in the economy. Oddly, this leaves out the fact that there was practically no inflation all through the 19th century and yet the world economies grew tremendously. And all this took place without the existence of a central bank. There was still a gold standard in place which controlled the growth of the money supply, but this was also controlled by keeping the money growth in line with industrial growth. Central Banks nowadays in collusion with private banks need to have some constant devaluation of currency to reduce the debt levels they face. Ultimately the population will be the mugs again as their money is either devalued or removed to prop up the banks and financial institutions.

Looking back to the time of the first US central bank, the Federal Reserve, it was established by the banks for the banks in collusion with the government in 1913. The supposed reason for this bank was that it could control funds sufficiently to avoid the large swings of bubbles and recessions by controlling the money supply, thus moving the issuance of money from the government to banks. Starting immediately in 1921 and 1929 this approach has proven a dismal failure by generating even more enormous swings in the economy throughout the 20th century and with the failure of Keynesian economics we are now approaching the end game. 2015, and the world debt is over 200 Trillion US Dollars and there is just no possibility in sight of ever getting the mounting debt under control. The implication here is that money has become just some bits in computers, actual cash represents only 7% of all the money created and flowing around the world, so in a way actual cash is of minor importance. But the freedom that remnant of cash represents must not be underestimated.

What would happen if there is a major break-down of the electricity system or even just the management system for these purely digital accounts is not being talked about at all. It is a good time to keep some of your assets at home in the form of cash, gold bullion or coins, and silver bullion for smaller denominations. Just in case.

A Minor Fantasy

It is always stated that for an economy to be viable it must expand continuously or face stagnation. If we were to take the situation of stagnation as a future development and compare the past, a questions begs immediately: What of an economy which grows without expansion? Birth rates are sinking in the entire world and at the same time people are living longer. Almost all economies of the world have suffered under interfering (mis-)management by their respective governments, who by now are totally clueless as to how an economy can be turned around, or are unwilling to do so. And yet, it is a future we have to deal with, and with a bit of optimism and good clear head for analysis surely an answer can be found.

Over the centuries each economic entity has slowly accumulated wealth, not only material, but also intellectual - people are better educated and have acquired more wealth, and countries have built infrastructure and educational institutions as well as supporting the population to better their lives. But all along the underlying premise has been growth through expansion. But can we have growth without expansion? Surely a static or even shrinking society can still increase their wealth if we stick to the original baseline of people keeping busy to look after themselves and in the process others as well.

To have growth without expansion means that all individuals of that society increase their wealth, and the society as a whole becomes wealthier as well on a public basis. Since in the early days the individuals produced goods and traded amongst themselves this was perfectly possible, under the condition that a majority of the participants slowly increased the quantity or the quality of their output. If you found ways to produce more and better tomatoes and beans eventually you could get a better horse cart, supporting the cart builder and encouraging him to improve the current model. It does not mean that we need more and more horse carts – just better and more useful ones. Some of the foundations of our current society will need to change.

Unfortunately many people succumb to the siren call of the environmentalists and economic doomsayers, the anti-capitalists and the 1%ers. These imbeciles want us not necessarily to return to a previous century, but they want to stop the world. They see consumerism and constant growth and expansion as the greatest threat to humanity and the environment. From way back, with the Club of Rome distress signals of ever decreasing resources and lack of food for a starving humanity, this approach has been proven wrong as food production per capita is actually higher than ever in history due to advances in technology and biology, and none of the resources have reached a point where we are facing a shortage. The most disappointing aspect of this trend is that some of the biggest capitalists in the world, Bill Gates, Warren Buffet and Richard Branson for example, having made their pile, now want the rest of us to go away. Fortunately there are generations of young people ready to carry the torch and innovate regardless, since that is in the nature of the human beast. The underlying basis of this is that capitalism and growth are inseparable; a capitalist attitude of self-made success automatically leads to wanting to improve the world around you. At what specific moment would we want to stop the world? Next week on Monday? Go back to 1957? The only direction away from capitalism is socialism and we have already elucidated where that leads, and that is to suffering and human misery for lack of goods. Economic growth is not due to governments or even economists, but simply to leaving people to do what they want, but within some legal and moral restraints, and no more.

Concerning the lack or depletion of resources, all the soothsayers, being economically ignorant, forgot the basic laws of transactions. As soon as a resource becomes scarcer its price will go up and demand will decrease, and further, some other good more readily available will take its place, while recycling will become more prevalent. This is why there is a market for futures of all goods and raw materials available in the world which sets the pricing for these items and makes the market predictable. Anyone who understands market economics will find comfort in this arrangement, while those who have not learnt will cower in anxiety before the future. World business is an open system which allows the freedom to produce things and sell them, and it has improved the lot of all the world's population as more people can take part. The alternative, to close the system and place restrictions, to 'save' the world, results in such solutions as public ownership, onerous and discriminatory taxation, strangulating red and green tape, wage and price controls, and income and wealth redistribution, all of which again lead us into poverty.

There is one other input that none of the old dismal computer models predicted and that is, as it has shown that as the inhabitants of the world become wealthier, their birth rate declines, and eventually we will face a population decline in society. This is already evident and problematic in several European countries and in Japan. In some countries the problem is still being masked by migration making up a decline in birth rates, but this too will end. So, what is needed is some thinking about a time when fewer houses will be required, no new roads and trains are necessary and established businesses will need to shrink. Luckily this will involve a long time frame and if planned correctly can be adjusted for.

Unfortunately, the underlying cause for constant expansion is the constant increase in debt, and growth has to be maintained so that the interest on that debt can be paid. The increase in debt is fuelled by the creation of fiat money leading to inflation as money becomes more abundant. One way in the past to control this was using the gold standard, but this is no longer possible. Another possibility would be taking a situation of the economic collapse of a country, such as we have seen in Argentina, Zimbabwe and more recently Greece to introduce a new, controlled currency. This would be issued in accordance with the actual production of goods as last known and issuing money in an equivalent amount. This is once again going back to the beginning where for every kilo of tomatoes or each shovel a value can be declared, based on the materials and effort required to produce that item. This would involve a lot of haggling and compromise, but nothing that couldn't be handled by some accounting programs. This 'virgin' money, undiluted by debt, would now be in circulation and keep everybody satisfied. What is required next is the opposite of what happens currently, which is inflation. Now the state will need to look out for deflation. If the money in circulation becomes insufficient to cover all the production happening, that is, an industrious people will produce more goods or higher quality of goods than last year, money would become scarce and prices would need to decline, so that the same amount of money should buy more goods, which is not the aim of the exercise. As deflation is detected more money can be injected in accordance with the increased production. It would be a little tricky, but there is no reason why it shouldn't work at least as well as the inflation control side. Now note the difference that under inflation – which was caused by the government issuing too much money – the required solution is the raising of interest rates. In our new situation interest rates become independent of government and would be determined by an open market. This must be in accordance with the amount of money someone wants to earn from an investment, versus the amount of money available in a business case to finance a new project, without any input by banks or the government controlling the rates. What can no longer happen is that a bank will sit on large piles of funds and invent new ways of making more revenue from the money alone without an increase in wealth. In a way this currency could still be backed by gold, but would need to be insulated from foreign exchange of gold to avoid currency manipulation by other countries.

There is one solution available, but may not yet be a practical solution, and that is Bitcoin. Bitcoin is a digital currency or a crypto-currency, existing without tangible cash components. All trades take place through a mechanism called the *blockchain*, which is the technology platform on which bitcoin is exchanged. Bitcoin fulfils all the requirements of a cashless currency, but is immune from government control and interference; it lives as a parallel market and supplants most government functions. It does not need to be Bitcoin exactly, as in the past many currencies have sprung up in different countries, but all unbacked currencies were done in by governments and debt until they collapse. A crypto-currency can only be used as it exists, no one can create debt and no more can be created. So for stability there is a solution in the system available.

In our mythical society there will still be a need for government revenue, but new ways of obtaining it have to be found. Revenue can be collected directly from services such as road tax, stamp duty for documents, sales tax etc., but not from an income tax, and the government would need to restrict its spending to the revenue received. If there is a requirement for roads or harbours to be built, the process must be the same as for a business: the business case is assembled, financing arranged and a fixed payment amount and time is set and included in the future budgets. If this is done under the auspices of an independent accounting firm, preferably from outside the country, it represents a legal and rational form of investment.

In the distant past, science fiction writers tended to picture a world where more and more machines have been introduced to do all menial tasks, and these setting free the population through shorter working hours or different types of work, maybe simply overseeing the mechanised work force for example. This to date does not seem to have happened. It is however true that machines and computers have replaced a multitude of jobs during the last few centuries and the trend is continuing, and yet, more people are now employed than ever before, only the preponderance is towards the service industry. Yet this focus on constant employment and busy-ness seems to be more of a 20th century aberration. In the time before the industrial revolution there was little employment as such and no term for unemployment. Most people worked on the land and another group would be artisans making things by hand in specialised trades.

Originally people lived in small communities and were much like an extended family. Everybody likes to have contact with other persons to exchange news or discuss the hunting season. When large numbers of people moved to the cities and worked in factories, these surroundings took over from the community and became not only a place to earn a living but also to interact socially. Even today, people will complain about their mundane jobs but become disconsolate when out of work. In areas where the industrial revolution did not happen or was minimal, such as the Mediterranean shores and the Middle East, life is still far more leisurely than in the Northern

European countries. Most people are engaged in trade of some sort or fishing and a lot of time is spent in cafes discussing politics or the neighbours. There is a different expectation to the contents of lives. In the wealthier countries people will use surplus income on toys: bigger cars, boats, vacations and computer equipment, and this leads to everyone wanting to work more hours rather than to have more leisure time. As rates of income climb, the employee sees a better utilisation of his time by working more hours, and also an engagement in the welfare of the company that supplies this bounty increases, leading to unpaid overtime and even carrying on at home in the evenings and weekends. Some companies have gone to the extreme of forbidding employees to take home their computers to ensure there is a break from work and some recuperation, what is now called work-life-balance.

The first signs of a change in this arrangement seem to be appearing in the new world of social media where extreme connectivity is leading to a *sharing economy*. It is defined as any marketplace that uses the Internet to connect distributed networks of individuals to share or exchange otherwise underutilized assets. Companies like Uber and Airbnb are offering a business model to people who don't want full time constant employment and are happy with a reduced income for work arranged to their time scale. If you don't want to do taxi service or room rental one day, simply don't answer to the offers. This removes the imperative found in normal taxi and hotel arrangements to have as much service sold as possible, and it allows the participant to determine how much time is spent on income and how much on leisure. Another trend showing up is the artisan's workspace where machinery and tools are provided on a rental basis, and quality products are made by a new breed of artisans and artists. These handcrafted products may be useful or decorative, but the purchaser ultimately can obtain desirable items that are not mass produced and may give more satisfaction to the owner without having to own a van Gogh. Along with this artisanal direction there is yet another development, and that is 3D printing, which may still be in its infancy but holds great promise of producing items without massive investment in machinery, and the ultimate potential of these printers is yet to be seen. One thing that is certain is that automation and robotics will advance and new ways of dealing with this next disruption to society need to be found.

Our Biggest Enemy? The UN!

Much as the European Union is establishing a single unelected bureaucratic Europe wide government that ultimately cannot be dislodged, so is the UN on its way to establishing an authoritarian world government and it can only achieve this by destroying the few remaining democracies.

The underlying agent for this is the UN's Agenda 21 and its annex. Habitat II and III, which outlines how this will be achieved under the mantle of environmental protection, sustainable development and fighting climate change – previously known as global warming. An excerpt from the outline: Read this carefully!

25. We, the States participating in the United Nations Conference on Human Settlements (Habitat II), are committed to a political, economic, environmental, ethical and spiritual vision of human settlements based on the principles of equality, solidarity, partnership, human dignity, respect and cooperation.

Agenda 21 was established at the Rio conference in 1992 and 178 countries signed up at that time. Its predecessor, and even more dangerous document, was the ICLEI - Local Governments for Sustainability, founded in 1990 as the International Council for Local Environmental Initiatives, and is an international association of national, regional and local government organizations that have made a commitment to sustainable development. The ICLEI has been concentrating on establishing green oriented local governments in all municipalities around the world, and so far over 1200 cities, towns and municipalities have joined. The point of this is to prevent individuals everywhere from exercising their own personal freedoms of movement, of consumption and of general behaviour, through restriction implemented for sustainability reasons. This will be achieved by progressively expropriating tracts of lands and declaring them as ecologically protected zones where no development may take place. The thus dislocated population will need to move into larger urban zones with very high population density. The main vehicle for this is The Wildlands Project. This is a treaty of land use and a lot of the effects will sound familiar to the reader. Land is taken over by: denying water and/or grazing rights to farmers; by denying clearing of vegetation for farmland; by expanding the legal definition of a wetland and making any trickle of water or puddle a wetland, preventing the development of the land and all the land around it; where it is declared a location of endangered species; declaring green non-development zones around cities where no subdivision can take place, even though these areas are devoid of any reasonable vegetation. The process involves large areas to be set up free of human habitation and later link these by corridors so the animals can move along them. As the animal population grows so would these areas and corridors, gradually forcing more and more people off the land and into cities. It is a most insidious project and seems to be well under way in North America and it has made a start in Australia.

The most effective way of controlling farming population is via control over water supply. The government will exercise authority over the amount of water farmers are allowed to use, charge them for it and at the same time prohibit any dams or retainings to be built. With total disregard for the supply of food for the population or for export income, the farming industry is diminished and subjugated.

In the words of Harvey Ruvin, Vice Chairman, ICLEI. (The Wildlands Project) *"Individual rights will have to take a back seat to the collective."*

Also:

"Current lifestyles and consumption patterns of the affluent middle

class – involving high meat intake, use of fossil fuels, appliances, home and work air conditioning, and suburban housing are not sustainable."

Maurice Strong, Secretary General of the UN's Earth Summit, 1992.

From the report from the 1976 UN's Habitat I Conference:

"Recognizing also that the establishment of a just and equitable world economic order through necessary changes in the areas of international trade, monetary systems, industrialization, transfer of resources, transfer of technology, and the consumption of world resources, is essential for socio-economic development and improvement of human settlement, particularly in developing countries.

And:

"Land...cannot be treated as an ordinary asset, controlled by individuals and subject to the pressures and inefficiencies of the market. Private land ownership is also a principal instrument of accumulation and concentration of wealth, therefore contributes to social injustice; if unchecked it may become a major obstacle in the planning and implementation of development schemes. Social justice, urban renewal and development, the provision of decent dwellings and healthy conditions for the people can only be achieved if land is used in the interest of society as a whole"

Essentially what is being forced here is a complete rollback of the Magna Carta, which set people free to own land, work it and generate goods for trading. What is being driven is for all ownership to revert back to the control of an authoritarian socialist feudal system.

The original signatories to the UN charter would be absolutely stunned if they saw the octopus that the UN has become. The original intent of the UN was simply to stop any further military conflicts between all its members and offer support for the development of the less developed countries. Since the majority of UN members these days are autocratic regimes, the whole purpose of the UN has been perverted to such an extent that there is little point in democratic governments even trying to have a say in world affairs. The situation is best summed up by some quotes from Madame Christiana Figueres who is the Executive Secretary of the United Nations Framework Convention on Climate Change (UNFCCC):

UN - 3 February 2015 - The Top UN Climate Change Official is optimistic that a new international treaty will be adopted at Paris Climate Change conference at the end of the year. However the official, Christiana Figueres, warns that the fight against climate change is a process and that the necessary transformation of the world economy will not be decided at one conference or in one agreement.

"This is probably the most difficult task we have ever given ourselves, which is to intentionally transform the economic development model, for the first time in human history", Ms Figueres stated at a press conference in Brussels. *"This is the first time in the history of mankind that we are setting ourselves the task of intentionally, within a defined period of time to change the economic development model that has been reigning for at least 150 years, since the industrial revolution."*

Figueres is also on record saying democracy is a poor political system for fighting global warming. Communist China, she says, is the best model. This is not about facts or logic. It's about a new world order under the control of the UN. It is opposed to capitalism and freedom and has made environmental catastrophism a household topic to achieve its objective. China is also able to implement policies because its political system avoids some of the legislative hurdles seen in countries including the U.S., Figueres said.

There is some encouraging news, however, and we will need to see how it plays out. A lot of previous signatories have now passed laws to opt out and prohibit being part of the Agenda 21 process, after seeing how pervasive the process of stopping local development really is.

The actual hook that is used to impose the UN agendas is the constant push on climate change and an emphasis on 'sustainable development', where all this takes place under a 'global governance'. Member countries that are better off financially will be bullied into sacrificing their wealth in the interest of poorer countries, a typical socialist redistribution scheme. Instead of dealing with the criminal governance of these poorer countries (speak dictatorships), it is easier to bring down the successful members and weaken them in turn.

The second front of this UN dominance has been established long ago via the World Bank and the IMF, in conjunction with all other banks that want to participate. For a long time these institutions have been loaning money to economically challenged countries to the extent where a normal repayment route is no longer available. This second hook is now that the banks will make further funds available if the offending country follows the exact instructions from the banks. This of course simply means that the running of the country's affairs has now been subordinated to the methods proscribed by the UN. The tentacles of this process are to be seen everywhere, whether economically or through the 'human rights commission' or arms control, to the level of the individual. The whole purpose of this exercise is to continuously reduce the freedoms of the member countries and also of the individuals by subjugating all to the authority of the UN bodies directly. The latest drive even strives to delegate the rights of children away from their parents under the guise of child protection, and thus making the State the primary 'duty-bearer', and relegating the parents to a secondary position.

The current step in the UN assault on sovereign countries is happening through the pretense of free trade. The vessel for this is the Trans Pacific Partnership (TTP) in the East and the Transatlantic Trade and Investment Partnership (TTIP) in Europe. In both treaties, which are being brought about in total secrecy, a so-called free trade agreement will deliver unheard of powers to private companies and global conglomerates in that they can challenge decisions made by sovereign governments, which will then face arbitration in an international forum. The driver behind this treaty is a combination of corporations and politicians in the United States with support from the UN on the legal front. The ramifications for both agreements would be extremely wide ranging, from pharmaceuticals and health care to control over food and health and control of internet and social media.

It is, however, not in the scope of this book to dissect the UN complete agenda and the reader may look up "UN world control".

The End of Democracy?

Before we get to the Philosophical Section later on we must evaluate where the preponderance of liberal thinking is leading us. As stated earlier the government must be responsible for certain aspects of the society that they are in charge of. So for example it makes sense that medical services are provided to ensure anyone who falls sick or has an accident can be supported to regain full functioning health and continue contributing to society. The same goes for workers who have lost their job and require some assistance until they have found a new position. The quality education of children is paramount to developing a knowledgeable and capable society where everyone can find their place and contribute to the welfare of all simply by looking after their own betterment. These areas of health, education and welfare are the core competences a government must deploy to manage a wealthy and supportive society, and initially in Western societies, where these areas were looked after and improved over the last 100 years or so it showed that against previous times incredible advances in technology, research and business acumen have generated a vastly improved and superior life for all people. This is not an easy arrangement to institute with fairness and balance, and most aspects should still be left in private hands through insurance schemes, with the government supplying direction and protection from fraud. Since all the funds have to be collected through taxes and are disbursed according to need, we run into the problem of the 'Tragedy of the Commons' again. This time it works in slightly altered version called *The Fallacy of Composition*. This occurs when a statement is true for a section of an economy, and this is then applied to the whole economy, when evidently it does not apply to some other sections of the economy, thus giving an incorrect conclusion. A simple example would be to observe unemployment in cities and then conclude unemployment is the same rate all over the country, while in rural areas it could be much higher.

If we consider the areas of government supporting separate groups for various reasons, which could be unemployment insurance, pensions, childcare, housing, Medicare, welfare payments, subsidies to certain segments of business, disbursements to charities or religious organisations and so on, a certain type of envy will be detected. So we can say that what benefits one section of society cannot be beneficial for the economy as a whole, because someone is always missing out on their particular version of benefits and come to feel victimised. After all they are paying the taxes and do not realise any return, while others reap large amounts of 'free' money. This can be observed daily in the newscasts, in the discussions in parliament and down at the pub. Depending on the size of the populace in various sections of society the government must - or will try to - keep them all happy through ever more disbursements of generosity. As said before there are only two ways for a government to obtain funds and that is to raise taxes or to print money. The reason the section is called 'End of Democracy' is that this situation applies only in truly democratic countries, never in a Democratic People's Republic. In order to be re-elected, one side of politics, usually called 'progressive' or 'liberal', will take the short term view and simply give away more and more 'free' money to more and more special groups to maintain their vote. The voters for the most part are not interested in where the money comes from – they have not read this book, nor any other economic study. The end of this occurs when the majority of the population resides in the receiving segment, and continually votes in the generous clique while racking up a larger and larger debt. This can now be seen in live action in countries like Greece, Portugal and Spain, and of late also in the USA. The opposing political party, who may instead be considering the welfare of the nation in the long run, has to focus on dealing with the impending crisis, and what measures to put into place to alleviate the situation. As recent history has shown the give-away side is very adept at dirty fighting and is also better organised, and thus the necessary difficult measures - with the co-operation of the main stream media - have been dubbed as *austerity measures*. It is an extremely clever use of words because it implies direct personal and unjust effects. The term is sufficiently generalised so that almost all segments of society feel they will be hard done by, and thus feel they need to oppose any such measures. And naturally, no group receiving benefits will ever voluntarily give up any portion of them, asking instead for more and more hand-outs. The result is a continuing majority vote for a free lunch without any qualms about the consequences, and the latest vote in Greece for the 'anti-austerity' party goes as the first government to be elected under a majority of hand-out takers.

So now we have a divided society, with one section of the population that pays essentially no taxes and receives only benefits, or benefits larger than their tax liability would be, and the other portion being the actual net tax paying public. This divides the community into two groupings, one of tax payers and one of tax spenders. The thought is not new and was addressed by John C. Calhoun, an American politician of the early 19th century, as well as Frederic Bastiat in Europe. The outcome of this division is simply that a government is tempted to increase taxes on the smaller proportion of the population, who pay the largest proportion of tax revenue and dispense this revenue to the far larger section of the society, who pay little or no taxes and receive the larger benefit. These people will of course vote increasingly for a government showing largesse, even to the extent that the state must borrow to maintain these running expenses, rather than keeping an administration that maintains a tight control over spending.

There is a quote still essentially unattributed which summarises the situation as follows:

A democracy cannot exist as a permanent form of government. It can only exist until the voters discover that they can vote themselves largesse from the public treasury. From that moment on, the majority always votes for the candidates promising the most benefits from the public treasury with the result that a democracy always collapses over loose fiscal policy, always followed by a dictatorship.

And:

"It is indeed difficult to imagine how men who have entirely renounced the habit of managing their own affairs could be successful in choosing those who ought to lead them. It is impossible to believe that a liberal, energetic, and wise government can ever emerge from the ballots of a nation of servants."
<u>*Alexis de Tocqueville*</u>

There are two further aspects to consider in conjunction with this scenario: The bureaucracy and the actual elections. Elections are a wonderful thing and would be even better if the people actually voted for policies instead of images and newspaper directions. The great waste that occurs with elections is the situation where one party is elected and begins to institute reasonable policies with balanced budgets and good social awareness, but within bounds. This may prove too boring for the population and they only last one term. In the meantime the opposition, in order to be able to oppose, needs to have policies that are different, and when in power will tear down all the previous government had instituted and replace it with more populist policies to better ensure its survival. In this endeavour the more populist party is usually fully supported by the bureaucracy through the simple fact that this group is in favour of constantly increasing the size of the public service, and is supported by the unions in this vast expansion. Secondly the bureaucracy is not an

218

elected body and thus over the years tends to accumulate employees of a similar political direction, even though they should not, and this endures, regardless of the party in power. The outcome of this situation can be that during times where a party has been elected that bureaucratic management disagrees with, they will actively (or passively) operate in the background to foil any new developments which do not fit their ideology. This is what Margaret Thatcher called the 'ratchet effect': When a 'progressive' party is in power the drive will be to push further into socialist territory and more spending/taxing, while the next more conservative party elected cannot undo all that has been introduced during this time, and gradually the pendulum swings more and more to the left.

Ultimately the socialist side will need to progress to a dictatorial position, since the general population will not accept the endless push to the left and stops supporting the measures, and any fully socialist regime can only maintain power by force. We have the examples in Cuba, Venezuela, Argentina, most African countries, and now Greece is heading there.

Personalisation

Having successfully ploughed through all the previous pages on a very subjective assessment of economics you may quite rightly ask yourself of what use all this could be to improve your life. Since there was no mention of economic theory or practice during the years of schooling you received, probably due to the fact that all pedagogues would be at each other's throat as to the curriculum, we will need to have a fairly simple and rational look at what an ordinary person can do to use economics effectively in their life.

Budgeting your Income

As a child, you first start becoming aware of money when you need to ask your parents constantly to buy this or that and the answer will be – to you at the time – more or less random. Some things you get, others you don't and you judge this as being simply the vagaries of parentism. Eventually you will start receiving pocket money and this changes the situation. The first times you are likely to spend the pocket money more or less immediately, and then have to wait until the next hand-out. After a few times you learn to pace your expenditures and start to become somewhat discerning in what you would prefer to buy. That is the whole point of the pocket money exercise, but a lot people have forgotten this lesson by the time they become adults. The next stage of the lessons is when you start earning money through work such as washing the car, mowing the lawn or some simple home endeavours, such as packaging stamps or delivering papers. For the first time you learn the connection between your time and effort and an appropriate reward. Now you'll also be able to plan for expenditures. You can save for a new cricket bat or a set of drums.

As you get older and graduate from high school you will face the first major choice of your life: whether to start working right away and earn money, or to carry on schooling for bigger rewards later on. What you don't realise at the time is that learning a serious trade may bring larger rewards later in life than a degree. Nowadays trades such as industrial plumbing or electrical work bring extremely high rewards, due to some of the difficult conditions and scarcity of qualified journeymen. A Bachelor of Arts or Science does not really endow the graduate with much of an enticement for good money to be spent on an employee. Now, along with the financial choice, comes a lifestyle choice as well, and the same will happen later in life when you have more money, affecting your choice of dwelling location, car and so on.

Now we get to the point at which you earn proper money for the first time, you can rent your own place and furnish it and generally have a good time. Being young of course the future is a long way off and in any case someone else will look after it.

This is exactly the point where any economics training from earlier schooling is missing, as we should be taught at least the basics of balancing your expenditures, and the pit falls that a free economy presents. No matter how distasteful it may seem, but a little bit of budgeting work right now can change your life, and for this some guidelines are required. Without some kind of an appraisal of available funds, some families seem to just tumble from crisis to crisis and quite often need to borrow to make it to the next paycheck. Since all well-run companies operate on an income and expense budget there is no reason why budgeting should not make your life a lot less stressful and more enjoyable. When starting out it is also very useful to have some appreciation of expenditures in the past. So collect bills and make note of cash expenditures for a few months to get a feel for the type of costs that are incurred. This does not imply that you should run around looking for every penny to be saved or any discount voucher to be maximized. We are after the bigger picture.

A number of inevitable expenses immediately rear their heads: rent (or mortgage) for an abode, insurance payments, regular utility bills, council rates, loan payments for your education perhaps and transportation. A general guide can be a split of 50% needs, 30% wants and 20% savings and debt payments, based on your net income (after taxes). Next a list is required of all the possible expenditures in life:

Housing – rent or mortgage plus maintenance expenses
Insurance – automobile, house and contents, health, life
Debt repayments – student loan, car loan
Utilities – electricity, water, gas,
Transportation – car fuel & repairs/maintenance, public transport, taxi, parking, tolls
Food – groceries
Regular medical expenses – dentists, medication

All these are part of the necessities you cannot get away from.

Next are wants:

Personal – clothing, hair care, make-up, exercise, club memberships

Entertainment – sport, hobbies, dining and drinking
Personal utilities – phone and internet,
Occasions – birthdays, weddings, presents etc.
Education – tuition, day care, books, office supplies

And last we need to have some funds set aside for later:

Savings – retirement, investments, house down payment, holidays, emergency funds.

There is more to this than people will have expected before writing it down and the best way will be with a theoretical example. Your first cost is accommodation and this should be about 25% of your net income. For a net income of, say $4000/month, this will be only $1000. Next, insurances run about $50/month each, perhaps $100/month altogether. Utilities are a bit dependent on where you live and how your preferences fall, but again $100/month should cover it. Transportation, depending on circumstances can also add up quickly: $50/week for fuel or other transport if you don't have a car is another $200/month gone. That leaves $600/month for food and drink. Not generous.

Now let's look at the wants with an allowance of $1200 and the largest expense these days is most likely your phone/internet connections probably eating up $200/month. Personal grooming and health expenses should be covered by $100/month, but the clothing budget is totally subject to your self-restraint. When you are still in your younger years you should enjoy yourself, so allow for sports and entertainment, going out with friends and looking good. The $900 is to be divided into these activities, but you do need to keep an eye on the money flow. The biggest risk at this time is the credit card, and many a young naïve person who thought this can easily be paid off later that year winds up in strife and financial shambles. As mundane as it may sound, please pay off your credit card every month. Or at most leave no more for the next month than the amount your current month's payment was able to manage.

This leaves an amount of $800 to be set aside for things you want in the future. Even though you may believe that the government will look after you in your old age, predictions are always dangerous, especially about the future. The earlier in life you start setting up even a small fund, say $200 per month initially, the better the long term outcome will be. Just as an example, the $200/month unchanged after 40 years and with a 3% interest rate would yield about $200 000. Obviously, as you earn more later in life the payments should increase accordingly and so will your reward. This takes discipline and determination but you will be ever so grateful when you are 60. The best way is to have an automatic deduction after every payday into an investment account, that way you don't even see the money and you get used to living on the rest. Even putting away 10% of your income will eventually make you quite wealthy.

The rest of the available funds should be put into a savings account or even a piggy bank at home so that, if you want to take a nice holiday for example, borrowing will be unnecessary. The same goes for a car. When you are younger some cheap used car will be adequate, but as your demands increase something more prestigious will no doubt rear its head and you will need a good amount to purchase this. If you already have a fund set aside to cover a large part of the cost for the whole thing, it will take the stress out of your budgeting. A little emergency savings must also be attempted here. Should you lose your work or have a more serious illness there should be a fund equivalent to 6 months of net pay at hand so you don't have to go into debt for daily living expenses. Depending what the medical insurance or system in your country of residence is, you may also need some money set aside to cover expenses for medical costs or other emergency situations.

Borrowing Money

Borrowing is probably the most difficult topic for most people because it is so easy. Banks are in the business of lending money and therefore are extremely clever how to get the most income from your desires. First and foremost we need to keep in mind what applied to governments: borrowing for ongoing expenses is a bad idea – borrowing should be confined to material improvements or extension of capabilities. This means for the individual that borrowing for a new bathroom or kitchen is a good thing as it actually maintains or increases value. The same goes for further education which will allow you to earn more money later on. Borrowing for a holiday or expensive entertainment events is not a good idea, since this will be a recurring expenditure and soon you'll need to borrow again.

The cost of borrowing comes in many layers, and some of them are well-hidden by the lenders. The basis of all borrowing is determined by the government's central bank which is used to lend money to the banks. Since banks don't hold sufficient funds at all times to cover the demand for commercial borrowing, they can borrow money from the Central Bank at a rate that is referred to as the *discount rate*. The central bank in turn can control the demand for borrowing by raising or lowering this discount rate. If the rate is higher fewer customers will be able to justify borrowing, and the economy will show a slowing down of activity. The commercial banks borrow from the Central Bank and add a mark-up for individual lending. This point is extremely important for mortgages. You need to plan for these rates to increase sometime in the future and you should make sure that such an increase of maybe 2 or 3 percentage points can still be covered in your budget. Sure, you can cut back on some other spending, but sufficient funds still need to be available.

The best and largest pool of private lending is found in mortgages and, since these are well secured with the property and there is a very large amount of money outstanding, these rates can be low and are usually within 2 percent of the Central Bank rate. Mortgages are considered long term borrowing, usually in the 20 – 30 year range. Generally, if you have a mortgage which has been paid down over some years, it is best to borrow additional funds against the mortgage through a Home Equity Loan, especially if these funds are also meant for the house in way of improvements, but you may want to buy a car or a fancy home entertainment system, but the security is always the house. There is no cheaper money available for the individual. The more adventurous will borrow against the equity in their property to acquire more properties and build up a portfolio of investment properties, which are rented out for income. This type of investment is somewhat hazardous if the Central Bank rate rises but your lease payments remain fixed. Although there is a temptation fueled by the banks overtures, do not refinance your mortgage to pay for holidays or other frivolities no matter how wonderful it sounds,

If the Central Bank rate is 3% then a mortgage rate should be in the 5 – 6% range and you need to shop around. There are other institutions apart from commercial banks such as Credit Unions, Savings & Loan Associations and other smaller pooled investment associations, who also lend money and may be able to offer slightly better rates. You will also need to decide whether to take a floating rate or a fixed term mortgage, this is up to you. If you have a floating rate mortgage, you can sell any time and not pay a penalty. With a fixed term arrangement you will need to pay what the bank's revenue might have been if you had continued for the full term, and this can be substantial.

The next level of lending is the personal loan. This carries a greater risk for the bank and accordingly the interest rates are much higher. Personal loans are considered short term borrowing usually in the 4 – 7 year range and this affects interest rates. From the 5 – 6% mortgage rate you will immediately face 10 – 14% or more, and again you need to shop around or you can also bargain for better rates if you can show solvency. But remember the bank's position is that past solvency does not equal future solvency. Also banks will try to disguise actual interest rates with low sounding monthly or quarterly percentages. The only true rate you will be paying should be the APR, the *Annualised Percentage Rate,* and this must include any charges and fees that also come in the small print and can vary enormously between offers.

This rate becomes even more important when you use credit cards to finance purchases. These are generally quoted as monthly rates and do not include any extra charges and annual fees. Banks are obliged to clearly state the APR along with any other format on offers, and this is the number you must use to compare deals. The better advice is to stay away from using credit cards for financing since the APR can be anything from about 18% to over 25%, money just simply wasted, unless you have the discipline to repay every month or at most spread a purchase over no more than 3 months. There is a way you can improve your purchasing power if you already have a credit card: find a company that offers 0% on balance transfers, make your larger purchase on your old card and then accept a new card with 12 months 0% interest and transfer the balance. Cancel the old card, pay off your purchase over the year, and then cancel the new card before the next annual fee becomes due. Sounds all a bit unethical, but it's their rules, just like the government's tax collectors have rules that can be exploited. Here you need to watch out for additional conditions, where for example there will be a 3% fee on the transferred amount, or where you would be locked in for so many years. Again you need to read the fine print several times.

Lastly we have what is called *Overdraft Protection.* This leads you into temptation since it is so simple to just keep spending and not worry about the balance in your account. But there is a price to pay: Depending on the type of arrangement you make with your institution, there may be a per payment charge of $5 – $25 (or more), there will be a fee for the arrangement and there may be a daily 'service' charge of $3 – 5 while the account is overdrawn. Additionally you will pay interest, probably daily, of as much as 25% APR. All in all, not a good way to manage your money. The problem exists mainly for those who have difficulty in managing their account in the first place, and they will not fare any better when all these additional charges arise, making things much worse.

As to arranging private loans from groups or individuals – just don't.

In this category is also one of the most insidious schemes yet devised and that is the pay check advance or payday loan. Here you would write a check for the amount of money you want to borrow plus a fee where the lender will cash your cheque when your next pay has been deposited into your account, usually a matter of two weeks. For a loan of $100 you may be charged a $15 fee for the two weeks. It may not seem much but it lies in an APR range of over 300%. Many times the money isn't there to cash the cheques, and it is rolled over with a new fee, so after one month you now have to pay back $130. Here is a typical table for a 14-day loan:

APR	Fee	Loan	Payment
312.86%	$6.00	$50.00	$56.00
286.79%	$11.00	$100.00	$111.00
278.09%	$16.00	$150.00	$166.00
273.75%	$21.00	$200.00	$221.00

As you can see this is really not good value. If you are in temporary financial difficulty, it is probably a much better idea to contact the creditor and discuss a deferment or revised payment terms, such as monthly billing instead of quarterly, which is easier to budget for. You can also approach your employer for an advance – which will cost you nothing, and as an added bonus will remind you to budget better next paycheck.

If you go back to the budgeting thoughts, it would serve you well to set up an emergency fund immediately after graduating from whatever level you have reached. During your study time you probably managed with a very small budget just to get through, so when you start earning money, stay a little on the side of the student budget and put away some money every month in a separate bank account, and you'll not have to worry about short term trauma again.

Obtaining Interest

The opposite of borrowing money occurs when you have a lot of money that you don't need immediately. Since you don't want to give it away or hide it under the mattress, which seems a bit insecure, you would like it to work for you, and that means to obtain some kind of an income. As soon as you have money to invest you'll be surprised to find how many people crawl out of the woodwork, quite happy to take it from you for investment purposes. This leads us probably to the first and most important single point for any investment: By all means listen to advisers if they appear, but collect all the information you can obtain and then make up your own mind how to invest. Never pass your funds into someone else's hands to invest it for you. They cannot possibly have your best interests at heart when their own interest would be better served. To make the point, this includes bank's advisers, mutual fund advisers and investment portfolio managers, all of whom would like control over your investment. Not every adviser is a bad apple, but you would not know beforehand which you are facing. Many a rock star, sports personality or movie actor has found out the hard way that those trusted people that managed their money for them had no interest whatsoever in their well-being, only how they could get the money away from their charge. So whatever investment decision you make, ensure all the funds and investments remain in your name under your control and respond only to your signature. With that out of the way let's see what options there are - and this could become a long chapter.

The first decision regardless of investment is the matter of liquidity. Can the funds be tied up for longer periods of time or do you want access anytime? The two extremes are for example government bonds, which can be for ten years or longer, against three-month certificates of deposit from a bank. There is no point mentioning bank's savings accounts since these interest rates are so minimal as to be ineffective.

For those who are fiscally conservatives to the extreme, bonds will be the safest investment. They come in two varieties: government and corporate. Fixed rate bonds are issued to obtain cash for the issuer. Governments are the most prolific borrowers and issue bonds on a continual basis, usually with low interest rates and fixed for 2, 3 or 5 years, during which time you receive a regular interest payment and then get back your money on maturity. Governments are unlikely to go broke, but corporations, no matter how large, can default, and therefore the interest rates for corporate bonds are a little higher, due to the higher risk. A second type of bond is the so-called 'gilt' which is issued for much longer periods of 20 years or more. These bonds also have fixed interest rates, but are traded on an open market. This is closer to trading on the share market in that the price for the bond can fluctuate. If general interest rates rise, and as the bond is a fixed rate, on selling you would need to offer a discount and receive less value than the issuing amount. Where interest rates fall during the life of the bond, the owner will see an appreciation in value as its rate then is above market return rates.

A more appropriate investment for interest is the fixed term deposit. Private banks will issue 3, 6, 9 or 12 months term deposit contracts at usually the highest interest rate available in the market and require checking out as to which bank offers the best rate. Depending on how urgently you may need the funds tied up in the term deposit, choose the best rate for the length of investment time available. At the end of the term it is best to roll over the total amount plus the interest to compound the income, if the funds are not needed at that time.

Mutual Funds, or Investment Funds, are the best way for the general investor to participate in the share market and other investment vehicles. These funds are professionally managed investment vehicles, using a pool of funds collected from many investors for the purpose of investing in securities such as stocks, bonds, money market instruments and similar assets. Most funds offer an investment mix for the investor to choose from, for example domestic companies, overseas companies, small companies, money funds or equity funds or a mix of different investments. Open ended funds will sell and buy back their shares at any time and are listed in the papers every day. Their value will be determined by the fluctuations of the particular assets they are invested in, and thus may increase or decrease, depending on the market. In the long term this is the best vehicle for the investor who does not have the time or does not believe to have sufficient knowledge for more direct investing.

Investing in the stock market directly should only be done by investors who have already other funds put aside through savings and have money to spare for a little more investment fun. Quite a lot of time must be set aside to learn about the stock market and some of the technical knowledge that is required. There are some basic tenets that apply for all and the basis of the market reads: Buy low and sell high. This is where most novice investors fall down. They may have bought a stock at an opportune time and it has risen, but now it becomes difficult to sell. Most of the time, rather than taking a profit, the person will hang onto the stock either to wait for it to rise some more, or for sentimental reasons, and eventually the stock will fall in price. Again, instead of selling quickly, the investor will hang on some more to wait for an improvement in price, but this could take a long time, as was shown after the 2008 melt down. The proper procedure is for your research to determine a stock that is liable to rise, decide on a sell level to give you good revenue and then sell at that point – unless you have some knowledge that there is more upside, but this is probably illegal.

Frequently stocks become famous in the headlines and everybody rushes in for a bit of the action, and when done early enough and sold quickly there may be some merit, but it requires discipline. A more promising approach is to seek out stocks that seem undervalued and have a low profile in the news. They will have regular dividends and good management and will seem unexciting, but at least you are not paying a premium for the publicity effect. Above all avoid tips from other people, especially taxi drivers and waiters – that way lies 1929. And do not ever borrow funds for investing in shares – read the first line of the previous paragraph again.

Next, it is imperative to understand that a share price contains all the information that is known about that company, plus a lot that is being assumed by other investors. Essentially one investor is betting against other investors at all times. When you purchase shares the seller will think they are going down, while you predict a rise in value. Therefore it is a good idea to learn a little about the company: check for regular dividends; has the price movement been steady or erratic and does it follow the market in general; are there news items on record showing future expansion or plans for rationalization in the company structure or products. But essentially you are always betting against someone else's interpretation of this same information.

The basic value of a share price is determined by its ability to provide a dividend. If the price is $100 for example and the dividend is $5 you have an investment return of 5%. Unless you are going into speculating on future value of a stock this should be your basis for investing. Some shares present a good upside potential and they will have only a 1 or 2% return, but this has been discounted because the market believes that future earnings will be much higher. Therefore, company earnings are the next most important aspect to investigate. Again, nothing is a simple as it seems: there are companies that pay out a large percentage of their earnings in dividends and some others, especially recently listed companies, will keep reinvesting their earnings and pay a low or no dividend, which does not make them any less attractive. One measure investors use to determine the value of a stock is the *Price to Earnings Ratio* or simply P/E. This is the value of a quoted stock divided by its last earnings per share listing. Thus a share worth $45 and showing earnings of $3 for the financial year has a P/E of 15. Traditionally a range of 12 to 18 has been accepted as a reasonable range for the ratio. A lower P/E may mean the stock has been neglected by the market, or it may be that earnings expectations are lower for the future. A higher ratio above 20 may mean the stock is flavour of the month and actually overrated, but it also may mean there is speculation of a higher earnings outlook. Many investors use technical analyses through the information from stock charts, developing graphs and predictive market extensions to establish future values. These are all based on past performance, and, as we all know, past performance is no guarantee for future performance.

For those who would like to learn more about the market there are many web sites to explain things and give advice, and two good ones to start would be *Yahoo Finance* and *Investopedia*. Most investing can also be done on line these days, so you probably won't need a stock broker of the traditional variety any more. For the serious investor it is imperative that time is taken to keep up with the market and to research the companies of interest. Probably 3 – 4 hours a week would be a minimum time to follow up on stocks you own or are considering to buy. And always keep in mind the market has to balance out: for every winner there is a loser.

The next level of investing would be in commodities futures, such as gold, copper, wheat and pork bellies. This is not for the amateur investor, since most of the trading is done using margin investing. The investor only pays a percentage of the total value of the contract, say $10 000 for a $100 000 contract, which gives a 10 fold leverage. If there is an increase in the product of 5%, this will give $5000 revenue, which is actually 50% of your investment, but it goes the other way, too. And you have to pay interest on the outstanding amount, $90 000 in this case, while the contract is open. An even more exciting level of risk is to apply margin buying to currency trading. More of this can be found on Investopedia again.

All high return investment schemes must be avoided entirely. The first maxim is that anything that seems to be too good to be true is.

Spending Money

Now that you have obtained money to live on – legally one hopes – you must actually put it to use and spend it. Having gone through the budget exercise above we pretty well know where all the money goes, but, as they say, you must get the most bang for your buck. On the fixed expenses such as rent/mortgage and utilities not a lot can be done. Where you live is partly a lifestyle choice and you probably want to live in a nice neighbourhood, and at the same time as close to your work or schools as is reasonable. One thing you need to consider right there is that your monthly rent/mortgage amount must be combined with the cost of transporting you to and from your place of work. This means as you live closer to your workplace you will expend less on travel, in fact zero if you can walk or use the bicycle. You can compare this to another area you could live in, but would be further away and you need to use the car every day, or pay for public transport. This difference can be applied to a slightly higher rent/mortgage payment without upsetting the budget calculations.

But let's put aside the all the basic needs for now. What we need to address is the 'wants' section above, since this is represented by what is called *discretionary spending*. This term refers to the fact that you can spend this money on whatever you would like, but bearing in mind the concept from the first chapter called 'opportunity cost'. This referred to the choices you have for expending funds, and it is these funds you want to spend most wisely, or at least to give you maximum enjoyment from your purchases. A good place to start is the old maxim *'Keeping up with the Joneses'*. It is the easiest trap to fall into and arguably the most expensive one.

Let's say you want a new TV and you have looked into the shops and read up a little and then start discussing with a mate what you are thinking. This person is bound to tell you what a wonderful TV he has and how much it was and how it was money well spent, even though it was quite expensive. If you now start thinking that you need the same or even a better TV, since you don't want to be ridiculed if he might come around and see your TV and judge it a lesser item than his own, then you have fallen into that trap. You have let another person make a judgment for you out of fear. There is nothing wrong with having a look at his TV and then deciding for yourself if this is what you want, or if you can actually decide for yourself that a lesser version will do. You must judge honestly for your usage if all the features of the more expensive model are for you, or if you really need the latest high resolution screen and that high profile brand name on the fascia. This decision should also be affected by an opportunity cost evaluation. If there is a $500 difference between the fancy set and one that will do you nicely, consider what use you can put that difference to. It may be the case that you actually watch a lot and have movies that you enjoy in the higher quality, then that is the decision. Just don't spend more than you need only to impress others (who probably could not care less about your image). At the other end of the transaction is the sales person who you need to watch out for. They will tell you this one is the best, they have one at home and all the reviewers in the papers and magazines agree this is what you should buy. Usually this only means it is the model with the best profit margin for their business. Also you need to consider that you might be falling for promotional hype sometimes: if you already have a TV, are you really unhappy with it or are you just feeling left out because everyone else has a bigger/brighter/curved/faster screen. It may turn out to be an unnecessary expense altogether.

For all these consumer goods one must very wary of promotional hype and clever marketing. Much effort is expended, especially by large corporations, to sell you goods that you don't really need, or that cost far more than their utility would indicate. Most common vacuum cleaners tend to cost about $150 - $200 and if you consider the product carefully a good product choice will be available to serve your need. At the other end of the spectrum are ones that exceed $800 by promising features which are probably irrelevant or that the less expensive vacuum cleaner delivers as well, but such is the power of marketing that these types sell simply because of the image created around the product. So to maximize your own welfare you will need to separate your actual satisfaction from the false satisfaction delivered by clever marketing.

The more extreme case can be made for cars. People are always buying new cars and this may be good for the economy, depending on what country you live in, but it may not necessarily be good for yourself. The same reasoning needs to be applied here, in that you have to assess the realistic need for a replacement. Most people will say that the repair costs and frequency is becoming a nuisance, in which case maybe another brand of vehicle is called for. There is no need to go through a penny-based calculation of the total lifetime costs of a car, as some motoring magazines or consumer choice reports will foist on the public. Keep in mind these magazines also have to make a living and this results usually in sensationalising the mundane and presenting it as absolutely vital to your financial well-being. When analysed correctly, the data will usually say you can save 35 Dollars a month, or a year, which is not what will give you the certainty of having obtained the most satisfactory product for your money. It is a better approach to decide exactly how much you are willing or able to pay for something you really like. To do this correctly look around and decide what sort of vehicle will make you happy while staying realistic in your expectations. There are people who really only want a good solid transport and don't really care what the neighbours think of them. This sort of person has the easier task of simply finding probably a slightly used fairly basic model with a good reputation. For the rest of you more work is required.

Saving Money – The Other Type

Every day flyers appear in the papers, through the door and ads flood the TV: SALE –SALE – SALE. The consumer does get a bit jaded because we just can't spend that much all the time. A lot of the fuss is created just to get the customer through the door, and lot of the offers are called loss-leaders, that is, the shop will reduce some items to the extent of actually selling them at a loss, but it entices people to come to the shops with the intent of just purchasing this sale item. The story, however, does not stop there. Once in the shopping environment temptation is all around, and the managers know that customers will spend more than they intended once they see all the wares around them. This all seems a bit cynical, but that's the way it is. What needs to be done is to make these occasions work for you. In particular on the food side there is much opportunity to maximize on the savings. First, keep a cupboard in your home aside for some major food storage – perhaps you have a pantry. Next keep a list of items you regularly purchase but are not perishable. There are things like rice, cooking oil, pasta, canned vegetables and also washing powder or toilet cleaner as well as toilet paper. When these types of items are on sale at a good price, usually close to half their normal cost, simply stock up and avoid buying other things at the same time. This gives you two advantages: you save the money from the lower price, and you don't have to worry about carting these things home every second week or so. The same goes for frozen foods. Get a larger freezer and store frozen goods, usually good for at least a year. When you use items like herbs the bundles are usually larger than what you need for one meal, so clean it and freeze the rest.

One doesn't need to be an absolute miser and worry about every cent or penny, but where it seems worthwhile the effort certainly does save some funds for you. Should you require something unusual sometimes, maybe a concrete drill or weed slasher, first try to borrow it from someone or just rent this sort of item for a day or two. Some items you may also pick up used from web selling sites, or from local pawn brokers if appearance is not an overriding factor. There are plenty of apps available to do comparison shopping, to locate Thrift shops and even for free stuff to a good home. For some other things, especially larger value purchases, you may be able to negotiate a cash price or simply an outright reduction in price if you purchase right there and then, it doesn't always work, but there's no harm in asking. Also try and time purchases correctly, some items go on sale regularly, or they are reduced on a runout sale just because a slightly updated model has appeared in the shop.

Although it may be a lot of fun, but try to avoid impulse purchases – wait a couple of days and ask yourself if it's really necessary or as much fun as it seemed at first look. No need to be a spoilsport, but many people do regret some major purchases after a while, usually because of the lost opportunity value: they would have preferred to buy something else instead that made more sense. Also, those who are constantly tempted to splurge on items that are on sale or offered as end of season or year specials need to keep in mind that what are called 'savings' are actually still 'spendings' and only make sense if the item fulfills a genuine need at that promised lower cost. Under no circumstances is spending money a 'saving' as the sellers would have you believe.

We don't want to harp on too much about scrounging, but you need to keep actively aware of how your money is spent and how to improve your take home value of stuff.

The Philosophical Section

The world is going to hell – and it's our fault.

Since the astute reader will be digesting the wisdom presented in these pages long after it was collected, it runs a risk of having been wrong. Nobody can predict the future with any confidence and we all have to take our risks. What we can deal with appropriately is the past, and not just the last couple of years, but more of an overall appreciation of events.

The Earth has been here for about 4.5 billion years and probably will be for another similar length of time. For most of that time the surface of the Earth was not exactly hospitable to life and not at all to humans. And keeping firmly in mind that we exist on some floating bits of temporarily solidified magma, that push each other around like drunken sumo wrestlers, pushing and shoving and sliding on top of one another, it is probably more surprising that it is so quiet here. Apart from the odd earth quake and volcanic display all seems to be at peace more or less.

Somewhere around 3 billion years ago the first signs of life appeared and then hung around in primitive forms for another billion years or so. These first forms of life lived in a primordial 'soup' of chemicals in a form of complex molecules, called Archaea, that learned how to replicate. By and by some improvements were made and Eukaryotes, cells with nuclei, developed. These were always very much loners that fed and divided and carried on for another billion years or so.

You begin to see the sort of timescales that nature within a universe operates in. Somewhere in that time frame the system started to produce oxygen, again over a billion years or so which finally allowed the type of life that we are surrounded by to establish itself. Then, about 800 million years ago, a lot of these single cell organisms tried many combinations and finally found a way of co-operating to become multi-cellular organisms. This in turn was the moment all of this development had been waiting for, and a veritable explosion of life occurred first in the sea and eventually on land.

More hundreds of millions of years passed and all the time the bits of earth floated around and rearranged themselves. Life forms appeared and disappeared, depending on various disasters and violent events that came along. At one point all of the earth seems to have frozen over completely and was referred to as "Snowball Earth". Large objects hurtled from space and smashed into the Earth. Enormous volcanoes erupted and blanketed the sky with soot, cutting out most sunlight and reducing vegetation to a minimum for continued survival. Polar reversals altered the protective envelope of the Earth and allowed massive cosmic ray downpours. Temperatures shot up and down depending on circumstances and the balance of atmospheric components changed over the course of these events. The dinosaurs reigned for a hundred million years and presumably would still be here if not for some major event, still in dispute, that wiped out the lot of them. We would probably remain as some very small mammal scurrying through the undergrowth or maybe in the tree tops to avoid being eaten by these beasts and could not develop much further under those conditions.

All that notwithstanding we are here, we have been a successful species, and we will continue to develop. Regardless of what individuals or groups of people believe, we have developed naturally and we are a part of the whole system of life. The dinosaurs never asked what their effect on the environment was and how they would influence other life around them. Humans have developed because unlike all other life on Earth we can manipulate the environment and we can foresee consequences. Early agriculture developed after some individuals noted that grasses that had edible seeds grew at certain periods, and that the seeds that were nourishing us also became new plants. As a single event this probably is the most important development in human society. It is the most dramatic display of actual consequential thinking and one no animal can duplicate, except accidentally. It also defined a sense of purpose. Life has been just running along nicely, but it was simply an existence for the sake of perpetuation under any circumstances, and without any particular direction. Thus life as such was immensely successful and absolutely no adverse condition could stop it. As we know now, even oxygen is not a requirement for life to continue, in fact first life most likely existed at undersea thermal vents using hydrogen sulfide, carbon dioxide and minerals expelled at these vents to establish itself. This implies that life is pretty well inevitable, once certain conditions are met.

There is something very seriously wrong with the approach of judging the human influence on the environment. Looking through pre-human history of life, you would discover that life arranged itself in proportions that were convenient for whatever life was successful just then. Before man had any influence at all you can take your pick: dinosaurs ruled, swamp ruled and then grass took over or most of the earth was covered in ice etc. Life was always there in one form or another and usually in some form of excess. What man represents is simply a different stage of the same process.

If humanity, as Greens would have it, were to just disappear from the face of the earth what would happen? Nature would carry on in its random fashion, life forms would develop and thrive or disappear again, volcanoes would erupt and destroy stuff, as would floods, fires and droughts.

This is how the world runs and how it will run until the sun explodes. We are but one tiny temporary part of this system and just happen to be here at this time with no guarantees of longevity. No matter what we do, we are in the system and we have to act by the same rules and circumstances. Do not believe philosophers, bankers, politicians or clergy who try to tell you differently. We can argue about it as much as we like, but everything comes back to simple power struggles between people who want to control your life, and this is the part all of us have to fight continually. Socialists want to redistribute your assets, Greens want you to stop breathing, Unions want you to support their elite and Climate Change proponents just want the money to keep coming.

This does not imply that it is all right to destroy the environment around us since we still need to live in it and we want it to be nice to look at and also we need to grow food that is reasonably clean and healthy. But out of sheer ideology and with the backing of the Agenda 21 participants, it now has become unacceptable to even build a dam, unless you are a beaver, or to rearrange nature to suit ourselves better. A lion does not apologise to the antelope when strangling it; a killer whale does not feel rueful about chomping a seal and who knows how dinosaurs treated each other in ancient times, but it probably wasn't pretty. In the words of a disappointed Alfred Lord Tennison:

For nature is one with rapine, a harm no preacher can heal;

The Mayfly is torn by the swallow, the sparrow speared by the shrike,

And the whole little wood where I sit is a world of plunder and prey.

Why there are no Aliens

Taking all the foregone into consideration we need to look at the futile preoccupation with certain sections of science in their quest for finding alien life forms. Even though the earth has had civilization of one form or another for several thousand years, only during the last 100 or so years would it have been 'findable'. That means the earliest forms of broadcasting, assuming they are discernible, would be around 100 light years from the sun ready to be intercepted. Since we (luckily) live in a very quiet corner of the galaxy there is not much opportunity for an alien to hear us yet. The closest star to our is Proxima Centaury at 4.2 light years, then there are about a dozen within 10 light years and none of these seem to have planetary systems that might support life. In fact, when the powers that run programs like SETI or the search for similar habitable planets, seek for results, they tend to be much further away and now we are talking about thousands or more light years. This of course means that the signals will have that age equivalent to the distance, and by the time we get to an interesting area of space we will be talking longer time slots than that. Now if we look again at the development of human technological society we have those 100 years and find that progress has been more or less exponential and accordingly difficult to predict. One thing we do know, unless the sun throws a hissy fit, we will develop technology at an ever increasing rate. The first obvious development will be in computing and nano electronics. Very soon computers will be operating on a quantum level and could be exceeding human brain capacity within 30 years. What! You say. Well thirty years ago there were no portable computers and next we will have them on our wrists like Dick Tracey. Once such a computer is developed we have no idea how it will react. It may have consciousness, which would be fatal for us. That computer individual will most certainly have not the slightest interest in human affairs and will follow its own direction which will be incomprehensible to us – even if it chose to communicate with us! Worst of all, this entity may find us still useful in expanding its own power and being extremely clever we wouldn't notice a thing until it was too late. Down this road in space we would find artificial intelligences with whom it would be impossible to even communicate.

One of the main effects is also how technology advances. When information was first recorded it was by mechanical means – cutting grooves into wax or metal. If a future observer found this relic they could actually devise a means to recover the information and replicate it. When later on this storage took place on tape recovery became more difficult, but could still be recovered by an advanced technology. With the advent of digital encoding such as CD/DVD and by now almost exclusively in solid state such as flash memory sticks, if no clue was available of the decoding process, it would be impossible to even determine that this was an information storage device. When this leads into molecular or even quantum storage of information it becomes even more obscure. Applying this to information we might want to retrieve from an ancient advanced civilization means that we may not even recognize stored information even if we were looking directly at it.

The other direction where human development is taking enormous strides is in biology. 100 years ago there was practically no useful knowledge of biology at all. Only in the 1950s did humans develop some idea of where to look for biological developments and found the existence of DNA and the meaning of this. Since then again development has been exponential but we are now probably where human flight was in 1910. From there to flying in a Boeing 747 took only 50 years. So expect an absolutely astounding future for biology.

One thing that would most urgently need to be addressed is human space flight. The human body is simply too frail to go into space. We are vulnerable to all sorts of radiation leading to sterility, cancer and so on. Secondly it has been shown that the human body is infinitely adaptable and unfortunately one of those adaptations is that the body under weightlessness immediately decides that it no longer needs bones and promptly dismantles these in space. So to travel in space for any length of time we would need heavy protection from particles and rays and also an artificial gravity environment. Both of these are heavy and costly and make it pretty well prohibitive to take human bodies into space in any numbers. What can be done, however, is a development commonly referred to as a Cyborg in Science Fiction. A Cyborg is a combination of human portions and a mechanism, ultimately leading to a brain, well protected, probably some biological sensing mechanisms and maybe even a touching section much like skin. The Martian rover vehicles have shown that even such a simple mechanism can survive for long periods in essentially hostile environments. The Rovers Spirit and Opportunity were launched in 2003 with the intent of exploring the surface of Mars for three months. They were well built and one is still roaming on Mars having covered many hundreds of meters every year. During winter when the sun shines less the Rover goes 'to sleep' and when more sunlight is available once again, it is woken up and, with batteries charged up, continues on its way. The only reason the second Rover has come to a standstill is the fact that it has become mired in sand. Another machine, Curiosity, landed on Mars in 2012 and is also doing a splendid job.

Back to why there are no aliens. We can reasonably foresee that human development hasn't stopped and will continue in directions that cannot now be foreseen, but we can say they will be radical. It is likely that society will still be reasonably similar to our current state in a hundred, maybe two hundred years, but, beyond that we are at a loss. To say that we will have the same or similar societies in a thousand years would be denying the reality of human exceptionality. So our temporal footprint is at most a few thousand years until our development will make us unrecognisable from our current state. Thus we must assume that wherever intelligent life develops the situation will be similar: a long period of basic development leading to an upward spiral of technological advancement leading to an elevated state of consciousness, probably uninterested in communication.

Thus when we look for intelligent life elsewhere in the universe we must first accept that the signals will be old. The signal we are deciphering will come from an intelligence that has long since developed into a different state or may no longer exist. Additionally, if we wanted to respond, the signal would take just as long again to be sent back to them, making actual two-way communication impossible.

Secondly we must accept that we may simply not be able to recognize these as signals containing meaningful information. Using mathematical formulations or universal physical constants for messages may have become just useless information to these advanced intelligences. It is also unlikely that they would send out signals with the purpose of contacting civilisations such as ours. Even Wittgenstein noted: If a lion could speak, we could not understand him. A lion's concepts and terms of reference would be truly alien to us and so would that of an alien civilisation. The closest simulation for the average person would be to listen to a talk within the medical or astrophysical society, or any highly specialised group of participants.

We can thus conclude that the quest for contacting extraterrestrial intelligence, unless it happens to be on Jupiter's moon Europa, is a futile exercise based on similar concepts as religious belief. The same can be said for the quest to find life on Mars. Untold amounts of money have been spent to determine whether actual living organisms are or were present on Mars. If we use our own environment as a guide it becomes immediately clear that no matter what the terrestrial conditions are, there will be life present. Life has been found under the sea at enormous depth, devoid of sunlight, devoid of oxygen, under permanent ice layers, at extremely hot and cold conditions: life has always managed to adapt and occupy a space available. So should any form of life have made it on Mars, we would find it everywhere. There is sufficient light, moisture and nutrients available to propagate endlessly, there is carbon dioxide and calcium, it could be a silicon based life form, but once life takes a hold it takes over everything. The interesting corollary here is that it would probably be quite easy to not exactly terraform Mars, but to introduce life forms specifically developed here on Earth to exist under these conditions and at the same time generate oxygen from carbon dioxide and from metal oxides in the soil. Instead of protecting an environment devoid of life, it could be made habitable. Morally there should be no compunctions since, as it now appears, even Earth was at one time 'seeded' with life introduced by falling meteorites carrying ice and the basic building blocks from which other forms developed.

What has been ignored in the search for alien messages is the fact of time spans. When dinosaurs romped through the environment all was in balance for a long time. Tens of millions of years in fact, because there were no events or developments to upset this balance during all that period. Only a random dramatic event ultimately changed the balance then to favour mammals instead. These extinctions may not have happened and mankind may not be here at all. In our current situation man is exerting an enormous influence on the environment and on himself, so the situation is in constant flux. If we interpolate current developments in electronics and information technology, it will not be too long before the hardware and the human biology merge and communications will become much more direct, almost telepathic. The human brain will be able to communicate with the electronic computer directly and then with all other individuals anywhere. It will eliminate all communication devices such as phones, PCs, even television as we know it and most likely books and magazines. At the same time full control of the human (and all other) biology will have arrived and we hit a singularity: It becomes impossible to predict what this world will look like. Man will metamorphose into a new being unimaginable now and with aims and priorities that would seem meaningless today. This development could easily have happened on another planet in our galaxy, but not necessarily in the same time frame as our development. These societies may have come and gone millions or even billions of years ago and none in the arena of time that mankind can survey. We may not be alone in the universe, but we may well be in this time slot.

Further Reading:

Clay, Henry – *Economics: an Introduction for the General Reader;* McMillan 1919

The Inter-War Years and Other Papers: a Selection from the Writings of Hubert Douglas Henderson, Edited by Henry Clay; Clarendon Press 1955

Mill, John Stuart – *Principles of Political Economy with some of their Applications to Social Philosophy;* Longmans, Green and Co. London 1848

Cantillon, Richard – *Essai sur la Nature du Commerce en Général (Essay on the Nature of Trade in General)* (1730?)

Von Böhm-Bawerk, Eugen – *Kapital und Kapitalzins (History and Critique of Interest Theories)* 1884

Von Mises, Ludwig – *Theorie des Geldes und der Umlaufsmittel (The Theory of Money and Credit)* 1912

Smith, Adam – *An Inquiry Into the Nature and Causes of the Wealth of Nations* (1776)

Say, Jean-Baptiste – *A Treatise on Political Economy* (1821)

Hayek, F. A, – *New Studies in Philosophy, Politics, Economics and the History of Ideas* (Routledge & Kegan Paul, 1978)

Hayek, F. A. – *The Road to Serfdom* (1944) The University of Chicago

Mill, James – *Commerce Defended. An Answer to the Arguments by which Mr. Spence, Mr. Cobbett, and Others, have attempted to Prove that Commerce is not a source of National Wealth* [1808]

Fisher, Irving – *The Purchasing Power of Money,* (New York: The Macmillan Co. 1911)

Hazlitt, Henry – *Economics in one Lesson* (Harper & Brths, 1946)

Smith, Peter – *Bad Economics* (Connor Court Publishing, 2012)

C.M. Reinhart & K.S. Rogoff – *This Time It's Different* (Princeton University Press, 2009)

Kates, Steven – *Free Market Economics: An Introduction for the General Reader*; Edward Elgar 2011

Spencer, Herbert – *The Man Versus the State*, Williams and Norgate, London and Edinburgh, 1884

Graeber, David – *Debt: The First 5000 Years*, Melville House 2011

De Tocqueville, Alexis. – *Democracy in America,* Doubleday/ Anchor, (1969)

Malthus, Thomas Robert – *An Essay on the Principle of Population* (1798)

Ricardo, David – *On the Principles of Political Economy and Taxation* (1817)